FOR DUMMIES

COMPUTER
BOOK SERIES
FROM IDG

cc:Mail For Dummies®

MW01488811

Sending Messages

1. Open a New Message window to create a new message (use Ctrl+M or choose Message⇨New Message). The New Message window pops up.

2. Click in the Address text box, type in the recipient's cc:Mail address, and press the Enter key when you're done.

3. Click in the Subject box, type in a subject and press Enter when you're done.

4. Click in the message window and type your message.

5. Choose Message⌐Send or press Ctrl+S to send the message.

Doing Something with Messages

 Reply to an open message by clicking the Reply icon.

 Move a message by selecting (or opening) the message, clicking the Store icon, and choosing a folder or archive in which to put it.

 Delete a message by selecting (or opening) the message and clicking the Delete icon.

 Forward a message by selecting (or opening) the message, clicking the Forward icon, and filling in an address.

Receiving Messages

1. Double-click on the Inbox container.

2. Marvel at all the messages people sent you.

3. Double-click on a message you want to read.

4. Double-click on the upper-left corner of the message (or click the Close button if you're using Windows 95) to close the message after you finish with it.

IDG
BOOKS
WORLDWIDE

...For Dummies: #1 Computer Book Series for Beginners

cc:Mail For Dummies®

COMPUTER BOOK SERIES FROM IDG

Cheat Sheet

The cc:Mail Application Window

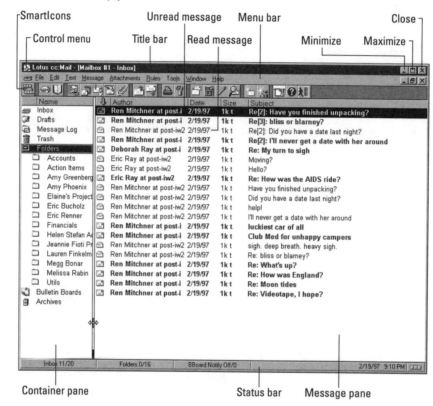

SmartIcons · Control menu · Unread message · Title bar · Read message · Menu bar · Minimize · Maximize · Close

Container pane · Status bar · Message pane

cc:Mail SmartIcons

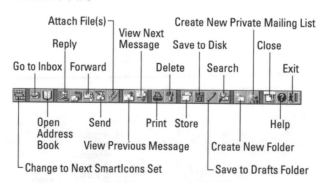

Attach File(s) · Reply · View Next Message · Create New Private Mailing List · Save to Disk · Close · Go to Inbox · Forward · Delete · Search · Exit

Open Address Book · Send · Print · Store · Help

Change to Next SmartIcons Set · View Previous Message · Create New Folder · Save to Drafts Folder

...For Dummies: #1 Computer Book Series for Beginners

®

References for the Rest of Us! ®

COMPUTER BOOK SERIES FROM IDG

Are you intimidated and confused by computers? Do you find that traditional manuals are overloaded with technical details you'll never use? Do your friends and family always call you to fix simple problems on their PCs? Then the *...For Dummies*® computer book series from IDG Books Worldwide is for you.

...For Dummies books are written for those frustrated computer users who know they aren't really dumb but find that PC hardware, software, and indeed the unique vocabulary of computing make them feel helpless. *...For Dummies* books use a lighthearted approach, a down-to-earth style, and even cartoons and humorous icons to diffuse computer novices' fears and build their confidence. Lighthearted but not lightweight, these books are a perfect survival guide for anyone forced to use a computer.

> *"I like my copy so much I told friends; now they bought copies."*
>
> **Irene C., Orwell, Ohio**

> *"Quick, concise, nontechnical, and humorous."*
>
> **Jay A., Elburn, Illinois**

> *"Thanks, I needed this book. Now I can sleep at night."*
>
> **Robin F., British Columbia, Canada**

Already, hundreds of thousands of satisfied readers agree. They have made *...For Dummies* books the #1 introductory level computer book series and have written asking for more. So, if you're looking for the most fun and easy way to learn about computers, look to *...For Dummies* books to give you a helping hand.

CC:MAIL™
FOR
DUMMIES®

by Victor R. Garza

IDG
BOOKS
WORLDWIDE

IDG Books Worldwide, Inc.
An International Data Group Company

Foster City, CA ♦ Chicago, IL ♦ Indianapolis, IN ♦ Southlake, TX

cc:Mail™ for Dummies®

Published by
IDG Books Worldwide, Inc.
An International Data Group Company
919 E. Hillsdale Blvd.
Suite 400
Foster City, CA 94404
http://www.idgbooks.com (IDG Books Worldwide Web site)
http://www.dummies.com (Dummies Press Web site)

Library of Congress Catalog Card No.: 96-78138

ISBN: 0-7645-0055-4

Printed in the United States of America

10 9 8 7 6 5 4 3 2 1

1E/QR/QV/ZX/IN

Distributed in the United States by IDG Books Worldwide, Inc.

Distributed by Macmillan Canada for Canada; by Transworld Publishers Limited in the United Kingdom and Europe; by WoodsLane Pty. Ltd. for Australia; by WoodsLane Enterprises Ltd. for New Zealand; by Longman Singapore Publishers Ltd. for Singapore, Malaysia, Thailand, and Indonesia; by Simron Pty. Ltd. for South Africa; by Toppan Company Ltd. for Japan; by Distribuidora Cuspide for Argentina; by Livraria Cultura for Brazil; by Ediciencia S.A. for Ecuador; by Addison-Wesley Publishing Company for Korea; by Ediciones ZETA S.C.R. Ltda. for Peru; by WS Computer Publishing Company, Inc., for the Philippines; by Unalis Corporation for Taiwan; by Contemporanea de Ediciones for Venezuela. Authorized Sales Agent: Anthony Rudkin Associates for the Middle East and North Africa.

For general information on IDG Books Worldwide's books in the U.S., please call our Consumer Customer Service department at 800-762-2974. For reseller information, including discounts and premium sales, please call our Reseller Customer Service department at 800-434-3422.

For information on where to purchase IDG Books Worldwide's books outside the U.S., please contact our International Sales department at 415-655-3023 or fax 415-655-3299.

For information on foreign language translations, please contact our Foreign & Subsidiary Rights department at 415-655-3021 or fax 415-655-3281.

For sales inquiries and special prices for bulk quantities, please contact our Sales department at 415-655-3200 or write to the address above.

For information on using IDG Books Worldwide's books in the classroom or for ordering examination copies, please contact our Educational Sales department at 800-434-2086 or fax 817-251-8174.

For press review copies, author interviews, or other publicity information, please contact our Public Relations department at 415-655-3000 or fax 415-655-3299.

For authorization to photocopy items for corporate, personal, or educational use, please contact Copyright Clearance Center, 222 Rosewood Drive, Danvers, MA 01923, or fax 508-750-4470.

is a trademark under exclusive license to IDG Books Worldwide, Inc., from International Data Group, Inc.

About the Author

Victor R. "Bob" Garza has been working and playing with computers since 1980 when he developed his first game for a computer class on an old SOL computer. Since then, he has worked in the computer industry as a writer and computer consultant.

Bob authored *cc:Mail For Windows For Dummies Quick Reference,* and this book is his third title for IDG Books Worldwide. He has also been a technical reviewer for IDG Books on over a dozen titles varying in scope from operating systems to hard disk drives.

Bob currently works for *InfoWorld* — the leading computer newsweekly — where he has worked for over seven years. He started this book as a Project Leader for the Enterprise Solutions team, where he managed a team of analysts and editors who tested and reviewed multiplatform, multiprotocol enterprise deployed solutions. Currently, he works on the Reviews Team where he tests and writes about new and emerging technologies (a heck of a fun job if you like to play with computers).

Bob has tested and reviewed a wide variety of products, including personal digital assistants, personal information managers, spreadsheets, Web servers, e-mail middleware, document management software, fax servers, project management management software, Unix clustering software, and more.

Bob has degrees in Humanities and Information Systems Management and is currently working on a graduate degree in Telecommunications Management. Bob lives in Sunnyvale, California, and when he's not working he tries to see as many new movies as humanly possible.

ABOUT IDG BOOKS WORLDWIDE

Welcome to the world of IDG Books Worldwide.

IDG Books Worldwide, Inc., is a subsidiary of International Data Group, the world's largest publisher of computer-related information and the leading global provider of information services on information technology. IDG was founded more than 25 years ago and now employs more than 8,500 people worldwide. IDG publishes more than 275 computer publications in over 75 countries (see listing below). More than 60 million people read one or more IDG publications each month.

Launched in 1990, IDG Books Worldwide is today the #1 publisher of best-selling computer books in the United States. We are proud to have received eight awards from the Computer Press Association in recognition of editorial excellence and three from *Computer Currents'* First Annual Readers' Choice Awards. Our best-selling *...For Dummies®* series has more than 30 million copies in print with translations in 30 languages. IDG Books Worldwide, through a joint venture with IDG's Hi-Tech Beijing, became the first U.S. publisher to publish a computer book in the People's Republic of China. In record time, IDG Books Worldwide has become the first choice for millions of readers around the world who want to learn how to better manage their businesses.

Our mission is simple: Every one of our books is designed to bring extra value and skill-building instructions to the reader. Our books are written by experts who understand and care about our readers. The knowledge base of our editorial staff comes from years of experience in publishing, education, and journalism — experience we use to produce books for the '90s. In short, we care about books, so we attract the best people. We devote special attention to details such as audience, interior design, use of icons, and illustrations. And because we use an efficient process of authoring, editing, and desktop publishing our books electronically, we can spend more time ensuring superior content and spend less time on the technicalities of making books.

You can count on our commitment to deliver high-quality books at competitive prices on topics you want to read about. At IDG Books Worldwide, we continue in the IDG tradition of delivering quality for more than 25 years. You'll find no better book on a subject than one from IDG Books Worldwide.

John Kilcullen
John Kilcullen
CEO
IDG Books Worldwide, Inc.

Steven Berkowitz
Steven Berkowitz
President and Publisher
IDG Books Worldwide, Inc.

IDG Books Worldwide, Inc., is a subsidiary of International Data Group, the world's largest publisher of computer-related information and the leading global provider of information services on information technology. International Data Group publishes over 275 computer publications in over 75 countries. Sixty million people read one or more International Data Group publications each month. International Data Group's publications include: **ARGENTINA:** Buyer's Guide, Computerworld Argentina, PC World Argentina; **AUSTRALIA:** Australian Macworld, Australian PC World, Australian Reseller News, Computerworld, IT Casebook, Network World, Publish, Webmaster; **AUSTRIA:** Computerwelt Osterreich, Networks Austria, PC Tip Austria; **BANGLADESH:** PC World Bangladesh; **BELARUS:** PC World Belarus; **BELGIUM:** Data News; **BRAZIL:** Annuário de Informática, Computerworld, Connections, Macworld, PC Player, PC World, Publish, Reseller News, Supergamepower; **BULGARIA:** Computerworld Bulgaria, Network World Bulgaria, PC & MacWorld Bulgaria; **CANADA:** CIO Canada, Client/Server World, ComputerWorld Canada, InfoWorld Canada, NetworkWorld Canada, WebWorld; **CHILE:** Computerworld Chile, PC World Chile; **COLOMBIA:** Computerworld Colombia, PC World Colombia; **COSTA RICA:** PC World Centro America; **THE CZECH AND SLOVAK REPUBLICS:** Computerworld Czechoslovakia, Macworld Czech Republic, PC World Czechoslovakia; **DENMARK:** Communications World Danmark, Computerworld Danmark, Macworld Danmark, PC World Danmark, Techworld Denmark; **DOMINICAN REPUBLIC:** PC World Republica Dominicana; **ECUADOR:** PC World Ecuador; **EGYPT:** Computerworld Middle East, PC World Middle East; **EL SALVADOR:** PC World Centro America; **FINLAND:** MikroPC, Tietoverkko, Tietoviikko; **FRANCE:** Distributique, Hebdo, Info PC, Le Monde Informatique, Macworld, Reseaux & Telecoms, WebMaster France; **GERMANY:** Computer Partner, Computerwoche, Computerwoche Extra, Computerwoche FOCUS, Global Online, Macweb, PC Welt; **GREECE:** Amiga Computing, GamePro Greece, Multimedia World; **GUATEMALA:** PC World Centro America; **HONDURAS:** PC World Centro America; **HONG KONG:** Computerworld Hong Kong, PC World Hong Kong, Publish in Asia; **HUNGARY:** ABCD CD-ROM, Computerworld Szamitastechnika, Internetto online Magazine, PC World Hungary, PC-X Magazin Hungary; **ICELAND:** Tolvuheimur PC World Island; **INDIA:** Information Communications World, Information Systems Computerworld, PC World India, Publish in Asia; **INDONESIA:** InfoKomputer PC World, Komputek Computerworld, Publish in Asia; **IRELAND:** ComputerScope, PC Live!; **ISRAEL:** Macworld Israel, People & Computers/Computerworld; **ITALY:** Computerworld Italia, Macworld Italia, Networking Italia, PC World Italia; **JAPAN:** DTP World, Macworld Japan, Nikkei Personal Computing, OS/2 World Japan, SunWorld Japan, Windows World Japan; **KENYA:** PC World East African; **KOREA:** Hi-Tech Information, Macworld Korea, PC World Korea; **MACEDONIA:** PC World Macedonia; **MALAYSIA:** Computerworld Malaysia, PC World Malaysia, Publish in Asia; **MALTA:** PC World Malta; **MEXICO:** Computerworld Mexico, PC World Mexico; **MYANMAR:** PC World Myanmar; **NETHERLANDS:** Computer! Totaal, LAN Internetworking Magazine, LAN World Buyers Guide, Macworld Netherlands, Net, WebWereld; **NEW ZEALAND:** Absolute Beginners Guide and Plain & Simple Series, Computer Buyer, Computer Industry Directory, Computerworld New Zealand, MTB, Network World, PC World New Zealand; **NICARAGUA:** PC World Centro America; **NORWAY:** Computerworld Norge, CW Rapport, Datamagasinet, Financial Rapport, Kursguide Norge, Macworld Norge, Multimediaworld Norge, PC World Ekspress Norge, PC World Nettverk, PC World Norge, PC World ProduktGuide Norge; **PAKISTAN:** Computerworld Pakistan; **PANAMA:** PC World Panama; **PEOPLE'S REPUBLIC OF CHINA:** China Computer Users, China Computerworld, China InfoWorld, China Telecom World Weekly, Computer & Communication, Electronic Design China, Electronics Today, Electronics Weekly, Game Software, PC World China, Popular Computer Week, Software Weekly, Software World, Telecom World; **PERU:** Computerworld Peru, PC World Profesional Peru, PC World SoHo Peru; **PHILIPPINES:** Click!, Computerworld Philippines, PC World Philippines, Publish in Asia; **POLAND:** Computerworld Poland, Computerworld Special Report Poland, Cyber, Macworld Poland, Networld Poland, PC World Komputer; **PORTUGAL:** Cerebro/PC World, Computerworld/Correio Informatico, Dealer World Portugal, Mac*In/PC*In Portugal, Multimedia World; **PUERTO RICO:** PC World Puerto Rico; **ROMANIA:** Computerworld Romania, PC World Romania, Telecom Romania; **RUSSIA:** Computerworld Russia, Mir PK, Publish, Seti; **SINGAPORE:** Computerworld Singapore, PC World Singapore, Publish in Asia; **SLOVENIA:** Monitor; **SOUTH AFRICA:** Computing SA, Network World SA, Software World SA; **SPAIN:** Communicaciones World España, Computerworld España, Dealer World España, Macworld España, PC World España; **SRI LANKA:** Infolink PC World; **SWEDEN:** CAP&Design, Computer Sweden, Corporate Computing Sweden, Internetworld Sweden, it.branschen, Macworld Sweden, MaxiData Sweden, MikroDatorn, Nätverk & Kommunikation, PC World Sweden, PCAktiv, Windows World Sweden; **SWITZERLAND:** Computerworld Schweiz, Macworld Schweiz, PCtip; **TAIWAN:** Computerworld Taiwan, Macworld Taiwan, NEW VISION/Publish, PC World Taiwan, Windows World Taiwan; **THAILAND:** Publish in Asia, Thai Computerworld; **TURKEY:** Computerworld Turkiye, Macworld Turkiye, Network World Turkiye, PC World Turkiye; **UKRAINE:** Computerworld Kiev, Multimedia World Ukraine, PC World Ukraine; **UNITED KINGDOM:** Acorn User UK, Amiga Action UK, Amiga Computing UK, Apple Talk UK, Computing, Macworld, Parents and Computers UK, PC Advisor, PC Home, PSX Pro, The WEB; **UNITED STATES:** Cable in the Classroom, CIO Magazine, Computerworld, DOS World, Federal Computer Week, GamePro Magazine, InfoWorld, I-Way, Macworld, Network World, PC Games, PC World, Publish, Video Event, THE WEB Magazine, and WebMaster; online webzines: JavaWorld, NetscapeWorld, and SunWorld Online; **URUGUAY:** InfoWorld Uruguay; **VENEZUELA:** Computerworld Venezuela, PC World Venezuela; and **VIETNAM:** PC World Vietnam.   3/24/97

Author's Acknowledgments

I'd like to thank my family and friends for all of their support while I was working on this book.

Special thanks goes to the Rays — Eric, Deborah, and little Ashleigh. I don't now how much Ashleigh wrote, but I do know that Eric and Deborah worked long and hard helping me get this book done on time, and I appreciate that heartily.

I would also like to say thank you to Karen Mitchell, Elaine Anderson, Jeannie Fioti, Megg Bonar, Amy Phoenix, Eric Renner and Helen Stefan. I could always count on them for help, support, and encouragement when I needed it.

I also want to thank Terry Goin and Michelle Mitchell at *InfoWorld* for helping me out when I wanted to accomplish some convoluted mail trick on a production server.

Thanks also to Tim Gallan, Gareth Hancock, and John Edwards at IDG Books. Finally, thanks to Amy Shaw, Judy Chang and Mark McHarry at Lotus for helping me get my cc:Mail questions answered.

Publisher's Acknowledgments

We're proud of this book; please send us your comments about it by using the IDG Books Worldwide Registration Card at the back of the book or by e-mailing us at feedback/dummies@idgbooks.com. Some of the people who helped bring this book to market include the following:

Acquisitions, Development, and Editorial

Project Editor: Tim Gallan

Acquisitions Editor: Gareth Hancock

Product Development Director:
Mary Bednarek

Copy Editors: James Edwards,
Felicity O'Meara, Constance Carlisle

Technical Editor: L. G. Parkhurst

Editorial Manager: Leah P. Cameron

Editorial Assistant: Jerelind Davis

Production

Project Coordinator: Sherry Gomoll

Layout and Graphics: Angela F. Hunckler,
Jane E. Martin, Anna Rohrer, Brent Savage

Proofreaders: Christine D. Berman,
Henry Lazarek, Robert Springer,
Karen York

Indexer: Liz Cunningham

General and Administrative

IDG Books Worldwide, Inc.: John Kilcullen, CEO; Steven Berkowitz, President and Publisher

IDG Books Technology Publishing: Brenda McLaughlin, Senior Vice President and Group Publisher

Dummies Technology Press and Dummies Editorial: Diane Graves Steele, Vice President and Associate Publisher; Judith A. Taylor, Brand Manager; Kristin A. Cocks, Editorial Director

Dummies Trade Press: Kathleen A. Welton, Vice President and Publisher; Stacy S. Collins, Brand Manager

IDG Books Production for Dummies Press: Beth Jenkins, Production Director; Cindy L. Phipps, Supervisor of Project Coordination, Production Proofreading, and Indexing; Kathie S. Schutte, Supervisor of Page Layout; Shelley Lea, Supervisor of Graphics and Design; Debbie J. Gates, Production Systems Specialist; Tony Augsburger, Supervisor of Reprints and Bluelines; Leslie Popplewell, Media Archive Coordinator

Dummies Packaging and Book Design: Patti Sandez, Packaging Specialist; Lance Kayser, Packaging Assistant; Kavish + Kavish, Cover Design

◆

The publisher would like to give special thanks to Patrick J. McGovern, without whom this book would not have been possible.

◆

Contents at a Glance

Cartoons at a Glance

By Rich Tennant • Fax: 508-546-7747 • E-mail: the5wave@tiac.net

page 207

page 9

page 143

page 37

page 255

page 79

page 317

Table of Contents

Introduction

*W*elcome to *cc:Mail For Dummies,* a book that looks at the lighter side of cc:Mail features and tasks. This book not only gives you the scoop on cc:Mail, but it assumes that you just want to get into cc:Mail to create or read an electronic mail message and then get out to do something important (like go to the beach or wash the car).

Why do you need cc:Mail anyway, you ask? Well, if you work for a small, medium, or large company, the old way of doing things was to pick up the phone and call your officemate or walk down the hall and hand-deliver that expense report.

Nowadays, your officemates may be down the hall, but more likely, they're probably across the country (and in a different time zone altogether). cc:Mail (and cc:Mobile, which I also cover in this book) allows you to move that information right from your desktop without having to take your hands off the keyboard. Send off that expense report (Zing!), get back to your boss with the details of the Zimmerman closing (Bam!), and whip off a witty agenda for tomorrow's meeting (Bang!).

That's the purpose of cc:Mail, to get you to be more productive. The same goes for this book — to get you up and off to a running start with cc:Mail with a minimum of fuss. Sometimes you may get tripped up by the nuances of cc:Mail (some may say nuisances, but you didn't hear that from me), and that's where this book comes in handy, untangling your fingers and letting you finish that message so that you can call it a day, go home, and relax.

Now, just so you know, this book focuses on Version 6 of cc:Mail. Although this is a relatively new version of the cc:Mail program, it's very closely based on it's Version 2 cousin. (If you didn't know better, you'd think that they were brother and sister). So where applicable, this book will explain the Version 6 way of doing things, and if the Version 2 way of doing that same thing is different, I'll explain how (and maybe even why) the older version is the way it is.

What's more, I devote an entire part to covering Version 8 of cc:Mail. (There used to be a Version 7, but everyone who has it is supposed to upgrade to Version 8.) This version of cc:Mail is very different from Versions 2 and 6, and because the people running your company may someday want to upgrade, I thought it might be helpful to show you what it's all about.

So now that you know that the point of cc:Mail is to enhance your productivity, sit back, stretch out your fingers, flip through these pages, and get ready to whip out those messages!

How to Use This Book

You know that you've got better things to do today than become a computer expert. So this book is designed to be used when you can't figure out what went wrong with that cc:Mail message you were just working on or when you can't seem to find the window for the message you were just responding to.

Along that vein, don't try to read this book in one sitting. (Although if you really feel like punishing yourself, who am I to stop you?) Instead, treat this book as you would any other reference book. The chapters are self-contained, and you don't have to read them in order. I've peppered every chapter with cross-references to related topics in other chapters.

When you get turned around by a particularly confusing piece of cc:Mail muddle, just pick up this book, and with the help of the index or table of contents, turn to the page with the information that you need to solve your problem (and then get on with your life!).

What kinds of topics do I cover? Here's a sample:

- ✔ How to create electronic mail messages
- ✔ How to send cc:Mail messages to an individual or group of individuals
- ✔ How to read, reply to, and forward electronic messages
- ✔ How to print and save messages
- ✔ How to send messages from the office, from home, or from a hotel room in Bulgaria
- ✔ How to find misplaced messages
- ✔ How to delete unwanted messages

Conventions Used in This Book

Sometimes I ask you to type stuff into your computer. When that time comes, I put the text in bold, like this:

Type this text stuff and then press the Enter Key.

(You've probably already figured out that in this case you'd type "Type this text stuff" but not "and then press the Enter Key".)

When I talk about commands on the menu bar, I refer to them like this: Choose File➪New➪Folder. This means that you click on the File menu (with your mouse), then click on New from the drop-down list of options, and then click on Folder from the next list. The underlined letters in the menu and command names are hot keys. Holding down the Alt key, pressing F, pressing N, and pressing F (Alt+F+N+F) is the same as choosing File➪New➪Folder.

Sometimes I refer to SmartIcons (which most programs call toolbar buttons). When I do, you should find a picture of the SmartIcon in the margin next to the text.

How This Book Is Organized

This book has seven parts. These parts have been broken out to give you specific information about different aspects of cc:Mail.

Part I: Genesis

This part of the book gives you an overview of the cc:Mail universe. What the cc:Mail screen looks like, what each of those odd looking icons at the top of the cc:Mail screen do, where to start when you want to compose a message to a friend or coworker, and how to use the online help system in cc:Mail.

Part II: Reading Your Mail

This part deals with all of the things that you'll want to know about when you start reading your messages, including telling the difference between an unread and previously read message, responding to an electronic mail message, printing out an electronic mail message, and dealing with those pesky files that come attached to your electronic messages.

Part III: Sending Mail

This part shows you how to send message from within cc:Mail to all the people you always wanted to (but didn't have this book to help you out). I also covers topics like e-mail etiquette, changing the properties of your text, using the integrated spell checker, and finding out about those things new to cc:Mail: forms.

Part IV: Bossing Your Mail Around

This part of the book talks about all of those things that you'll have to deal with at one time or another when you're using cc:Mail, such as finding a lost message, storing all of your received messages in an electronic filing system, deleting unwanted messages when you feel like doing a little spring cleaning, and doing all of that other Felix Unger stuff. (You remember *The Odd Couple,* right?)

Part V: Remotely Accessing Mail

In this part, I discuss cc:Mobile, the cc:Mail program for people on the move. I show you how to install cc:Mobile, tell you the differences between LAN and Mobile mode, help you deal with synchronization, and even provide troubleshooting tips.

Part VI: Extra! Extra! Read All about It!

In this part, I show you the ins and outs of cc:Mail Version 8, which is very much like Version 7, except that it has fewer bugs. I give you a tour of the new interface and cover the basic features of this newest member to the cc:Mail family.

Part VII: The Part of Tens

This part of the book is filled with assorted tidbits that are meant to make your life easier while using cc:Mail. In Letterman-esque fashion, the information is organized in lists of (about) ten items.

I end the book with four appendixes containing optional and referential information. You'll find a list of menu commands and what they do, a list of keyboard shortcuts, some troubleshooting advice, and even some help installing cc:Mail.

What I Assume about You

You have cc:Mail installed on your computer (Versions 2, 6, 7, or 8) and you want and/or need to use it productively.

I'm also going to assume that you have a working familiarity with the Windows operating system, whether it be Windows 3.1, Windows 3.11, or Windows 95. (Pick one, any one, but please pick the one that is installed on your computer.)

If none of these names ring a bell to you, or if you don't feel as comfortable as you'd like to with your operating system, I recommend that you pick up a couple of books at your local bookstore to make yourself more relaxed: *Windows 3.1 For Dummies*, 3rd Edition, by Andy Rathbone or *Windows 95 For Dummies,* 2nd Edition, also by Andy Rathbone. (Does this guy have a corner on the market or what?)

The Cast of Icons

Just like in cc:Mail (where the little icons represent actions that the program can perform), the following little visual queues will notify you of important information.

A tip to make you a more clever and agile cc:Mail user.

This signpost means that detailed technical information is nearby. If you want to know some of the technical ins and outs of cc:Mail, read the text next to this icon. If you want to stay sane, you may just want to drive on past this little roadblock.

Just a little note to remind you of some useful info that may someday save your bacon.

This icon lets you know that I'm about to explain a difference between Version 6 of cc:Mail and Version 2. This icon isn't quite as bad as a Technical Stuff icon, but if you don't have a Version 2 of cc:Mail (it's still quite popular), feel free to just skip this little side trip down memory lane.

Look out! There's some little something here that can get you into trouble or possibly make your day more difficult.

Some Stuff You Probably Already Know

Just in case you're brand new to the whole concept of e-mail, this section can help.

What is electronic mail?

Electronic mail (a.k.a. e-mail) is just a way of getting correspondence between two computers, whether those computers are separated by a distance of five feet or five thousand miles. You can think of e-mail as an electronic means of sending a paper letter to a friend or colleague. One of the advantages of sending e-mail is that it can be considerably faster than snail mail (what the U.S. Postal Service is lovingly referred to on the Internet).

E-mail can sometimes get a letter across the nation or the world in as fast as two minutes!

Imagine sending a note off to a coworker in China and getting a response within the hour. If that's not enough for you, imagine getting an e-mail from across the country containing a written proposal, an up-to-date spreadsheet, and a picture of a new product all in the same message. That's what's so great about e-mail: It allows you to move information almost instantaneously.

Now, to get electronic mail from one place to another, you need an electronic mail program. That's what cc:Mail is.

Within cc:Mail, you compose and receive e-mail messages. When you send a cc:Mail message, it goes to the local cc:Mail post office (just like dropping a letter in a mailbox gets the letter to the local U.S. Post Office via your local postal carrier).

cc:Mail then figures out where your message is going and sends it along the appropriate path (to maybe the computer of a coworker down the hall or to the e-mail box of your friend who uses America Online).

Who or what is a cc:Mail administrator?

This book makes references to the person you may know as the cc:Mail *administrator*. This person is responsible for maintaining the cc:Mail system as a whole. The administrator adds new users, deletes users, makes sure your personal messages are not taking up a disproportionate amount of space on the cc:Mail server, and above all, fixes problems with cc:Mail.

The administrator has a huge responsibility, and being nice to your administrator can mean making this person's job easier. Being nice to your administrator can also mean that this person is quicker to solve a serious problem with cc:Mail if you should ever have one.

There are certain functions in cc:Mail that the administrator has control over (enabling the Trash folder and the Message log, for example). Talk to your administrator about turning these options on if you want to use them (and perhaps you will after you read about them in this book).

What about installing cc:Mail?

You may be lucky enough never to have to install cc:Mail on your computer, or you may have a really cool cc:Mail administrator who took the time to install it for you. If that's the case, pat yourself on the back and grab a candy bar because the worst is over.

If you're not one of the lucky few who has the program preinstalled for you, don't despair. Just check out Appendix A. Here, I go through a quick installation that'll have you working with cc:Mail in no time.

What Now?

That's all you need to know to get started playing with cc:Mail. Whenever you hit a snag with cc:Mail, just look up the problem in this book. You'll have the problem solved in no time — or you'll know how to find the answers to your questions.

Part I
Genesis

The 5th Wave   By Rich Tennant

In this part . . .

1 remember when I used to watch Carl Sagan's *Cosmos*. He was always referring to how many stars there were in the heavens. "Billions and billions," he said. I used to think to myself, "Where do you start counting when you have that many stars?" Did he just start in the lower-left and go from there? Did he get out a great big crayon and play connect-the-dots? Or perhaps he just knew.

The point is that Carl Sagan had to start somewhere. The same holds true for cc:Mail, so let's get started — at the beginning.

Chapter 1

Starting at the Beginning

. . . .

In This Chapter

▶ Starting cc:Mail

▶ Logging-in to cc:Mail

▶ Getting familiar with the cc:Mail Interface

▶ Quitting cc:Mail

. . . .

*1*t's 11:57 on a Saturday night, and you're still working your buns off at the office — for the second night in a row. What better way to earn brownie points — er, um . . . at least keep your job, these days. So you had better find some subtle way to tell your boss that you worked all weekend — but how? Why not call your boss at home? Or send your boss a singing telegram? Or write a note on the rest room wall? Or mention it in Monday's staff meeting?

Why not just send your boss a cc:Mail message? Hmmm. That has some potential. I can see it now:

```
11:57 pm
Dear Boss:
Did you know that the janitor comes and
empties trash at 11:32 pm on Fridays and
Saturdays? I didn't think anyone else
worked this late. Do they get overtime?
Just wondering.
(Your Name Here)
```

But first, you'll have to figure out how to start cc:Mail, get logged-in to cc:Mail, get familiar with the windows, and eventually exit cc:Mail. Lucky for you, all these tasks are covered in this chapter.

Cranking Up cc:Mail

Cranking up cc:Mail is as easy as starting any other Windows program. Start with your computer on and Windows (either 3.1*x* or 95) running.

1. **Look for the cc:Mail icon on your desktop.**

   Windows 95: If you don't have a cc:Mail icon visible, you can start cc:Mail by going to Start➪Programs➪Lotus Applications and looking . . . Ahhh, there it is, that little critter that looks like a sideways envelope on a stand with the words *Lotus cc:Mail 6.0* next to or underneath it.

   Windows 3.1*x*: If you don't have a cc:Mail icon visible, double-click the Lotus Applications folder in your Program Manager to open it. Aha! *Lotus cc:Mail 6.0* complete with the icon that looks like a sideways envelope.

2. **Double-click the cc:Mail icon on your desktop (or Program Manager) or click once on the critter in your Start menu.**

   After your computer grinds for a few minutes, you should see something very similar to Figure 1-1. Your cc:Mail log-in name should be in the Log-in Name list box, and the flashing cursor should be at the Password: prompt.

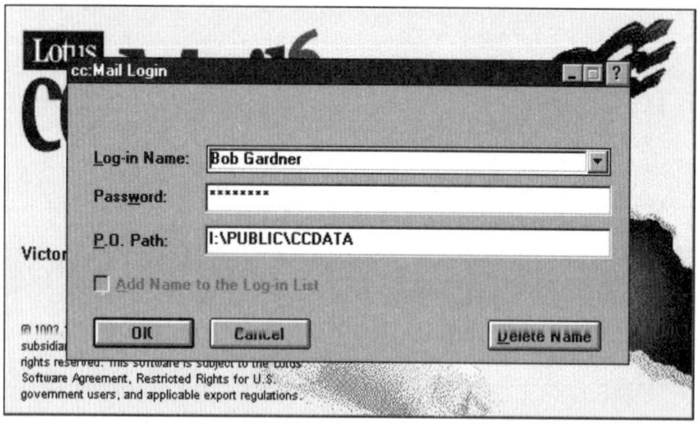

Figure 1-1:
The Login
dialog box.

Lotus
cc:Mail Login
Log-in Name: Bob Gardner
Password: ●●●●●●●●
P.O. Path: I:\PUBLIC\CCDATA
☐ Add Name to the Log-in List
OK   Cancel   Delete Name

3. **Verify the Log-in Name and Post Office path in the dialog box and then type in your password.**

   To move from field to field, just use the Tab key (or use Shift+Tab to go back to a previous field). Or you can just click your mouse where you need to type.

   By default, Log-in Name and P.O. Path should already be filled in, but check them to make sure they're correct. You need to type in your password each time you log-in to cc:Mail.

About this trivia you have to fill in:

- **Log-in Name:** Your log-in name, as assigned by your cc:Mail administrator, should appear in this box. If you don't see it, try clicking the down-arrow and selecting your log-in name. If you don't see your name in the drop-down list, try just typing it in yourself if you know *exactly* what it is. Guessing won't do here — just the difference between using and not using your middle initial is the difference between success and temporary frustration. (You might check out the sidebar called "How'd cc:Mail Know My Name?" in this section.) If you're not sure, you'll need to ask your cc:Mail administrator.

- **Password:** Your initial password is also assigned by your cc:Mail administrator. Your password is a way-secret word that allows you — and only you — to log-in to your cc:Mail account. For more information about changing your password and selecting good passwords, check out Chapter 15.

- **P.O. Path:** The P.O. path tells cc:Mail where the Post Office is. It'll be something like M:\ccdata\, but only your cc:Mail Administrator knows for sure.

4. Click OK or press Enter when you're done.

Because safeguarding your electronic mail from prying eyes is a *very* good idea, always choose a password that you won't easily forget or lose. Be sure to select a password that can't be easily guessed, either.

One of the really cool things about this version of cc:Mail over the 2.*x* versions is that Version 6.0 will automatically go out and try to find your Post Office path and place it in your P.O. Path text box. (If cc:Mail can't find the path, you'll have to type the path yourself.) This excellent feature saves you time that you would normally spend tracking down your administrator and asking what type of DOS cryptic mumbo-jumbo should go in the P.O. Path text box.

Okay, now you're in. Before you move on to typing that message to your boss, go ahead and get acquainted with the cc:Mail interface.

How'd cc:Mail know my name?

Hmmm. Maybe it's magic. Maybe cc:Mail knows more than even Nostradamus. Or maybe your cc:Mail administrator put in your name for you. Seriously, until you log in at a given workstation, your name won't show up in the list. But after you log in (and think to put a checkmark in the Add Name to the Log-in List check box), cc:Mail will remember your name and Post Office path for the next time. How's that for convenient?

Getting Acquainted with the cc:Mail Interface

Now that you have cc:Mail open and ready to go, you need to get acquainted with the cc:Mail interface. cc:Mail is composed of two windows: the Application window and the Mailbox window (which is really just part of the Application window). The next sections introduce you to the Application and Mailbox windows as well as panes, pane sliders, column widths, and containers.

The Application window

The Application window, shown in Figure 1-2, is the big window you see when you open cc:Mail. Really, the Application window just holds the icons and all the rest of your cc:Mail paraphernalia, including the Mailbox window(s), which are discussed in the next section.

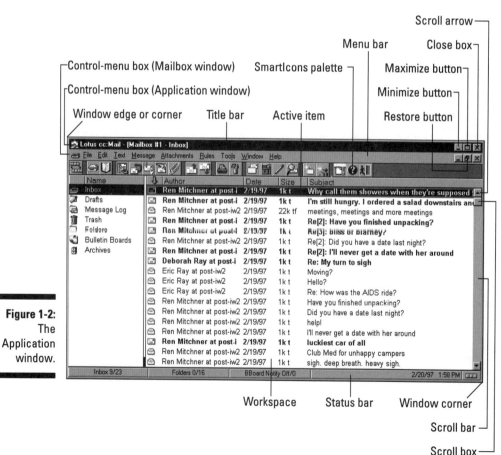

Figure 1-2:
The Application window.

Active item

The active item has a black bar with a white border completely around it like a mat surrounding a picture in a frame. When an item is active, you can take action on it. This is like the "You are here" X on a map. If you see two items with black bars on your screen, the one with the white border is the active item, and the one with no white border is an inactive item.

Control-menu box (Application window)

This pull-down menu has several options that enable you to change the size of the application window, to get to the Clipboard (to see what you may have recently copied) and the Control Panel (to change system settings — although why you'd need to do this from cc:Mail is beyond me), and to close cc:Mail. To close cc:Mail, double-click the control-menu box. If you click this box to open the menu and have second thoughts, press Esc to close the menu.

Control-menu box (Mailbox window)

This pull-down menu has several options that enable you to change the size of the Mailbox window, and the control-menu box is where you can close the Mailbox window. You can also save cc:Mail window settings and sizes (either immediately or when you exit cc:Mail) from this pull-down menu. To close the Mailbox window, double-click the control-menu box. If you click and open this menu and then change your mind, just press Esc to exit the control menu.

Menu bar

This collection of pull-down menus lets you get at all the available commands cc:Mail has to offer. At the same time, when the pull-down menus are not being used, they remain out of sight and your workspace stays nice and neat. You can access menu items using three different methods. First, you can click a word in the menu bar (with the mouse), and a list of options rolls down (just like pull-down window blinds). Second, you can press Alt plus the underlined letter of a word on the menu bar (for example, press Alt+M). Third, you can use the arrow keys to move around the menu bar after you've tapped the Alt key.

Maximize button

This button in the top right of a window makes that window occupy the maximum real estate possible. For the application window, that maximum is the whole screen. You can also press Alt+spacebar+X to maximize a window.

Minimize button

This button causes the window to shrink to a small fraction of its former self and become an icon (or a tab on the task bar in Windows 95). You can also press Alt+spacebar+N to minimize a window.

Restore button

This button restores — hence the name — a maximized or minimized window to its former size. You can also press Alt+spacebar+R to restore a window.

Scroll arrow

On the right side of the screen are two arrows, one at each end of what's called a vertical scroll bar. The upward-pointing arrow on this bar moves your view to the top of the file (or list, or whatever). The downward-pointing arrow moves your view toward the bottom of the file or list. You can use the up-arrow key and down-arrow key or the PgUp and PgDn keys to do the same things without using the mouse.

Scroll box

This little elevator-like box inside the vertical scroll bar lets you know whether you're at the top, middle, or bottom of your text within the window. You can tell your relative position based upon the position of the scroll box within the vertical scroll bar. You can move up and down in a window by clicking the scroll box and dragging it up or down. You can use the up-arrow key and down-arrow key or the PgUp and PgDn keys to do the same thing without using the mouse. If you want to move up or down by a screen at a time, just click the scroll bar between the scroll box and an arrow.

Vertical scroll bar

This bar is where that elevator-like vertical scroll box hangs out. You can move text up or down within a window by clicking the vertical scroll bar, by clicking one of the arrows on each end of the vertical scroll bar, or by clicking and dragging the vertical scroll box.

SmartIcons palette

The SmartIcons palette serves as a quick way to accomplish many common tasks in cc:Mail. If you use SmartIcons, you won't need to fuss with the menu bar or keyboard shortcuts. Just click a SmartIcon with your mouse to have that task accomplished. Don't know what the little SmartIcon graphics represent? Just click and hold your right mouse button when your pointer is over a SmartIcon, and the SmartIcon's description and keyboard shortcut are displayed in the cc:Mail title bar. If you don't have the SmartIcons palette displayed when you're in cc:Mail, or if you don't get a short description of the SmartIcon after you click the right mouse button, check out Chapter 15.

Status bar

At the bottom of cc:Mail is the status bar. It holds information about how many read and unread messages are in your Inbox, how many read and unread messages are in all of your folders, and how many read and unread messages are in all of your bulletin boards. You can click any of these buttons with your mouse to have cc:Mail update the number of currently read and unread items. On this bar, farther to the right, is the current date and time (unless the clock on your computer is wrong, in which case both the time and date shown will be wrong, too). At the far right is a representation of the SmartIcons palette that lets you change displayed palettes quickly.

Title bar

The stately title bar sits atop each window and serves as a handgrip for the window, enabling you to pick up and move the window around the Windows desktop with the mouse. The title bar lists the current application or window name. If you are working within a window, the title bar of this window is a different color from that of any other open window. This different color indicates that the window is active, so you know which window you are currently working in. By double-clicking the title bar, you maximize the window or restore the window's size.

Window edge or corner

Moving the mouse-pointer arrow to any corner of a nonmaximized window changes the normal mouse arrow to a genetically altered, two-headed arrow. This two-headed arrow lets you resize the window either vertically or horizontally. If you move this two-headed arrow to a window edge, it lets you change the window edge or corner window both vertically and horizontally at the same time. Click and hold down the left mouse button with this arrow to change the window's dimensions.

Workspace

This is the inner part of the window where you move, copy, make, or break mail.

The Mailbox window

As you probably noticed already, the Mailbox window is just a part of the Application window. (You might say that the Mailbox window sort of has a parasitic relationship with the Application window.) This Mailbox window, though, is where you'll do your real work in cc:Mail. Take a look at Figure 1-3, which shows elements of the Mailbox window.

Pane slider   Column widths

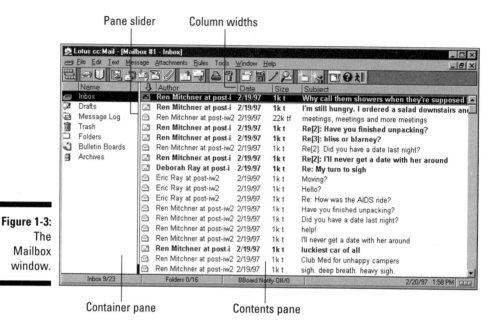

Figure 1-3:
The
Mailbox
window.

Container pane   Contents pane

The Mailbox Window is composed of two panes: the Container pane and the Contents pane. You can move between the two panes by clicking in the panes or by pressing F6. You'll notice that it seems as though both the Container pane and the Contents pane are selected because they both have a black bar in them. Au contraire! If you look carefully, you'll see that only one pane is selected (the active item); the active item is the black bar with a white border around it. Be sure you've selected the correct pane before you issue any other command, or you may find yourself somewhere you didn't intend to be!

Above each pane is a set of movable columns (called column widths) that contain information about the column beneath it. Panes are separated by a movable border called a pane slider.

If you have problems with using panes, don't sweat it. They can be real PITAs (Panes In The Application). Seriously, they're more specifically discussed in the following sections, at which time everything will become clear.

The Container pane

Think of the Container pane, shown in Figure 1-4, as a file cabinet that has seven drawers (or containers) — Inbox, Drafts, Message Log, Trash, Folders, Bulletin Boards, and Archives.

Container names — Unread messages

Icons — Totals — Path

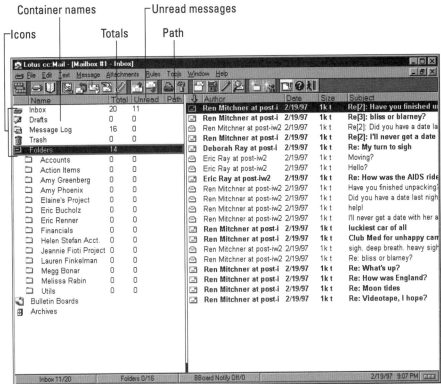

Figure 1-4:
The
Container
pane.

You'll notice that some of the container icons might show a plus (+) sign or a minus (–) sign. The plus sign indicates that a container is hiding other containers. For example, the Folders container might have other folders within it, or the Archives container might hold several categories of archived information. These folders might also have a minus sign, indicating that everything within the container is showing.

You can expand or collapse these containers either individually or all at one time:

✔ To expand or collapse one of these containers, double-click the container icon. From the menu bar, you can also go to View⇨Expand (to expand a single selected container) or View⇨Collapse (to collapse a single container).

✔ To expand all the containers inside of the Container pane simultaneously, select View⇨Expand All from the menu bar or use the Ctrl++ (Control + plus) key combination. To collapse all the containers simultaneously, select View⇨Collapse All from the menu bar or use the Ctrl+– key combination.

✔ When you expand the Folders container, the closed-folder icon changes to an open-folder icon with all the folders it contains neatly arranged underneath it. When you expand the Bulletin Board container, the icon changes slightly, and all the bulletin boards are displayed neatly beneath it. When you expand the Archives container, the file cabinet icon displays a bunch of file cabinets neatly beneath it representing archived folders.

✔ After you expand a container, you must open the folder, bulletin board, or archive underneath it to see the messages contained therein. Just think of opening a filing cabinet, finding the folder you want, opening the folder, seeing the memo you want, pulling it out, and reading it.

Each container serves a specific purpose, described in detail in the following section.

The Inbox container

The Inbox container lists all the new messages that have arrived (either read or unread). When you start cc:Mail, the Inbox icon should look empty, and its contents should be displayed in the Contents pane of the Mailbox window. Why? Because the Inbox (to use the desktop metaphor) is the place where all your work piles up until you have a chance to get to it. At any time, you can double-click the Inbox icon (or press Ctrl+I on the keyboard) to open it and refresh the contents of your Inbox.

Next to each message in the Inbox container is an icon that will help you determine the contents of the message.

✔ An unopened envelope represents an unread message with normal priority. The icon is yellow, and the line that the icon sits on is blue to let you know that the message hasn't been read yet. The message contains either good news or bad news. Because you're at work, well, you get the idea.

✔ An open envelope represents a previously opened message of normal priority. At this point, you probably know whether the news it contains is good or bad.

✔ An open envelope with a letter sticking out represents an open letter.

✔ A high-priority message, if it's unopened, appears as a red letter with a black exclamation point in the center. If the letter has been opened, the exclamation point is red. This is hot, hot, hot, and the message probably should be read right away. On the other hand, the message could just contain a burning question about last night's *Seinfeld* rerun.

✔ A low-priority message, if it's unopened, appears as a gray envelope with a blue downward-pointing arrow at its center. You can hold off on reading this message until you're done with lunch — or longer, depending on who sent it.

It's a good idea to move your messages to other containers after you've had a chance to read them. As with the real-world inbox on your desk, if you don't do something with the messages in your cc:Mail Inbox, you'll end up with an overflowing mess. Keep reading to see which containers are right for your old messages.

The Drafts container

The Drafts container is where you store messages that you didn't quite finish composing. It's very handy when you're working on a mail message, and in the middle of your grand creation, your boss walks in to remind you that you're late for the 2 p.m. meeting. You can save the message to the Drafts container, look at the message later to see if you want to send it then, or wait and send it after you've had a chance to finish it.

The Drafts container has to be turned on by the administrator at your cc:Mail post office, and you must also have the Drafts container turned on at your computer for it to work.

For the complete lowdown on the Drafts container, see Chapter 12.

The Message Log container

The Message Log container keeps track of all the messages that you have sent by keeping a copy of every outgoing message. The Message Log container is like having your very own copy machine to copy every message that leaves your desk. It can be very handy when there may be differing points of view about whether the Zebra contract went out on time. All you have to do is look into your Message Log container to see whether the Zebra contract was sent by you, when it was sent, to whom it went, and what it said. In other words, the Message Log container is the ultimate Cover-Your-Butt agent.

The Message Log container has to be turned on by the administrator at your cc:Mail post office, and it must also be turned on at your computer. For all the notes on the Message Log container, take a look at Chapter 12.

The Trash container

The Trash container is also known as the circular file, the basketball hoop, and the void of no return. The Trash container is similar to the wastebasket under your desk in that it is where the trash goes, but there's one big difference: If you suddenly realize you really do need that message Bill sent you last week with the numbers on the Zebra contract, you can resurrect that message from the cc:Mail Trash container.

The Trash container has to be turned on by the administrator at your cc:Mail post office, and you must also have it turned on at your computer for it to work. For all the dirt on the Trash container, take a look at Chapter 12.

The Folders container

The Folders container is like one big folder that holds other folders. It holds all the folders you may create over time for certain projects, jobs, and contracts, just to name a few. Just think: You can have one folder for all the mail received about the Zebra project, another folder for all the mail regarding the Zimmerman contract, and yet another folder to store all those jokes from Zed down the hall.

One drawback to cc:Mail folders is that you can't create what's called a nested folder, a folder within a folder. Nested folders would be nice, but cc:Mail 6 just can't create them. For all the info on the Folders container, see Chapter 13.

The Bulletin Boards container

Just like real bulletin boards that hang in the lunchroom, the Bulletin Boards container is designed for posting information that is for general consumption. Bulletins regarding employee benefits, classified ads, and company meetings are usually posted here. Bulletin boards are created and maintained by the cc:Mail administrator. Depending on how they're set up, you might be able to post to bulletin boards, or you might only be able to read them.

The Archives container

The Archives container is usually used for storing messages that, although old, are necessary (or at least you thought so at the time you saved those messages). The only difference between the Folders container and the Archives container is that the messages stored in the Folders container are on the cc:Mail server (that machine that the cc:Mail administrator takes care of and keeps locked up in a room all its own), whereas the messages that are in the Archives container are on your local computer at your desk, or on a disk (your choice).

The same problem that plagues the Folders container also plagues the Archives container: You can't create a nested folder within an Archives folder. Archives have some other drawbacks as well, but they're good for their intended purpose. For all the stored info on the Archives container, peek at Chapter 13.

The Contents pane

The Contents pane is where the real day-to-day action occurs — it's where your mail is kept and where you view the contents of all the containers. Like the Container pane, the Contents pane has five columns, shown in Figure 1-5.

✔ Icon column shows the icons for the messages and also sorts messages.

✔ Author column shows who sent the message.

✔ Date column shows when the message was sent to you.

✔ Size column shows the size of the file in kilobytes; also shows what kind of attachment may be tagging along with the message.

✔ Subject column shows the subject of the message (that is, if the author of the message entered a topic in the subject line of the message).

Column widths

Above both the Contents pane and the Container pane are the column widths. The column widths are just that — they determine the size of the columns of information within the Contents pane and the Container pane. You may want to change the size of the columns at a given time to see more or less of what's in that column.

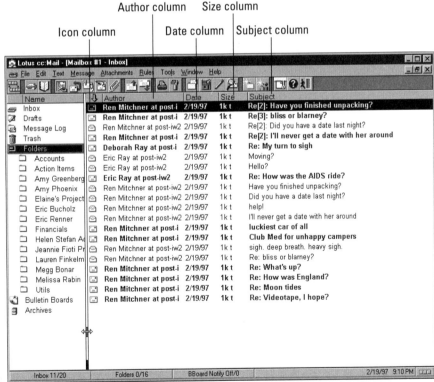

Figure 1-5:
The
Contents
pane.

To change the column width, just follow these quick steps:

1. **Move your mouse pointer up to the column bar that separates two column headers.**

   Your arrow should change to a double arrow (two opposing arrows with a vertical bar in between) when you're in the right spot.

2. **Click and hold the left button on your mouse and move the mouse either left or right.**

   When you do this, a vertical bar will appear so that you can position the column exactly where you want it.

3. **Release the mouse button.**

If you like where you've put the column widths, you need to save that information in cc:Mail by pressing Shift+F2. Or you can also use the mouse to click the control-menu box in the upper-left corner of the Mailbox window. Then click either Save Window Defaults <u>N</u>ow or Save Window Defaults <u>o</u>n Exit.

The pane slider

Between the Container pane and the Contents pane is what is known as the pane slider. (Sounds slick, huh? Impress your friends with this bit of arcane knowledge.) The pane slider is used to give you more of a gander into either the Container pane or the Contents pane. (I usually have it so that the pane slider sits about a quarter of the screen over from the left.)

To move the pane slider around, move the mouse over to the pane slider until the regular arrow turns into a kind of two-dimensional representation of one of the jacks used in a kids' game. (Now wasn't that a long time ago? Unless, of course, you have kids, and you recently stepped on one — a jack, not a kid.) Just click and hold the left mouse button and slide the slider either to the left or to the right until you can see enough of the pane you want, and then release the mouse button.

If you like where you've put the pane slider, you need to save that information in cc:Mail by pressing Shift+F2. Or you can also use the mouse to click the control-menu box in the upper-left corner of the Mailbox window. Then click either Save Window Defaults <u>N</u>ow or Save Window Defaults <u>o</u>n Exit.

Okay. That's the scoop on the cc:Mail interface. Read on to find out how to quit cc:Mail.

Quitting cc:Mail

When you're finished using cc:Mail, you close it the same way you close any other Windows program.

 ✔ Press Alt+F4.

 ✔ Double-click the control-menu box (in the very-most-upper-left-hand corner of cc:Mail).

 ✔ Click the close button (in the very-most-upper-right-hand corner of cc:Mail, if you're using Windows 95).

After you use one of those methods to close the program, cc:Mail prompts you to be sure you really want to exit. Click Yes or press the Enter key to exit. If you're having second thoughts, just click No.

Sometimes when you're trying to exit cc:Mail, you may get a pesky Modified Message dialog box, shown in Figure 1-6, telling you that a message has been changed and offering you the choice of Save Draft, Send, or Close Message and Discard Changes. The error messages just mean that you have an unfinished cc:Mail message (one that you started writing but didn't send) floating around.

Figure 1-6:
The
Modified
Message
dialog box.

Here's what to do:

1. Choose one of the following:

  • Click Cancel to stop cc:Mail from closing. The dialog box will disappear and cc:Mail will still be running, with your message probably hidden under some other window.

  • Click Save Draft to keep the message for completion later. You'll find the message in the Drafts folder.

  • Click Send (to do the obvious).

  • Click Close Message and Discard Changes if you really want to kiss all of your work good-bye without saving it. (I personally wouldn't do this, but hey, it's your work.)

2. Click the Window menu (or press Alt+W to activate the <u>W</u>indow selection on the menu bar).

At the bottom of the drop-down list is a list that shows the names of all the currently active windows. One of these listed names will be the message you were working on; select the message and close (or send or store) it. Continue to select windows and close them until you've closed all the open windows. That would leave the Inbox as the only selection left, confirming that all the open windows have been closed.

3. Try again to close cc:Mail.

Never, *but never,* quit cc:Mail or Windows by just turning off your computer's power switch. In Windows etiquette, just turning the system off is like knocking the boss's drink into his or her lap at a cocktail party. It's not a pleasant sight, and it's not good for your career. If you first exit cc:Mail and then choose Shut Down from the Start menu (exit Windows) before you turn off your computer's power switch, you, your boss, and your cc:Mail administrator will all lead happier lives.

By the way, if you have unfinished messages at the end of the day and you just don't want to deal with them at that time, save them to the Drafts container before exiting cc:Mail. Then exit Windows and turn off your computer.

Now, about that late night "Oh, by the way, I've been working really really hard" message to your boss . . .

Chapter 2
Getting Help

In This Chapter

▶ Using online help

▶ Getting help from your cc:Mail administrator

▶ Getting help on the Web

▶ Getting help from a listserv list

*W*hat is a good help system, you ask? Well, it answers your questions with a minimum of fuss and doesn't get your shirt dirty in the process.

This chapter describes different ways of getting cc:Mail help features (when you can't find this book, of course). You'll find information about the cc:Mail online help, help from your cc:Mail administrator, help on the World Wide Web, and help through a listserv list. Everything except "Help Me Rhonda."

You can always get to the help system in cc:Mail by pressing the F1 key when cc:Mail is the active, highlighted application on your Windows desktop.

Using Online Help

When you find yourself dealing with one of those problems that has you scratching your head (like Gilligan after the Skipper tells him that he needs to work with the Professor on building a small, portable cold fusion reactor), check out cc:Mail's online help.

Quick note here — after you start help, you'll probably eventually want to get out of it, so here's the scoop: You can exit the Help window by double-clicking the control-menu box in the upper-left corner of the Help window or by using the Alt+F4 key combination when the Help window is the active window. If you're using Windows 95, you can also click the Close button in the upper-right corner of the window to close it quickly.

To get cc:Mail help, go to Help on the menu bar, and you'll see a drop-down menu, shown in Figure 2-1.

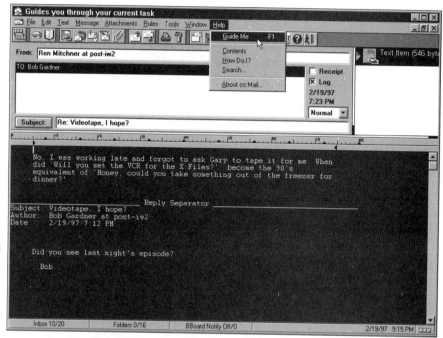

Figure 2-1:
The drop-
down Help
menu.

This menu gives several different ways of getting to help, but the actual information is the same throughout. It's kind of like entering your house through the front door, garage, or kitchen window. Once you get in, the same old stuff is there. The following sections describe each of the menu options.

Using Guide Me

Selecting Help⇨Guide Me brings up a help screen, shown in Figure 2-2, with help topics that you can choose. These help topics are pretty generic and focused on what you will most likely need to do. They're also less fun and less comprehensive than what's in this book (although they address basically the same information). Guide Me is also the first screen you see when you press F1 for help.

To use Guide Me help, just click one of the topics to link to more information.

Using Contents

Selecting Contents brings up a list of general cc:Mail topics to choose from, shown in Figure 2-3. It's a table of contents (hence the name) for the whole cc:Mail help system.

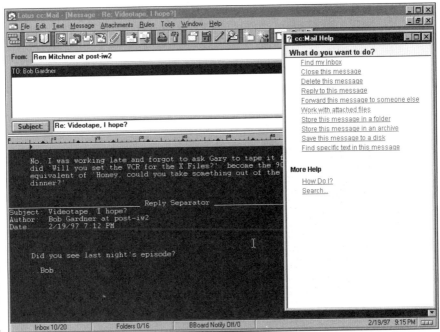

Figure 2-2:
The Guide
Me screen.

Figure 2-3:
The
Contents
dialog box.

All you have to do is choose a topic you want more information about, click the icon once, and then click the topic from the list that appears. If you don't see a promising topic and want to get rid of the little pop-up menu, just click outside the pop-up menu or click a different icon.

You can also get to the Contents page by clicking the Contents button on any help screen.

Using How Do I?

The How Do I screen, accessed through Help➪How Do I, is just another help screen with information about common cc:Mail tasks. Take a look at Figure 2-4.

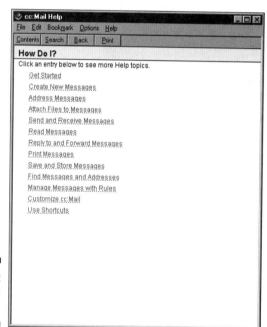

Figure 2-4:
The How Do
I screen.

Using Search

The Search screen is accessed by — you guessed it—going to Help➪Search. This screen, though, is a bit different because it lets you search for information by using an index of topics or by entering keywords and searching for them. Figure 2-5 shows the Search screen.

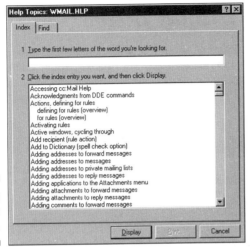

Figure 2-5:
The Search
screen.

In the Index tab, just Type the first part of the word you're searching for. In the bottom section of the window (Click the index entry . . .) you'll see the list of topics that match what you've typed. Scan through the list for something that looks promising and then double-click it (or click once to select it and click the Display button).

The Index tab lets you search through the text in the help files, rather than key on specific words, so it's likely to be slightly more complete and to offer many more choices. Try Index first and then Find if Index doesn't get you the information you need.

In the Find tab, just type the word or words you want to find. Then select appropriate terms from the middle pane to narrow the search. Finally, double-click topics from the bottom of the dialog box (or click once on a topic and click Display).

Using About cc:Mail

Help⇨About cc:Mail shows information about your particular version of cc:Mail as well as the post office and directory you use. Your help desk or cc:Mail administrator might ask you to go to this dialog box to verify and report on some information. Unless you're just curious, there's nothing else here that's of interest.

Navigating Help Dialog Boxes

When you select one of these menu items, you'll be whisked away to a Help dialog box that will give you further Help options to choose from.

Anyway, at the top of all these dialog boxes are a menu bar and a button bar, shown in Figure 2-6.

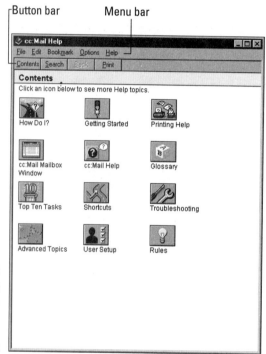

Figure 2-6:
The menu
bar and
button bar.

The menu bar functions similarly to menu bars in other Windows applications. You might take a peek at them if you want, but it's pretty standard. The command buttons, on the other hand, serve specific purposes that are worth a few words, at least. Take a look at Table 2-1.

Table 2-1	Help Command Buttons
Button	*Function*
Contents	This command button brings up the table of contents for the help file. (See "Using Contents" earlier.)
Search	This command button brings up a Search dialog box. (See "Using Search" earlier.)

Button	Function
<u>B</u>ack	This command button lets you backtrack through the help system after you have lost your way on the help path. This option is grayed out if you haven't gone anywhere in the help system yet.
<u>P</u>rint	This command lets you — well — print the topic that's on your screen.

Reaching Your cc:Mail Administrator

Your cc:Mail administrator is probably the next best resource if you have questions. Many situations that come up when you're using cc:Mail are controlled by your local configuration, so generic help won't be as useful as the personalized variety from your administrator. You might tack a note on your wall that has the following information on it:

- ✔ cc:Mail administrator's name
- ✔ Phone number
- ✔ Fax number
- ✔ Pager number
- ✔ Preferred snack
- ✔ Good times to call

Finding Help on the Internet

First, even putting in this section is evidence that I'm a belt *and* suspenders type of guy. It's highly unlikely that you'll encounter any cc:Mail situations that this book won't cover in exhaustive detail. It's even more unlikely that a situation will also stump the cc:Mail help system and your cc:Mail administrator (a.k.a. Your Personal Demi-Deity of All Things cc:Mail). However, if you end up needing more information, you can probably find everything you need on the Internet.

Using the cc:Mail Web site

The cc:Mail Web site, officially sanctioned and sponsored by Lotus/IBM, is the definitive source for cc:Mail information. In addition to the normal propaganda and news and demos that usually populate Web sites, Lotus is kind enough to provide an easily searchable interface to its Knowledge bBase (with product support questions and answers).

To try out the Web site and browse through the (generally useful and always voluminous) information, just fire up your Web browser and connect to http://www.ccmail.com/.

Note: If you don't have an Internet connection and Web browser, you won't be able to get to this Internet help. No problem. Just ask your cc:Mail administrator (but point out that you'd have been helping yourself if you'd only had Web access).

If you don't want to bother with the fluff and just want to head straight for the good stuff, try http://www.ccmail.com/support/base.htm.

This site lets you use real English to search for information from the cc:Mail support archives. Pretty cool, huh? As of press time, the search page looked like Figure 2-7.

All you have to do is type your question into the Ask Your Question field and click Search. Then click to select any of the possible answers from the following screen.

Keep in mind that Web sites change as often as most people change their underwear, so the addresses might change slightly and the information available might differ from what was available at the time of this writing.

Figure 2-7:
Search for
cc:Mail
help at
this site.

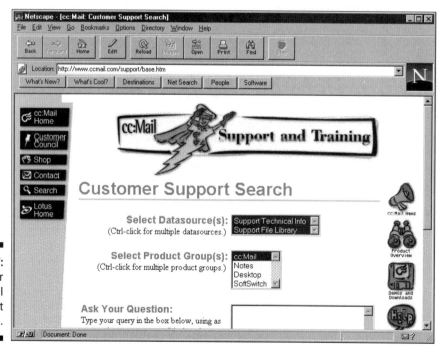

Using the cc:Mail listserv list

If you have a problem that just seems to defy solution, or, more likely, if you take something to your cc:Mail administrator and stump him or her too, there's a great brain trust out there on the Internet. It's a listserv list (fancy Internet-ese for discussion group) for cc:Mail. In general, probably because cc:Mail is so easy to use, the list focuses primarily on administration and configuration issues, but it is a good resource for those really confusing questions. For the full scoop, you might search the archives (strongly recommended) or just browse through the messages. Just point your Web browser to

`http://listserv.okstate.edu/archives/ccmail-l.html`.

If you've decided that you just have to get your cc:Mail listserv fix every day, you can subscribe to the list. All the messages sent to the list will end up in your e-mail box. The name of the list is `ccMail-L@listserv.okstate.edu`.

Refer to Chapter 8 for the full scoop on sending e-mail messages.

Here's some general information about using the cc:Mail listserv list:

- To subscribe, send an e-mail message to `listserv@listserv.okstate.edu`. You can just leave the subject line blank. In the body of the message, write

  ```
  subscribe ccMail-l Billy Shakespeare
  ```

  You would, of course, put your name in place of Billy Shakespeare. Don't put any other information — a computer reads the message, and words like *please* just confuse the bejabbers out of the computer.

- To send questions or answers to the list (yes, you can answer questions too), just send e-mail to `ccMail-l@listserv.okstate.edu`.

- If you've had all the cc:Mail list you can stand, sign off the list with another message to `listserv@listserv.okstate.edu`. In the body of the message, put

  ```
  signoff ccMail-l
  ```

- If you have questions or problems, you can contact a real person at `ccMail-l-request@listserv.okstate.edu`.

Part II
Reading Your Mail

The 5th Wave   By Rich Tennant

"No thanks. But I would like to check my e-mail."

In this part . . .

Although the excitement of getting new messages in cc:Mail doesn't quite compare to the excitement of getting letters (and I'm not talking about junk mail or bills here!) from your postal carrier, it's still kind of fun — like unwrapping presents or buying the miscellaneous junk bags at a rummage sale. This part introduces you to all of the different unwrapping techniques you could want. You won't be missing anything except paper cuts and Christmas bows stuck in your hair.

Chapter 3
Bringing In the Mail

· ·

In This Chapter

▶ Finding your Inbox

▶ Opening and reading messages

▶ Navigating your piles of messages

▶ Selecting multiple messages to read

▶ Using bulletin boards

· ·

*B*y now, you may have figured out that cc:Mail is practically invaluable at the office. It's paperless; it doesn't take up much disk space; it's fun to look at. It's odorless, colorless — and even tasteless if you happen to send a rude message to someone (which, of course, you never heard me say). Heck, cc:Mail can even help you look busy when the boss walks by.

This chapter focuses on getting messages — rude and otherwise — that other people send to you.

Getting to Your Inbox

The advent of the cc:Mail Inbox is even more remarkable than your United States Postal Service mailbox. With the Postal Service, you still have to go out to your mailbox, open it, retrieve your mail, and go back to your house. With cc:Mail, you don't even have to leave your office to get mail. Your mail is delivered right to your computer, where you don't have to brave the wind, rain, and snow to get your messages. Well, if you do have to brave the wind, rain, and snow to get your cc:Mail messages, you may want to place an emergency call to the maintenance department.

The first step in reading your messages is getting to your *Inbox*. Think of your cc:Mail Inbox as being similar to the real one that sits on the corner of your desk. People who want to give you messages, files, or other information sneak into your office when you're not looking and plunk their missives into your inbox for you to deal with. The cc:Mail Inbox works in the same way. It's a receptacle for e-mail messages; it's where the little e-mail fairy puts electronic messages and files addressed to you.

To get to your Inbox, you have to start cc:Mail and get past that annoying Unread Messages dialog box, shown in Figure 3-1.

Figure 3-1
The Unread
Messages
dialog box.

The Unread Messages dialog box announces how many messages are in your Inbox that have not been read. This number includes messages that have been delivered to your box since you closed cc:Mail as well as previously delivered messages you didn't read. The Unread Messages dialog box is particularly handy for those of us who like to know how many messages they're going to have to wade through. And I'll bet that the same people who developed the Unread Messages dialog box also own cars that say, "Your door is ajar" every time they open the door — you know, the kind that just make you want to scream, "No! It's a door — not a jar!"

In any case, all you have to do to get past the Unread Messages dialog box is click OK. Then, finally, you'll be at your Inbox, which looks something like Figure 3-2.

Notice that your Inbox is divided into two panes. The left (container) pane contains all the folders and files that help you sort your mail. The right pane lists the messages you have in your Inbox, which is what we focus on in the rest of this section. If you want specific information about panes, see Chapter 1.

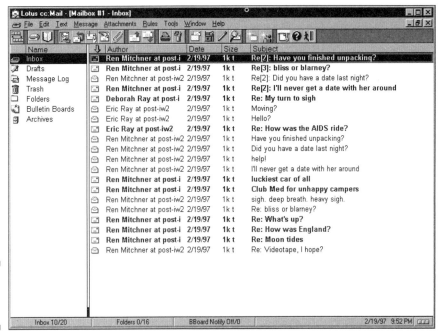

Figure 3-2:
The cc:Mail
Inbox.

Getting rid of that pesky
Unread Messages dialog box

Tired of cc:Mail reminding you that you have 2,347,890 unread messages? Well, one option would be to read your messages. Or if you don't want to do that, you can fool yourself into thinking that you don't have any unread messages by disabling the Unread Messages dialog box. Here's how:

1. **Go to Tools⇨User Setup.**

   The User Setup dialog box appears.

2. **Under Preferences:, scroll down to Notify and double-click the Notify icon.**

   The Notification options appear on the right side of the User Setup dialog box.

3. **Click (uncheck) the check box next to Notify Dialog.**

4. **Click OK.**

Now when you start cc:Mail, you won't be notified of how many unread messages you have. If you're really sick and tired of being notified of new messages — period! — you could just disable the whole new message notification business by unchecking the box next to Enable New Message Notification. Doing so will keep cc:Mail from dinging, flashing, or giving you dialog boxes informing you about new messages. However, if you do that, cc:Mail won't even check to see if you have new mail. A reasonable compromise might be to *uncheck* each form of notification (Notify Dialog, Flash Window, and Tone) but leave the Enable New Message Notification checked.

Unread messages look a bit different from read messages. Unread messages appear with yellow envelope icons at the left of the pane, and the message's author, subject, and similar information in boldface type. Read messages still appear in your Inbox — until you file them or delete them — but their little envelopes are white, and the typefaces are normal.

In addition to being able to see whether you've read a message or not, you also have some other information. You can tell who sent the message (Author), when it was sent (Date), how big the file is (Size), and what the message is about (Subject). Having this information is handy, for example, when deciding which message to read first. Many people take a look at the author and subject to decide how important a message is — after all, messages about the golf game on Saturday are far more pressing than messages about the staff meeting time change. Some people, though, look at the size and date to determine which message to read first. For example, you may wait until your lunch hour to read a message that's 35K (which is really long — about 17 pages), or you may read yesterday's messages before you read today's messages so you don't miss anything.

The Size column offers additional information about the message. If you look closely, you see a letter or two next to the file size, such as the ones shown in Figure 3-3.

Size column

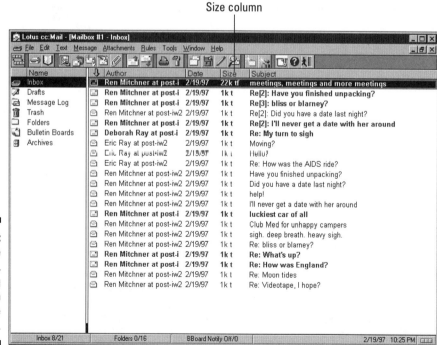

Figure 3-3:
The Size
column,
indicating
information
about the
message.

Here's what the letters mean:

- ✔ *t* means that the message is a text message. If someone has attached a file, for example, but didn't type anything in the message area, the *t* won't be present.

- ✔ *f* means that there's a file attached to the message.

- ✔ *g* means that there's a graphic attached.

- ✔ *x* means that there's a fax attached.

After you've found your way around your cc:Mail Inbox, you probably want to read your messages. The following sections tell you how to select and read messages as well as organize your Inbox window. In the meantime, here are some thoughts to ponder about the cc:Mail Inbox:

- ✔ cc:Mail checks for messages (this is called refreshing your screen) at a specified interval, provided you haven't disabled new message notification. If you have disabled new message notification and want to retrieve any new messages, double-click the Inbox in the Container pane (it's in the upper left of your cc:Mail real estate).

- ✔ You can change the interval at which cc:Mail refreshes your screen by going to Tools⇨User Setup and clicking the Notify icon. Under Options, you can change the number in the text field to reflect how often you want to check for messages (make sure that Enable New Message Notification is checked).

- ✔ If you want to check for messages in between the intervals at which cc:Mail checks for you, all you have to do is double-click the Inbox in the Container pane (in the upper left).

- ✔ If you're using cc:Mail Mobile and want to check for messages in between intervals, you have to reestablish a connection. Remember that when cc:Mail Mobile refreshes your Inbox, it connects, retrieves your messages, and then disconnects. Take a look at Part V for more information on cc:Mail Mobile.

- ✔ If you've been cruising through different cc:Mail features and seem to have lost your Inbox, click the Inbox icon in the toolbar or go to the menu bar and click Window⇨Go to Inbox.

- ✔ You can adjust the width of the container panes — for example, you may want to make the right pane wider so that you can see more of the subject information. All you have to do is hover your cursor over the border between the panes. You see the pointer turn into a double arrow. Click (and hold the mouse button down) and drag the pane to the location you want. That's it! Likewise, you can change the size of the Author, Date, Size, and Subject columns by hovering over the line between each of the sections, clicking and holding, and dragging the border over to where you want it. Press Shift+F2 to save your settings.

Reading Messages

Reading messages in cc:Mail is easy — way easier than ripping open an envelope and unfolding the pages. You'll probably start by reading messages from your Inbox (because that's where new messages arrive), but you can do the same thing to read messages from folders or archives or even bulletin boards.

All you have to do is double-click the message you want to read. A message window appears on your screen, such as the one shown in Figure 3-4.

From the message window, you can tell a lot about the message without even reading it. Among other things, you can see who got copies of the message, whether the author was sent a return receipt, what priority the message is, and how many bytes long the message is. In short, you have a lot of information about the message beyond the message text itself — for example, if you see that your boss got a copy of the message, you may assume that the sender was using CYA (Cover Your Appendages) tactics. Similarly, if you see that the message is high-priority, you'll probably want to go ahead and read the message. You get the idea.

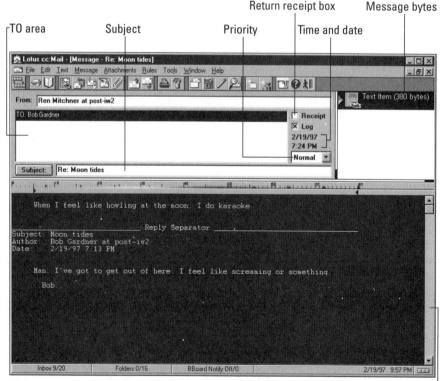

Figure 3-4:
The
message
window.

Here are some other magnificent tidbits of information about reading cc:Mail messages:

- ✔ If the message is longer than a screen's length, you can use the vertical scroll bar or the PgDn key or even the down-arrow key to read through the message.

- ✔ If the message is wider than the message area, you can use the horizontal scroll bar to read the long lines. Or, you can click your mouse on a long line and press the End key, then press the Home key to return to the beginning of the line.

- ✔ If you're reading messages from an archive or bulletin board, you won't be able to delete messages, although everything else will be normal. See Chapter 13 for more information about archives.

Navigating Messages

When you're slogging through a bunch of messages, you have several options that can help make your life a bit easier. In fact, cc:Mail provides you with a slew of different ways of navigating your messages. The best way to experiment with these is to open up (by double-clicking) a message from somewhere in the middle of your Inbox.

What, you say? There's more to reading mail than just opening an individual message, reading it, closing it, and then opening up another message? What will they come up with next? Actually, the open, read, close method is tried-and-true, but tedious, particularly if you get lots of messages.

Those in the know about cc:Mail get clever with their reading process by first selecting the Read Message SmartIcon set. Click the SmartIcon button on the status bar (that's in the very lower right of your cc:Mail program window) and select Read Message, or click the Switch SmartIcon Set SmartIcon button until you see a SmartIcon bar like the one in Figure 3-5.

Figure 3-5:
The Read
Message
SmartIcon
set.

Equipped with these SmartIcons, you'll go through your messages faster than a hot knife through butter.

Before you dive into reading your messages, I have a suggestion, born of experience. cc:Mail has a trash can feature that holds onto messages after you delete them. If you find that you accidentally deleted something you really need, you can retrieve it from the trash can. For some strange reason, cc:Mail's default setting is to *not* have this trash-retrieval feature enabled, so anything you delete is gone. Really gone. Like a snowball in Arizona in July. I'd suggest that you go to Tools⇨User Setup, click Special Folders on the left side of the dialog box and under the Trash section, click Ena<u>b</u>le. For the time being, just leave Ne<u>v</u>er Empty — the default — selected. Click OK to return to the regularly scheduled program.

If trash retrieval doesn't seem to work or the Ena<u>b</u>le menu item is grayed out, see your Administrator. The Administrator may have disabled this function at the server (hey, stranger things have happened).

Now that we've got the preliminaries taken care of, it's time to read your messages.

A quick way to navigate messages is to open a message, read it, then immediately view the next message in the Inbox — hence, skipping the going-back-to-the-Inbox step. To do this, double-click a message you want to read, read the message, then click the View next message SmartIcon once or press Alt+→(that is, Alt+right-arrow key).

If you want to backtrack, you can read a message, then click the View previous message SmartIcon once or press Alt+←(that is, Alt+left-arrow key).

Many times you'll find, as soon as you read a message, that it should be consigned to the trash can forthwith. (I've always wanted to use that word in a sentence, ever since ninth-grade English.) If it's time to go, it's time to go. Just read the message, then click the Delete SmartIcon once. You then return to the Inbox, where the next message will be highlighted.

If you get on a roll throwing that mail away, you can also open a message, read it, delete it, then immediately go to the next message in the Inbox — again, skipping over the going-back-to-the-Inbox step. All you have to do is double-click the message you want to read, read it, then click the Delete this message, view next one SmartIcon once or press Ctrl+Alt+→ (that is, Ctrl+Alt+right-arrow key).

Of course, you can also backtrack in the throwing-everything-away mode by clicking once on the Delete this message, view previous one SmartIcon or pressing Ctrl+Alt+←(that is, Ctrl+Alt+left arrow key).

Zowie! Those SmartIcons will have you done with your mail and ready to get to real work in no time flat. Here are a few additional thoughts about navigating through your collection of mail.

✔ If you like that delete-and-move-to-the-next-message business, you may consider disabling the Confirm to Delete dialog box. Because you enabled the trash can (you did, didn't you?), you have a second chance if you mess up, so why let a little dialog box slow you down? Go to Tools⇨User Setup, Confirmation on the left, and uncheck Confirm to Delete a Message. Click OK.

✔ If you get so much mail that even these tips don't give you a respite, you need to check into more-automated ways of managing your mail in Chapter 16. Just as a hint, you can set rules to automatically process incoming mail — for example, anything with "Project X" in the subject goes in the Project X folder, anything from your boss makes the computer beep at you and remind you that you just got a message from the Big Cheese, and anything with "donation" or "United Way" in the subject line goes straight to the trash without passing Go.

✔ By default, cc:Mail sorts messages by date with the last one in on the top. If you'd rather have the oldest at the top and the newest at the bottom, just click the arrow at the top-left corner of the Inbox message pane to reverse the order. Click again to re-reverse the order. If you like the reverse order better, press Shift+F2 to save it.

Selecting Multiple Messages to Read

The developers at Lotus built in this nifty feature that lets you select multiple messages. This feature is particularly handy, say, if you get a ton of messages every morning but only want to read a few right off. All you have to do is read through the list of messages and select messages as you're going through. Here's how:

1. **Scroll to the top of your Inbox.**

2. **Click once on a message you want to read.**

   The message is highlighted.

3. **Press (and hold down) the Ctrl key.**

4. **While you're holding down the Ctrl key, click another message you want to read.**

   You now see two highlighted messages.

5. **Repeat Step 4 until you've selected all the messages you want to read.**

   Figure 3-6 shows a sample of multiple messages selected.

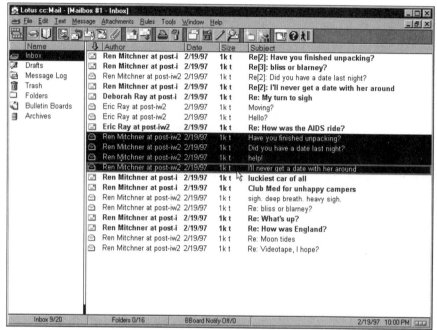

Figure 3-6:
Multiple
messages
selected.

6. **Place the mouse pointer somewhere on one of the selected messages and double-click (while you're still holding down the Ctrl key).**

   The messages open, with the first message from the list on top and the subsequent messages following in the same order as they were on the Inbox list.

   Figure 3-7 shows multiple messages opened.

   ✔ If there are several consecutive messages that you want to open and read, click once on the first message in the group, press (and hold) the Shift key, and then click once on the last message in the group. (You could start with the last message in the group, press and hold the Shift key, and then click once on the first message in the group, too.) This shortcut lets you select several consecutive messages with only two mouse-clicks rather than selecting the messages individually.

   ✔ Just like Windows, cc:Mail can have multiple windows open at the same time. (You can even minimize the Mailbox or Message window if you so desire.) When you open a message to read and then press Ctrl+I (to refresh the Inbox), you can see that the icon for the message that you just opened has an envelope sticking out of it. That means that the message is still open somewhere beneath the Mailbox window. To find the opened message, click Window, Cascade (on the menu bar) and find all those stray messages. You can also press Alt+W+C to do the same thing from the keyboard, and Shift+F5 is even faster.

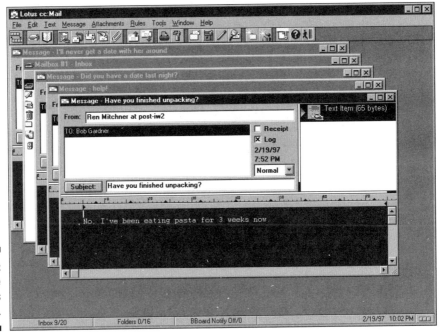

Figure 3-7:
Multiple
messages
opened.

✔ Because of the way that cc:Mail works, it's possible to have multiple copies of the same message hiding beneath the Mailbox window. (Having multiple copies of the same message open can cause a small crisis if you're responding to a message and there's another copy of the same message open.) If you're reading or composing messages, be sure that you don't reopen a message that you've already opened once. The icon for an already-open message is an open envelope with a letter sticking out. And check Window on the menu bar to see if there are multiple copies of the same message open. At the bottom of the Window pull-down menu is a list of all open windows; just click the one you want to go to.

Using Bulletin Boards

A *bulletin board* is like a folder that everyone on a post office shares. Messages of interest to a group or to the whole organization get posted there — for example, your administrator may set up bulletin boards for your weekly staff notes.

If your administrator set up bulletin boards for your use, you'll also periodically get messages in your bulletin board folders. Just double-click the Bulletin Boards item in the container pane to open the list, then double-click the bulletin board of your choice. You'll be able to read, store, and print messages from the bulletin boards just as you can from folders or your Inbox. The only difference is that you can't delete messages out of a bulletin board, because the messages are shared for everyone on your post office to use; only the administrator can delete the messages.

Replying to Messages

Replying to a message means to respond to a message that someone sent to you. For example, after your boss sends you a message and requests a response, you have a couple of choices: quit, or reply. Not much of a decision there, huh? You don't have to address the message or anything — cc:Mail takes care of that.

Here's how you reply to mail messages:

1. **Double-click a message in your Inbox or another folder to open it up.**

   Unlike with forwarding, you have to have the message open to reply to it.

2. **Select Message⇨Reply, click the reply icon, or press Ctrl+Y.**

   The Reply dialog box appears, ready for you to provide additional information about the reply, as shown in Figure 3-8.

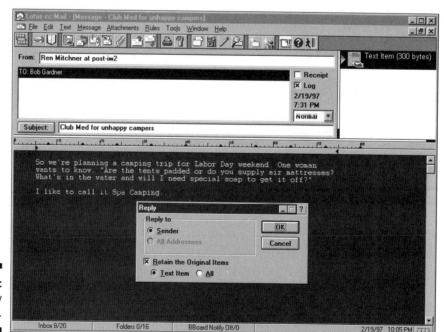

Figure 3-8: The Reply dialog box.

3. Under Reply to, select Sender or All Addressees.

If the original sender sent the message to other people in addition to you, selecting All Addressees sends your reply back to everyone. If you want to send your reply to the Sender only, you can do that too.

4. Select Retain the Original Items to include parts of the original message in your reply.

If you select Text Item, your reply includes only the main body of the message; selecting All retains all attachments from the original message as well.

5. Click OK to get to the reply itself.

6. Add or delete attachments to the message if you choose.

All attachments to the original message may have been retained in the reply, depending on your choice in Step 4. If you want to delete one of the attachments, click the attachment once in the Attachment pane and press Delete.

To add an attachment, use Attachments⇨Files, the Attach icon, or Ctrl+F, and select the file you want to attach. If you want to attach files using other methods, refer to Chapter 6.

7. Add additional text to the message, either above or below the reply Header.

Just sending a reply with no additional text at all can look a little odd, all things considered.

8. When you're finished, send the message by choosing Message⇨Send, Ctrl+S, or the Send icon.

Additional comments about replying to messages:

✔ You can set cc:Mail's reply defaults by selecting Tools⇨User Setup and choosing Message in the left pane. Click to set the default setting to Include Reply Separator (or not), Retain Attachments (or not). If you want to keep those attachments hanging around, you choose Text or All. Additionally, you can set the standard reply to go to Sender or All recipients. These selections determine the default settings in the Reply dialog box, but you'll still be able to choose to include or not to include settings for each individual message.

✔ An important thing to keep in mind when replying to a message is that if you make any changes to a received message while you're reading it but before you click the reply button (to reply to the message), the reply separator line will not appear in the body of the message. This can provide for some confusion when people are replying to each other's messages but don't know where one message ends and another begins.

✔ If you're in the middle of a reply to a message and you decide to just forget about replying (or you get called into an important meeting), you can press the Esc key or use the Ctrl+F4 key combination. When you do this you get a Modified Message dialog box, which lets you choose one of three options by clicking on the option of choice and then pressing the Enter key. You can save the message to the Drafts folder for later completion, just go ahead and send the message anyway (what the heck, it was a bad day to begin with), or choose to go ahead and trash the message and let all of your creative changes go by the wayside. You can also click the Cancel button and complete your reply masterpiece.

✔ Using the Reply command is a great way to get a message back to someone who is on the Internet (but is not a cc:Mail user) without having to know his or her mail address. Just ask that person to send you an e-mail message, reply to the message (replacing the original text in the message with your own), and send it off. You can keep the original message in the Inbox or a folder and just open it and make a reply whenever you want to send a new message.

✔ When you send or receive messages from other cc:Mail users, you'll find that using different colors for text and backgrounds makes it really easy to mark in and comment on messages. You can just scroll down to the middle of the included text in a reply and insert your own comments using, say, black on magenta. Your comments will stand out and everyone will associate you with that garish magenta color. Seriously, different colors do make it much easier to see who said what in messages. See Chapter 10 for more information about color highlighting.

✔ Messages that go from your cc:Mail system to addresses on the Internet lose all of their color attributes. That is, if you make colorful comments within included (reply) text and send the message to the Internet, your recipients are likely to think that your comments are just part of the original text — they won't be able to tell the difference at a glance.

✔ Many mail systems on the Internet provide cool little indicators with replies so that you can see what text was in the original message. Those little indicators look like this:

```
> Some electronic mail programs on the Internet
> clearly indicate what text was quoted.
```

Some even do cute little symbols like this:

```
:-) In the really user-friendly programs
:-) you find reply indicators like these.
```

cc:Mail doesn't do any of that. At all. Sorry! The best you can do is to type in the > manually.

✔ Beware Reply to All! It would probably be a good idea to set your default reply to go to Sender, not to All. The most inconvenient messages tend to be the ones in which your reply to the sender accidentally goes to everyone. For example, suppose your coworker sends you a message telling you about her current project, with a copy to the boss. You reply, commenting that only an idiot would assign anyone such a stupid project. Reply to All, accidentally or not, would clearly be a CLM (Career Limiting Move).

Chapter 4

Using cc:Notify

So you think that the messages you get through cc:Mail are so darned important that you want your computer to jump up and yell at you whenever you get mail? Do you want cc:Mail to jump up and yell at you when you get mail even if cc:Mail isn't open?

If you answered Yes to either of these questions, cc:Notify is the program for you. Just think of cc:Notify as an answering service of sorts. When you use an answering service, you can have someone page you and tell you that you have a call, even if you're not in the office and officially taking calls. cc:Notify is similar — you can tell it to ding you, beep you, or flash you every time you get a message, even if you're not using cc:Mail at the time.

Starting and Configuring cc:Notify

If you're a cc:Mail user, you also have a program called cc:Notify on your computer. cc:Notify is an application that notifies you of incoming cc:Mail messages without having to have cc:Mail open.

Using cc:Notify has a couple of advantages. First, just like cc:Mail, it takes care of notifying you of new messages, but it doesn't take nearly as much memory or space as cc:Mail does. You can easily run cc:Notify in the background and do your regular work — whereas cc:Mail is bulky enough that many users have problems using it at the same time that they're using a couple of other big programs, such as Lotus Notes or Microsoft Word.

Second, you can tell cc:Notify to inform you when other users get mail. This might be a good feature for a departmental secretary to use to manage some of the mailboxes in the department: "Yes, Mr. Smith, your wife did get that picture you sent — it's in her cc:Mail box right now. No, she's in a meeting now. Can she call you at home later?" Used in this way, cc:Notify can help improve e-mail communications within the cc:Mail group.

You start cc:Notify just like you'd start cc:Mail. That is, you can either

- ✔ Double-click the cc:Notify icon in the Lotus Applications program group if you're a Windows 3.1*x* user, or

- ✔ Select Start⇨Programs⇨Lotus Applications⇨cc:Notify if you're a Windows 95 user.

After cc:Notify starts, you see the blank cc:Notify screen, like Figure 4-1.

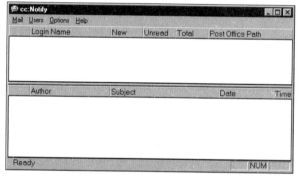

Figure 4-1:
The
cc:Notify
screen.

The first thing you need to do is tell cc:Notify which mailboxes to check on. You do this by adding users to cc:Notify, just as, say, you'd add names to your address book. Here's how:

1. Choose Users⇨Add or press Ctrl+A.

The Add User dialog box appears, as shown in Figure 4-2.

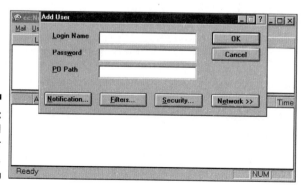

Figure 4-2:
The Add
User
dialog box.

2. Enter the Login Name, Password, and PO Path, just as you do on your cc:Mail login.

You can probably get the login name and P.O. path from the regular cc:Mail Login dialog box for the person whose name you're adding. You'll have to ask the other user for the password. See Chapter 1 for details about logging into cc:Mail.

3. Click Notification to set notification options.

The Notification dialog box appears, as shown in Figure 4-3.

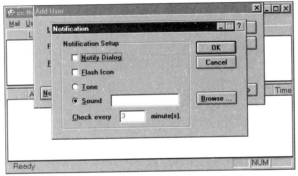

Figure 4-3: The Notification dialog box.

Just as you can set cc:Mail to notify you through a dialog box, by flashing or beeping, you can tell cc:Notify to do the same thing. Click the Notify Dialog or Flash Icon check box to activate either or both of those forms of notification.

If you want, you can even add sound to the Notify Dialog or Flash Icon. cc:Notify gives you choice of either hearing a tone (boring!) or a sound file that you pick out (cool!). If you want the tone, click the Tone radio button. If your computer has a sound card and you want real music, select the Sound radio button. You have to tell cc:Notify which sound file to use, though, by entering the filename in the text field. Of course, if you don't remember the filename, you can browse for it by pressing Browse and finding the sound you want the computer to play.

The *1812 Overture* will get pretty old if you use it as your notification sound and you get more than about two messages a day. Your neighbors will be pointing the cannons at you by noon. I'd recommend simple and quiet sounds.

Finally, you need to enter a number to specify how often cc:Notify should Check for new mail. Generally, every five or ten minutes is a good choice, but you can pick whatever interval you want.

4. Click OK to dismiss the dialog box.

5. Click Filters to further specify which messages you want to be notified about.

Figure 4-4 shows the possible choices.

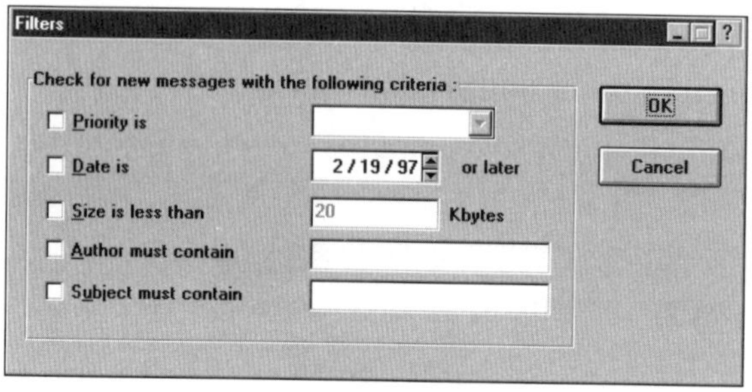

Figure 4-4:
The Filters
dialog box.

If you don't select anything in this dialog box, cc:Notify will inform you about every single message. Here's what the options let you do:

- Notify by Priority lets you be notified of messages that are of "Urgent" or "Urgent or Normal" priorities. Just select the Priority is check box and then choose a level of urgency from the drop-down list.

- Notify by Date lets you be notified of messages based on the date of the message. Just select the Date is check box and then specify the date in the text field. (Don't ask me — I couldn't find a use for this one, but maybe you're more inventive than I am.)

- Notify by Size lets you be notified of messages that are smaller than a file size you specify. For example, you can choose to be notified of messages that are less than 20K, so you can save reading the real biggies for your afternoon break. Just select the Size is less than check box and specify the file size in the text field.

- Notify by Author lets you be notified about all messages from a specified sender. For example, if you want to be notified about messages from a certain person (spouse, boss, whomever), select the Author must contain check box and fill in the text field with the name (for other people on your post office) or Internet address (for people who aren't on your post office). In this field, you could also include the name of a cc:Mail post office to ensure that you're notified about any mail from other users on your post office.

- Notify by Subject lets you be notified about messages that have certain words in the subject line. Just select the Subject must contain check box and add words into the text field. Any word or words are fair game.

In case this array of selections isn't sufficient, remember that you can choose these items in combination as well, to specify only high-priority messages with a subject of Top Secret, or something like that.

6. Click OK.

7. Select the Security button to indicate what information should be available to cc:Notify, as shown in Figure 4-5.

Figure 4-5:
The
Security
dialog box.

- Verify Password to Launch cc:Mail is probably a good idea — every little bit of security helps. This selection, of course, forces you to enter a password every time you open cc:Mail, rather than being able to flip right into it from cc:Notify.

- Show Message Headers lets you see the subjects of incoming messages. This might help you figure out whether you want to fire up cc:Mail for the message or not.

- Store Password tells cc:Notify to remember your password from session to session. It'd be slightly more secure, as well as a slightly bigger hassle, to have to enter it each time — so don't select Store Password.

8. Click OK to dismiss the dialog box.

You should return to the Add User dialog box. Notice that you still haven't yet explored the Network button. Your cc:Mail or network administrator will tell you if you should enter Dynamic Drive Mapping information under this button. Otherwise, don't worry about it.

9. Click OK to complete the user setup.

10. Select Users⇨Save Now or Ctrl+S to save the user setup — you don't want to have to redo this after a power outage, do you? cc:Notify saves everything when you exit, but it's better to be safe than sorry.

Following are some additional thoughts about this notification business:

✔ If you'll be setting up several users in cc:Notify, you might go to Options⇨Default Settings to set any of the characteristics that are common to most of the users you'll be adding. By setting the options here in the Default Settings dialog box, you won't have to set them for each additional user you add. However, nothing you enter here will change the setup for existing users.

✔ Remember that you can set up multiple users in cc:Notify and get notified about the new mail for each one of them. This could be useful for departmental secretaries or for nosy people with time on their hands. (Not, of course, implying that departmental secretaries *are* nosy people with time on their hands. With a couple of exceptions. You know who you are.)

✔ To change a user's setup, just click once to highlight the user name in the cc:Notify window and then choose Users⇨Edit or Ctrl+E to edit the configuration.

✔ If you want to stop being notified about mail for a specific user, click once to select the name in cc:Notify and then press Del or choose Users⇨Delete.

Using cc:Notify

There's really not much to using cc:Notify. You just start it up and let it do its thing. Though you could start it manually each time you want to use it, you might also consider starting it automatically. If you want cc:Notify to fire up automatically every time you start Windows, holler at your local computer guru and ask them to fix you up. The process isn't terribly difficult, but you'll need more specific information than I have the space to provide.

After you're all set up and configured, you'll probably just leave cc:Notify running in the background and peer in at it whenever it beeps, flashes, or otherwise irritates you to let you know that you have mail.

If you're the impatient sort, you can select Mail⇨Update Now or Ctrl+U to check right now for new mail. (By the way, do you always check twice, in case something was overlooked the first time? I find it similar to setting the alarm clock at night, or checking to see that I turned off the iron, or making sure the back door is locked, or . . .)

If you've already seen the messages about which cc:Notify continues to remind you, select Mail⇨Clear New Message Count to reset cc:Notify to a clean slate again, both in terms of the message numbers and the message headers.

Anyway, after something appears, just press Ctrl+ R or select Mail⇨Start cc:Mail to launch cc:Mail the quick way and read that message.

That's all there is to cc:Notify. A whole program in a single chapter. Not too shabby, if I do say so myself.

Chapter 5
Printing Mail Messages

. . . .

In This Chapter

▶ Printing your messages

▶ Printing lots of messages at one time

▶ Printing message headers

▶ Printing attachments

▶ Connecting to a different printer

. . . .

*A*nd you thought that electronic mail and all this computer networking and stuff would lead to the paperless office? No more paper, no more dead trees, no more lines at the copier? Wrong! Sometimes it seems like all cc:Mail does is shift the burden from the memo sender standing at the copier to the memo recipient standing at the laser printer.

If you have a mail message that you just have to keep a paper copy of, this is the chapter for you! (If you're an advocate of the paperless office, just remove this chapter from all the books you can find. It might help. And don't forget to recycle!)

Printing Messages

Printing messages from cc:Mail is a little different from printing messages from most other applications because you have extra choices of what to print. With cc:Mail, you can print the message, its attachments, or even lists of messages.

If you're in a volatile corporate environment, you might consider printing anything that's critical — notes of commendation, receipts to prove that the engineering supervisor really did receive your message, or the e-mail notification of your 27.5-percent raise. Although it isn't nice to think about it, human error can destroy all the messages in your cc:Mail account, leaving you with no record of any of them.

Another belt-and-suspenders tactic to keep from losing anything critical is to use archives liberally — see Chapter 13 for details.

Printing individual messages

Printing individual messages is pretty straightforward — tell the computer to print, and answer a couple of questions. As a matter of fact, it's too easy for some people. I've known people who printed *every* cc:Mail message they ever received, and kept them in a folder. That's possibly a little too compulsive, not to mention hard on the printer, trees, and whoever is in charge of file cabinet procurement. With that warning in mind, here's the process, in a nutshell.

1. **To print the message that you're reading, just click the Print icon, select File⇨Print, or press Ctrl+P.**

   You'll see the Print Options dialog box, something like Figure 5-1.

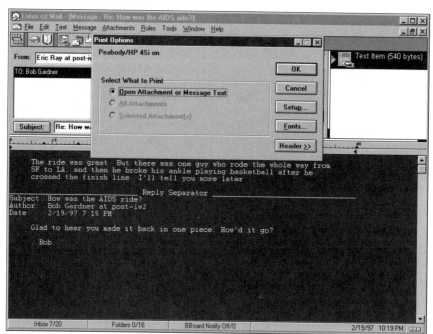

Figure 5-1:
The Print
Options
dialog box.

The Print Options dialog box tells you what printer you're using and offers you some choices on selecting what to print.

2. **Click the radio button to print Open Attachment or Message Text (whichever is visible in the bottom part of the window), All Attachments, or Selected Attachments.**

   If you really want to print all of the attachments, go ahead, but printing the Open Attachment or Message Text is usually adequate for most needs.

3. Click OK.

The dialog box disappears and cc:Mail sends your print job directly to the printer. That's all there is to it.

Printing multiple messages

If you want to print multiple messages, or perhaps just print the list of messages straight from your Inbox, you can very easily do so. To print multiple messages (or parts thereof), do this:

1. In the Inbox (or any folder or archive), select the messages you want to print.

Hold down Ctrl and click each message you want to print. Or if several of the messages are lined up in a row, click the top message, hold down Shift, and click the bottom one. Voilà! All the messages from the first to the last are selected.

You can even do the Shift-click trick to select a lot of messages; then use Ctrl-click to unselect the ones you don't want to print.

2. After you've selected the messages, just click the Print icon, select File⇨Print, or press Ctrl+P.

You'll see the Print Options dialog box, something like Figure 5-2.

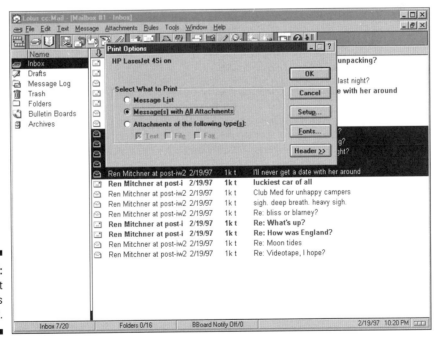

Figure 5-2:
The Print
Options
dialog box.

The Print Options dialog box tells you what printer you'll be using and offers you some choices on selecting what to print. You might notice that the choices are somewhat different if you've selected multiple messages than when you were printing a single message.

3. Click the radio button to print Message List, Message(s) with All Attachments, or Attachments of the following type(s). If you select Attachments of the following type(s), you can choose Text, File, or Fax.

If you're looking to print just the message headers from the list you see in your Inbox, choose Message List. If you really want to print all the text and attachments of all messages or only specific types of attachments, choose accordingly.

4. Click OK.

The dialog box disappears and cc:Mail sends your print job directly to the printer. If you're printing quite a few messages, or messages with a lot of attachments, it might take a while.

Following are some additional items of note about printing from cc:Mail.

✔ To change the font used to print out message text, just select Tools⇨User Setup and then click Fonts on the left side of the dialog box. Choose Printed Message from the Select Font drop-down list and click Change Font. Because the messages have to be printed in a fixed-pitch font (one in which all characters take up the same space — as with an old typewriter), you won't have many choices. Choose a font style and size and then click OK. Click OK again to get out of the User Setup dialog box.

Just in case you were wondering, you can get to the same User Setup dialog box used to change fonts from the Print Options dialog box and the Fonts button.

✔ In the Print Options dialog box, you'll see a button for Header >≥. If you choose Header >≥, you'll see that cc:Mail lumps several evils under Header, with several options to print part of the Message Header, including None, Partial (complete with check boxes for which items), or Full. The message header includes that administrative stuff, like the Author, Subject, Date and time, Recipients, and Priority level. Additionally, if you choose Full, you can also print the Forwarding History and can specify to Print Recipients on Separate Lines. You probably didn't even know that there was that much information about a single cc:Mail message.

✔ Additionally, and this is the random lumping part, this part of the dialog box is where you can tell cc:Mail to reformat the text to fit the page (recommended, in my opinion), and to include header text (as a running header to appear at the top of every page of your printout).

Selecting a Different Printer

You might want to select a different printer before you send those messages to print. For example, you might choose one closer to you so that those personal messages don't get printed out halfway across the building.

To choose a different printer, use the following procedure.

1. **Choose File➪Print Setup.**

   You'll see the Print Setup dialog box, as shown in Figure 5-3.

2. **Under Printer, choose from any printers you have installed by clicking the down arrow on the list under Specific printer.**

3. **After you've selected a printer, verify that the radio button in front of Specific printer is selected.**

4. **If the Orientation and Paper selections aren't correct, change them to the proper values.**

   Generally, Portrait orientation and Letter size paper, from Standard Source, will work fine.

5. **Click OK to finish selecting the printer.**

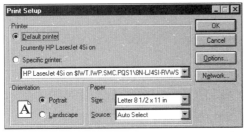

Figure 5-3: The Print Setup dialog box.

Chapter 6

Attachments, or What to Do with All That Baggage

. . . .

In This Chapter

▶ Understanding attachment terminology

▶ Receiving attachments

▶ Viewing attachments

▶ Running attachments

▶ Saving attachments

▶ Customizing attachment options

. . . .

*Y*ou've just been to visit the Grand Canyon, and you even remembered to take your new camera. You returned from the experience with fantastic pictures of the Canyon at sunset, replete with lovely shades of purples and blues, reds and maroons. You sit down at the computer, fire up a cc:Mail message to your best golf buddy, and describe how beautiful it was.

"It was so beautiful. The colors were stunning. Really. Beautiful. You had to be there."

What's wrong with this picture? No picture, that's what! Describing the sight just can't compare to showing your correspondents the beauty (not to mention showing off your skill with the new-fangled camera). The classy, high-tech, impressive, effective way to do it is to attach your pictures to the message and send the whole thing, just as you'd paper-clip pictures to a real letter and send it.

This chapter introduces you to the magic of attachments (otherwise known as stuff held on a message with virtual paper clips), including how to attach them, read them, and save them. Lest you think that the chapter will only be useful if you take great pictures (and have a scanner to get them into the computer), never fear — you can also attach documents, spreadsheets, or anything else in your computer. With that, grab your paper clips and have fun!

Getting the Attachment Terminology Down Pat

An *attachment* is a separate file that you attach to a regular cc:Mail message. You can attach practically anything to a message — things like word processing documents, spreadsheets, pictures, movies, and sound clips. In short, if it's on the computer, you can attach it.

If you get an attachment and want to look at it within cc:Mail, you want to *view* it. If you get an attachment and want to look at it through a different program, you want to either *run* it or *launch* it. Running and launching have the exact same meaning, but different parts of cc:Mail use different terminology. (I suspect that they felt that cc:Mail was just so darn user-friendly that it may not even be allowed to run under Windows. Adding strangeness back into the program assures continuing Windows compatibility, or so it seems.)

Even if it's a picture or spreadsheet, and what you really want to do is fire up Excel so that you can look at it, you still want to *run* or *launch* it. For example, if someone attaches a Microsoft Word document and sends it to you, *viewing* the attachment brings it up within cc:Mail. *Running* the attachment brings up Word and opens the file so that you can read it much more easily (and it looks better, too).

Microsoft Word documents, along with many others, cannot be completely viewed through cc:Mail. If you receive a Word document that is longer than one page — as most of them tend to be — you only be able to see the first page through the cc:Mail viewer. To see the whole document, you'll have to run or launch the attachment.

Receiving Attachments

So, what do you do about getting attachments, and how do you know if you've gotten any recently — attachments, that is? Messages with attachments are like any other messages. They show up in your Inbox when they arrive, and you double-click the individual messages to view the body of the message. If you're already comfortable with reading regular messages, this shouldn't come as a surprise.

If you get a cc:Mail message with attachments, you'll be tipped off by a little **f** in the Size column of the message pane, indicating that a File attachment (or attachments) awaits your attention, as in Figure 6-1.

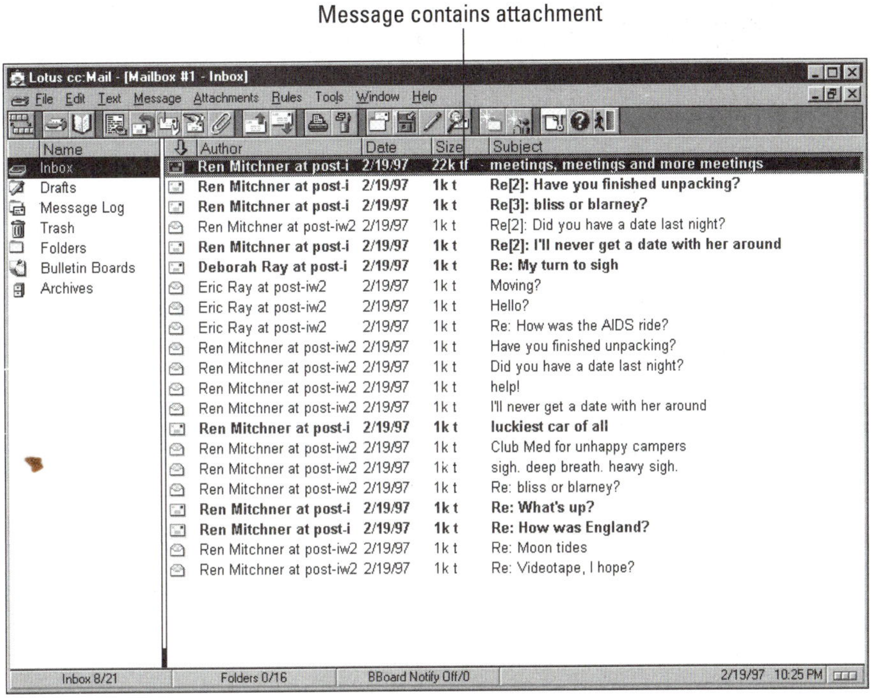

Message contains attachment

Figure 6-1:
The tip-off
to a file
attachment.

After you open a message that has an attachment, you see both the regular text of the message, just as you usually do, and one or more icons in the Attachment pane of the message window — at the top-right corner. The icons in the Attachment pane represent the files attached to the message.

Each of the icons represents a different chunk of attached information. There's a text item icon up there by default — that's the regular part of the message. If you get a text file attachment, for example, it'll have the old trusty Notepad icon, whereas a Windows bitmap file will probably have a Paintbrush (or Paint) icon. If Windows doesn't recognize the file type, you just get a generic icon. Figure 6-2 shows examples of each of these icons.

After you've received your attachment, you'll probably want to look at it, right? Try double-clicking the attachment icon — if that doesn't seem to do what you wanted, check out "Viewing Attachments" later in this chapter. But first, some additional thoughts about receiving attachments:

✔ You may get a message that has no message text at all. Before you call the sender to ask just what the deal is with wasting your time with empty messages, check the Attachment pane and see if there's an attachment up there.

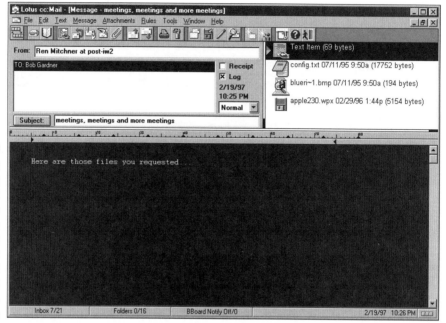

Figure 6-2:
The
Attachment
pane with a
text item, a
text file, a
Windows
bitmap, and
an unknown
file.

✔ Some attachments may come through with funky filenames — that is, something like playth~1.wav. The tilde (~) is what cc:Mail sticks in when it encounters a long filename. Windows 95 and Windows NT users can use long filenames to really describe files, as in **play that funky music** for a sound clip. cc:Mail, however, doesn't much like long filenames because it's designed to be compatible with all of the Windows 3.1x users out there. Therefore, regardless of your platform, after your buddy sends a Windows sound file of **play that funky music** to you, you'll see an attachment with playth~1.wav appear. That's fine, though, because it will still work.

✔ If the message claims that five files were attached but you can only see a couple of icons up in the Attachment pane, try scrolling down in the Attachment pane scrollbar to see the rest. You can make the Attachment pane bigger by moving your mouse cursor slowly down and out of the Attachment pane. When the pointer becomes a double arrow, click and hold the mouse button and drag the bar down until the Attachment pane is as big as you want it to be.

Viewing Attachments

Viewing attachments is the quick-and-easy way to find out what's in them. Sometimes you'll find that viewing attachments is all you need, but viewing attachments is often like holding an envelope up to the light — you can get a pretty good idea of what's in there, but the specifics are kind of blurry.

Here's the process for viewing an attachment:

1. **Open the mail message with the attachment you want to view.**

   Just double-click the message in the Inbox window. Remember, messages with attachments have a little **f** in the size column of the Inbox window.

2. **Double-click the attachment icon in the Attachment pane (upper-right corner) of the message window.**

   After a couple of seconds, the contents of the attachment appear in the message window.

   Depending on how your attachment setup may be customized, you may see a Viewing Options dialog box asking you to choose a viewer. Generally, just going with the default is fine. (If you want to turn the dialog box off and just let cc:Mail go with its best guess, check out "Customizing Your Attachment Options" later in this chapter.)

   When you're finished viewing the attachment, you can close the message (Ctrl+F4) or run, save, or view another attachment.

Some files cannot be completely viewed — you may only get to see the first page. Microsoft Word documents are a good example of this. There won't be any indication that you're not seeing the entire document, but if you launch the attachment or if you save the file and open it in the regular program, you find there's much more to the file than you could see through the cc:Mail view mode. Therefore, I'd strongly recommend that you run attachments or save them as files if they contain important information — you don't want to accidentally miss out on anything.

Running Attachments

Running an attachment simply refers to opening the attachment in the program the attachment was created in. For example, your boss may send you a schedule of next week's staff meeting. When you run the attachment, you're just viewing the document in the program it was created in.

The advantage of running an attachment, rather than just viewing it, is that you see the full contents of the file. Take your boss's meeting schedule as an example. If you don't run the attachment, you may only get to see a portion of the schedule and miss out on the information on the second page, including the little tidbit about your presentation to the corporate vice president who will also be in attendance at the meeting.

The main disadvantage to running an attachment is that it takes a little longer than just viewing it. Not a big deal, really. Another possible difficulty could be if your computer doesn't know what program to use for a specific attachment. In that case, you can just save the attachment and manually open it in the program of your choice. For information on saving attachments, see "Saving Attachments" later in this chapter.

Anyway, here's the process for running an attachment:

1. **Open the mail message with the attachment you want to run.**

   Just double-click the attachment in the Inbox window. Remember, messages with attachments have a little **f** in the size column of the Inbox window.

2. **Hold down the Shift key and double-click the attachment in the Attachment pane, or select the attachment and choose Attachments⇨Launch Attachment.**

   You may need to scroll down in the Attachment pane to see all the attachments.

   After a flurry of disk drive activity and a pause, your attachment appears in its own program, rather than in cc:Mail.

3. **After you're finished with the attached file, close the program, probably with File⇨Exit or Alt+F4.**

   You won't be able to do anything else with cc:Mail until you've closed the program that was opened to run your attachment.

You'll probably need to restore cc:Mail from its minimized (iconified) state at the bottom of your screen before you can do anything else. Running attachments generally leaves cc:Mail minimized, even though that causes extra work for you. How inconvenient!

Other notes about running or launching attachments:

✔ Running attachments without knowing what they are or what they do can be risky. Though a regular e-mail message cannot transmit a computer virus, running an attached executable file may transmit a conventional virus, and Word or Excel files could carry other, specialized viruses. Ask your system administrator about virus scanners for attached files and think twice before running attachments from people outside your company and running attachments that you didn't expect to receive.

✔ If you (or someone else) changed the attachments setup options, Shift-double-click may just open up the file within cc:Mail so that you can view it. If this happens, try double-clicking the attachment icon and see "Customizing your Attachment Options" later in this chapter.

✔ If you launch an attachment and are looking at the attachment in its associated program, that's the best time to print it. Though it's possible to print attachments directly out of cc:Mail, that tends to be fairly time-consuming. It's generally easier to just print from the program that claims that attachment.

✔ After you've looked at the file in the associated program, you may decide that you need to keep it for reference or decide to use it. Though you could always keep it in your cc:Mail box and rerun it as needed, you can't save changes, and your system administrator will start yelling at you about the amount of space you take up in the post office. Or, you could return to cc:Mail and save the attachment (as discussed later in this chapter), but that's kind of a hassle. The easy solution is to just select File⇨Save As from whatever program you're in and save the file. No muss, no fuss.

✔ If the attachment you want to run has a generic disk icon, Windows and cc:Mail can't figure out what to do with it. Attempting to run it will generate a remarkably user-friendly error message like the one shown in Figure 6-3. The generic icon means that the file is not associated with any compatible program. See the sidebar "Known by the company you keep: associations at work" later in this chapter for more information. In the meantime, save the attachment as a file, start the program of your choice, and try to open that file in the chosen program.

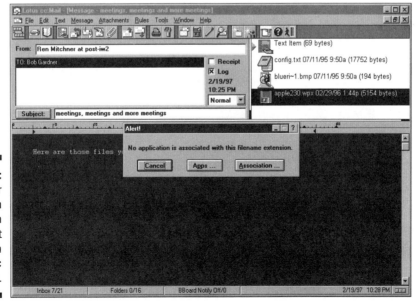

Figure 6-3:
An error from running an attachment with a generic icon.

Saving Attachments

Some people save bits of string. Some people save junk mail. But did you know that you can even save your cc:Mail attachments without saving the messages they came with? Saving attachments without the message can be handy, say, if the message itself was long-winded or useless. For example, suppose that company party attachment came with a six-page discussion of why you need to attend. I mean, of course you want to attend. Company parties are always great, right?

Just toss the message and save the attachment. Here's how:

1. **Open the mail message with the attachment you want to save by double-clicking the message in the Inbox.**

2. **Click the attachment you want to save once to select it.**

3. **Press F2 or select <u>A</u>ttachments⇨<u>S</u>ave Attachments to bring up the Save As dialog box.**

   The Save As dialog box, as shown in Figure 6-4, lets you choose what to save and where to save it.

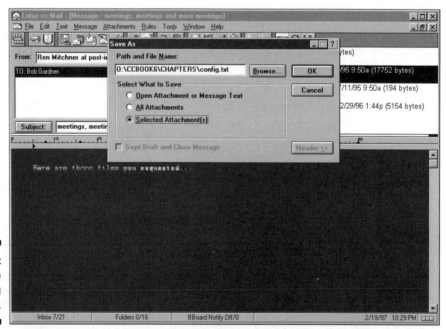

Figure 6-4:
The Save
As dialog
box.

Path and File Name specifies where you want to save the file. You can type in or edit the path and name that cc:Mail suggests, or you can use the Browse button to shuffle through your hard drive (and the network, if you have one) to find a good place to store the file.

Under Select What to Save, you can choose Open Attachment or Message Text to save whatever is visible in the message window. If you choose to save All Attachments, cc:Mail files away all the attachments in this particular mail message. Finally, the default choice is Selected Attachment(s). You'll probably want to stick with Selected Attachment(s) so that you don't clutter your hard disk with unneeded stuff.

4. Click OK.

That's it! Now, all you have to do is remember where you put it and use that attachment like any other file on your computer. (And you'll be able to recycle that persuasive message about the company party next summer when you're on the picnic committee.)

Customizing Your Attachment Options

As if you don't have enough cool things to do with cc:Mail, you can even customize your attachment options. Specifically, you can customize your View/Run options, which specify how you'll launch or view attachments, and you can customize your View File options, which help control viewing attachments.

Customizing View/Run options

By default, double-clicking an attachment icon brings the attachment up within cc:Mail; holding down Shift and double-clicking starts the associated program and opens the attachment there. So far, so good, right? However, you can change some of these options to make it easier and faster to use cc:Mail.

You adjust your attachment options by selecting Tools⇨User Setup and choosing Message in the left pane of the User Setup dialog box.

You'll see a dialog box like the one in Figure 6-5.

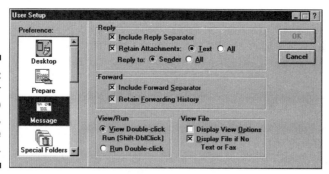

Figure 6-5:
The User
Setup
dialog box,
Message
options.

If you find yourself continually Shift-double-clicking so that you can run a separate program to see the attachment, select Run Double-click under View/Run. After you make this change, a double-click will run the attachment (bring it up in the associated program), though you will have to Shift-double-click to view it within cc:Mail.

Customizing View File options

View File options let you make sure that cc:Mail gives you something to look at when you open a message, rather than just presenting you with a blank screen and an attachment icon in the upper-right corner. Additionally, you can tell cc:Mail what viewer to use each time you view an attachment, if you really want to exercise that much control. (Me? I let cc:Mail just do its thing — that's what it's there for.)

You adjust your attachment options by selecting Tools⇨User Setup and choosing Message in the left pane of the User Setup dialog box.

Under View File, select Display File if No Text or Fax to make sure that cc:Mail brings up something for you to look at when you open a message with an attachment. If someone sends you a document all by itself, with no other text or anything, you'd generally just see a blank message window in cc:Mail with the attachment icon hanging out in the Attachment pane. However, it's more fun and less confusing if you tell cc:Mail that you want to see whatever is there by default.

On the further-customization topic, viewing some attachments doesn't work for a variety of reasons that depend on your particular configuration and the attachments you were sent. If you find that you can't generally double-click attachments and have them work correctly, you still have some choices. (By the way, this is likely to happen only with certain types of attachments, such as sound or graphic files.)

Known by the company you keep: associations at work

Warning: This section will delve shallowly into the very superficial surface of how Windows and cc:Mail try to guess what program should be used to view your attachments. If you're waiting for a meeting and have a couple of minutes, or if you're experiencing confusion with attachments randomly flaring up in different programs at different times, take a gander at the following few paragraphs. We'll start at the very beginning.

If you've used Windows for any length of time at all, you've probably discovered extensions. Extensions are the little three-character additions to the end of a filename, as in thesis.doc or budget.xls. The .doc and .xls parts are the extensions, and they help Windows know what kind of program is associated with that file.

For example, when Microsoft Word was installed on your system, it informed Windows (95 as well as 3.1x) that it claimed all files that end with .doc. Likewise, Excel claimed the .xls files. Generally, programs will claim all file types that could conceivably be used with them.

When you first get an attachment and open up the message, cc:Mail checks with Windows to find out what program claims the attachment files. If you get a file that ends with .txt, Notepad will probably claim it. Likewise, a file with .htm will be claimed by your Web browser.

You'll see the icon of the program that claims the attachment up in the Attachment pane. Unclaimed files show up with a generic little off-blue disk icon, and the rest of the icons will probably look familiar.

When you Shift-double-click to run (or launch) an attachment, cc:Mail hands the attachment to the associated program. You get to see the file in the associated program, and when you're done, you exit out of the associated program and wind up back in cc:Mail.

Problems can arise due to mistaken identity or unclaimed files. Mistaken identity often happens when you install a new program, and the program claims more file types than you really want it to have. A good example would be many photo-editing programs. These programs claim most graphic files, but they take forever to start up. Even if someone just sent you a little snippet of wallpaper for your Windows desktop, running the attachment brings up that whole massive program. Or you may have an unclaimed file, for example, if someone sent you a document created in a program that you don't have.

If you wind up with one of these unclaimed or mistaken-identity files, the easy and fairly reliable solution is to just save the attachment to your disk as a file, open the program of your choice, and then open the file. If you feel that you've just got to get the problem of mistaken identity resolved immediately, you may try bribing your local computer guru, reinstalling the program that should claim the files, or referring to *Windows 3.1 For Dummies* or *Windows 95 For Dummies*, both by Andy Rathbone and published by IDG Books Worldwide.

If you insist on controlling what program is used to present the view, you can do so by selecting Display View Options under View File. Generally, you don't want to select this — the only exceptions would be if you're having real problems viewing attachments. This tells cc:Mail to bring up a dialog box whenever you try to view a document so you can choose the program that will be used to view the attachment. Because you're *viewing* the attachment, it will still appear within the cc:Mail window.

Part III
Sending Mail

"In this part . . .

"**D**eliver the letter, the sooner the better." But it can't be delivered until you address it, write it, and send it.

Sending mail from cc:Mail is like sending a regular letter, only different. You don't have to write out the address; you just click it in. You don't laboriously scrawl your letter; you type it, spell check it, and change the colors if you want. You don't walk down the block and put the letter in the mailbox; you just click and wave good-bye to your message.

Beats the heck out of the old ways of doing things, huh?

This part takes you through addressing messages (necessary to send them, don't you know) and everything you ever wanted to know about preparing and sending messages. I then jump into some other sending-related cc:Mail features that you just can't live without.

Chapter 7

Addressing Addresses

In This Chapter

▶ Addressing a message — the quick way and the not-so-quick way
▶ Getting the scoop on directories
▶ Addressing public and private mailing lists

*A*ddressing messages is a necessary prerequisite to sending a message — if there isn't an address, the message doesn't have anywhere to go. This chapter shows you how to tell messages where to go.

Addressing a Message

An address in cc:Mail identifies a particular person (or group, as discussed later) so that your e-mail message can find that person. Rather than having to remember the addresses of everyone in your group or company, you can just select your intended recipient from a *directory*, or list of addresses. No big deal, right?

Even if you want to address messages to people who aren't in your company, you can do so. You need to add a couple of steps to the process (because the cc:Mail directory in your company presumably doesn't include the addresses of outsiders), but the additional steps aren't a big deal.

Quick addressing

The following is the process for addressing a cc:Mail message the quick and easy way:

1. **Start a new message by choosing Message⇨New Message, by clicking on the New Message icon, or by pressing Ctrl+M.**

   You then see a new, blank message appear on your screen, as shown in Figure 7-1. Your cursor is shown blinking in the address box.

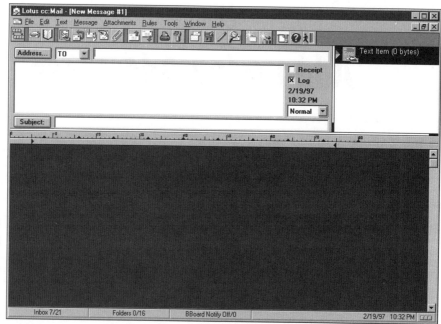

Figure 7-1:
The cc:Mail
New
Message
window.

2. Start typing the name of your first recipient.

As soon as you start typing, you see names appearing in the address box. cc:Mail matches the letters that you type with the names that are in the directory. If you're addressing a message to Jim Smith and there's only one Jim in the directory, you have Jim Smith in the address box after typing only **Jim.**

Some cc:Mail directories are organized with first name and last name, in that order. Others are last name, first name. Try one way and see how it's organized (or flip ahead a few pages and look at the directory directly).

3. Press Enter to add the recipient to your message.

The recipient's name is added to the address window, and your cursor stays where it was so that you can add additional addresses. Repeat Steps 2 and 3 until you've addressed the message to everyone who should receive it.

4. Click the down arrow in the drop-down list beside TO.

You then see a drop-down list with TO, CC, and BCC as choices.

By default, cc:Mail sends messages with a standard TO line, just like in a traditional memo. However, there may be times that you would prefer to send a courtesy copy (CC) or a blind courtesy copy (BCC) (which isn't very courteous at all).

If you're following up on an important matter with a client, you may send a CC to your boss to eliminate worry and nagging and to make it clear that you're on top of your game.

Use a BCC if you need to keep someone in the loop on certain discussions without everyone else's knowledge. Blind copies are occasionally necessary, but they can backfire on you. If your boss finds out that you've been blind copying *his* boss on messages, that could sink your ship.

5. **Select CC and place the cursor back in the address box by pressing Tab or by clicking with the mouse.**

6. **Type the name of a CC recipient, and press Enter to add the name.**

 That's it for the quick-and-easy way of addressing a message. Just add some text to your message, and choose Message⇨Send, press Ctrl+S, or click on the Send icon to send your message on its way.

Not-so-quick method of addressing a message

If you're yearning for more control, more recipients, and more options when addressing a message, you've come to the right place. Lurking behind Button Number 1 (actually, the Address button), you can address messages to regular recipients, folders, mailing lists, or bulletin boards. You only get the last two options if mailing lists and bulletin boards are supported by your post office.

The following is the complete scoop on addressing, the longer but more comprehensive way.

 1. **Start a new message by choosing Message⇨New Message, by clicking on the New Message icon, or by pressing Ctrl+M.**

You then see a new blank message appear on your screen.

2. **Click the Address button (in the upper-left corner of a new message), choose Message⇨Address, or press Ctrl+A.**

You then see the Address Message dialog box, as shown in Figure 7-2.

The top part of the dialog box looks and works just like the addressing options at the top of a cc:Mail message. You can just start to type the name of a recipient, and the name is completed by cc:Mail. Then press Enter to add the name to the list.

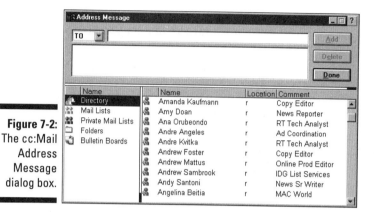

Figure 7-2:
The cc:Mail
Address
Message
dialog box.

If you want to send either a CC (courtesy copy) or a BCC (blind courtesy copy), click the down arrow beside TO and select the addressing form that you prefer. Move your cursor back into the address box and continue addressing the message.

In the lower-right portion of the dialog box, you see all of the addresses from the directory. You can select addresses directly from this area and add them to the address window of your message. Just click on a name to select it and then click Add or double-click the name.

3. **Add the names from the cc:Mail directory to your message by selecting the name and clicking Add. You can also type the name until cc:Mail completes it, and then press Enter or click Add.**

You can also address messages to mail lists or bulletin boards (if your cc:Mail administrator has established any), private mail lists (if you've created some), or to folders (if you have any).

See Chapter 13 for information about creating and using folders.

Suppose that you file all of the funny sayings and Dave Barry copyright infringements that you can find in a folder called *funny.* If you find a good one and want to send it to your friends, you can also send a copy directly to your funny folder at the same time.

4. **To address your message to a folder, double click on the Folders icon in the Containers pane at the lower-left area of your Address Message dialog box.**

Double-clicking on the Folders icon expands the folder so that you can see the folders that you created.

Click the folder that should receive the message and then click Add.

5. **To address your message to a Private mail list, double-click on the Private Mail Lists icon in the Containers pane to expand it. Click the list of your choice and then click <u>A</u>dd.**

   Keep selecting potential addressees from the bottom of your Address Message dialog box and continue clicking <u>A</u>dd until you're finished.

6. **Click <u>D</u>one.**

   Now that message is as addressed as they come.

7. **You can cancel the message by pressing Ctrl+F4, by pressing Escape, or by double-clicking the top-left corner of the message window. Choose <u>C</u>lose Message and Discard Changes and then click OK.**

    On the other hand, you could enter a subject and text and send the message by choosing <u>M</u>essage⇨<u>S</u>end, by pressing Ctrl+S, or by clicking on the Send icon.

These additional tips may make addressing messages even easier, if that's possible.

✔ If you notice that one of your intended recipients who is listed in the address window does not have the type of address (TO, CC, or BCC) that you had intended, just double-click on the name in the address window. You then see the type of addressing change. Double-click again to change it again. Stop when it's right.

✔ When you are typing a name and cc:Mail is completing it, you don't have to type the whole name. Here's a shortcut. Consider a directory that is arranged as last name, first name. You want to address a message to Alexander, James. As soon as you type **Al**, cc:Mail matches the rest of the name and shows you Alexander, Jack. Just press the down-arrow key to get to the next Alexander in the sequence. This way, you don't have to type the rest of the name until cc:Mail matches the correct one.

✔ Remember, when you are addressing a message, whatever shows in the address mode area (TO, CC, or BCC) determines the mode for the next address that you add.

✔ Look at the addresses as you add them to your message. If one address has a pound sign (#) beside it, the addressee is probably a group of people and not an individual. Make sure that you really want to mail your message to all of the people in the group. You can click a name and press Delete to remove an entry from the message's address.

✔ If your post office has either bulletin boards or mail lists, you can send messages to them, too (assuming that your cc:Mail administrator allows you to). In the Address Message dialog box, double-click on either the Mail Lists or Bulletin Boards icon to expand those lists. Select the bulletin board or mail list to which you want to mail, and then click <u>A</u>dd to add it to your address window.

✔ Adding multiple recipients at once is a snap from the Address Message dialog box. To select and add a series of adjacent addresses (for example, all of the names that start with A), click the top message, hold Shift, and click the bottom address of the sequence. Presto! You just selected the whole group. Now click <u>A</u>dd to add the group to the address window. If you want to select multiple, nonadjacent addresses, hold Ctrl as you click each address that you want to include. If you accidentally click an extra address, just click it again to deselect it. Click <u>A</u>dd when you're done.

✔ The only things hanging out in the Container pane that cannot be message recipients are Archives. You need to move messages into Archives by dragging them or by selecting <u>M</u>essage⇨<u>S</u>tore. See Chapter 13 for more information about archives.

Addressing messages to the rest of the world

Addressing messages to recipients in your cc:Mail directory is a snap, but you have a ready-made list. What happens if you want to address a message to Great Aunt Mabel, who has discovered the Internet and is likely to blow the rest of her pension in phone bills and her online service account collection?

If your cc:Mail post office has a connection — technically known as a *gateway* — to part of the great beyond, you could probably send Aunt Mabel a message. The Internet gateway is what you use to send Aunt Mabel a message; you also probably use it to send most other messages to recipients that are outside of your directory.

Some cc:Mail installations don't have external connections or gateways; therefore, you can't e-mail Aunt Mabel from work. Goodness knows why a company would choose not to have an Internet connection, but if yours doesn't, you can't do much except to find someone who cares and complain about it.

For the rest of us, here's the scoop on addressing messages to people on the Internet and elsewhere:

1. **Start a new message by choosing <u>M</u>essage⇨New <u>M</u>essage, by clicking on the New Message icon, or by pressing Ctrl+M.**

2. **Address a message to your Internet gateway address, which may be INET, INTERNET, or something as obscure and techie as SMTP.**

   As soon as you add the message to your address window, you see the Post Office Addressing dialog box appear, as shown in Figure 7-3.

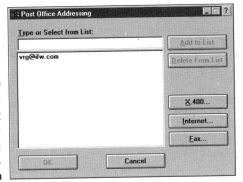

Figure 7-3:
The Post
Office
Addressing
dialog box.

3. **Type Aunt Mabel's address in the Type or Select from List text box.**

4. **Click Add to List if you don't want to type her address again.**

   Repeat Steps 3 and 4 for any additional addresses that you want to add.

5. **To add more addresses in X.400 form, click X.400, complete the dialog box, click More if you need to add more information, and click OK when you're finished. Definitely click Add to List so that you don't have to do that again.**

   If you're not familiar with X.400 addressing, it's no problem. If you need it, someone should tell you. I've never had to use it.

   By the way, depending on the way that your cc:Mail administrator configured the post office, you may have to address X.400 messages by selecting X400 from the directory (rather than by selecting INET or INTERNET).

   You could use the Internet button to add additional Internet addresses, but it's easier to just type the address.

6. **To add Fax recipients (assuming that your post office supports a fax gateway), click the Fax button.**

   You would send faxes to e-mail–impaired friends and colleagues.

   Complete the dialog box according to the example in Figure 7-4 with Name@FAX#Number.

   Depending on how your administrator configured cc:Mail, you may have to address a message to FAX (rather than to INET or INTERNET) to send to fax recipients.

   Again, click Add to List so that you don't have to re-enter this information.

7. **Now, to add those new external addresses to the message, rather than just entering and saving them for posterity, click an address once to select a recipient, and then click OK to add the recipient to the address window in your new message.**

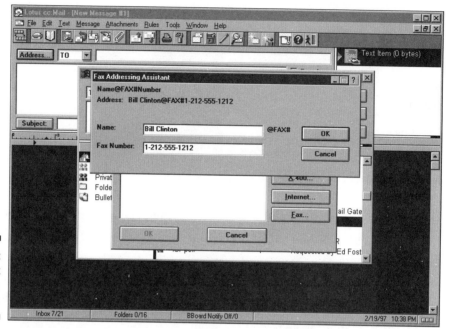

Figure 7-4:
The Fax
Addressing
Assistant.

If you hold Ctrl and click each intended recipient, you can add several at once. If you want to add several adjacent recipients, click the first one, hold Shift, and click the last one.

Click OK when you're done.

8. Great! Now just enter a subject and text of the message, and send that puppy, or just cancel it.

Cancel by pressing Ctrl+F4, by pressing Escape, or by double-clicking in the top-left corner of the message window. Choose Close Message and Discard Changes, and then click OK.

 Send by choosing Message⇨Send, by pressing Ctrl+S, or by clicking on the Send icon.

The following are a couple of additional tips to keep you sane when addressing messages to the Internet:

✔ If you're a cc:Mail Mobile user, every time that you get a message from someone who isn't listed in your directory, you have the option of automatically adding him or her to the directory.

✔ If you're trying to send a message to an Internet address and you have problems, you can always ask your cc:Mail administrator how to do it. Or you can take the easy way out: Have your Internet buddy send you a message via the Internet, and save that message in one of your folders (see Chapter 13). Then you can simply reply to the message every time that you want to send a message to that person and not worry about creating the address. This procedure is commonly called *capturing an address.*

✔ You can also easily address messages by dragging an address from the address window of an existing message into the address window of the new message that you're creating. Just open both messages, make sure that you can see both address windows (choose <u>W</u>indow⇨Tile Horizontal or press Shift+F4), and drag to your heart's content.

✔ Be wary when a CompuServe member gives you his address. Within CompuServe, addresses consist of two numbers that are separated by a comma (for example, **5555,713**). For Internet access to this account, you must change the comma to a period and add *@compuserve.com.* Therefore, this member's Internet address is **5555.713@compuserve.com**.

✔ Your cc:Mail administrator must install Internet access as well as a fax gateway and an X.400 gateway before you can use them. You should check with your administrator about any of those options that you may need. Additionally, individual cc:Mail sites occasionally configure these gateways differently, so the addresses that you choose from your directory may be slightly different. Again check with your administrator, who knows for sure.

About Directories

The cc:Mail directory is the comprehensive list of everyone on cc:Mail in your company or organization. Fortunately, someone else was kind enough to put all of these addresses into the directory so that you don't have to remember them. For that matter, you don't have to do anything except read them.

Technically speaking, if you have a real aversion to a directory, you don't have to use it. You could just try to recall every address in the company and type it without errors every time. Sold on directories? Good, I thought so!

You probably only need to bring up your directory to look for a specific person's name (to verify spelling, perhaps), to verify that someone is in the directory, or if you want to try the drag-and-drop addressing method.

To call up your directory, follow these steps:

1. Select Window⇨New Address Book Window.

Your directory or address book appears, as shown in Figure 7-5.

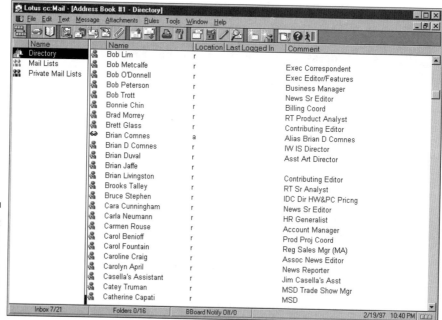

Figure 7-5:
The cc:Mail
Address
Book -
Directory
window.

You can scroll through it and look at it. You can also use it to help address a message — read on!

2. Start a new message by choosing Message⇨New Message, by clicking on the New Message icon, or by pressing Ctrl+M.

3. Choose Window⇨Tile Horizontal or press Shift+F4 to arrange the Address Book window and the New Message window so that you can see both of them at once.

4. Click on an address from the Address Book, hold the mouse button, and drag the address into the address window of your new message.

To select and add a series of adjacent addresses (for example, all of the names that start with A), click the top message, hold Shift, and click the bottom address of the sequence. Presto! You just selected that whole group.

If you want to select multiple, nonadjacent addresses, hold Ctrl as you click each address that you want to include. If you accidentally click an extra address, just click it again to unselect it.

After you've selected all of the addresses that you want, click one of them, and drag the whole pile into the address window of your new message. Pretty slick, isn't it?

5. **Now enter a subject and the text of the message and mail your new message, or just cancel it.**

Cancel by pressing Ctrl+F4, by pressing Escape, or by double-clicking in the top-left corner of the message window. Choose Close Message and Discard Changes, and then click OK.

 Send by choosing Message⇨Send, by pressing Ctrl+S, or by clicking on the Send icon.

An additional note about using the cc:Mail directory: If you're a cc:Mail Mobile user, you must maintain your own cc:Mail directory. When you're working in Mobile mode, you do not have a constant connection to the LAN post office; therefore, you cannot summon the directory at a whim like your LAN-based counterparts can. No problem! Chapter 19 tells you everything that you need to know about building and maintaining your own directory, and never fear, you don't even need to retype all of those addresses.

About Mailing Lists

Mailing lists are just collections of addresses. Using these lists, you can send a message to Sales Team or Senior Level Managers or Everyone rather than having to address the message to each person.

cc:Mail supports two kinds of mailing lists — public and private. Public mailing lists are set up by the cc:Mail administrator for everyone to use. Sales Team, Senior Level Managers, and Everyone are examples of public mailing lists. Private mailing lists would include lists such as Bob's Friends, Lunch Crew, or that Quality Productivity Team that your boss asked you to form.

Addressing to mailing lists

The following section shows you how to mail to a mailing list, either public or private.

1. **Start a new message by choosing Message⇨New Message, by clicking on the New Message icon, or by pressing Ctrl+M.**

   You then see a new blank message appear on your screen.

2. **Click Address, choose Message⇨Address, or press Ctrl+A.**

3. **Double-click on the Public Mailing Lists icon to expand the container in the Container pane of the New Address window.**

   You then see the Address Message dialog box with the list of Public Mailing Lists visible, as shown in Figure 7-6.

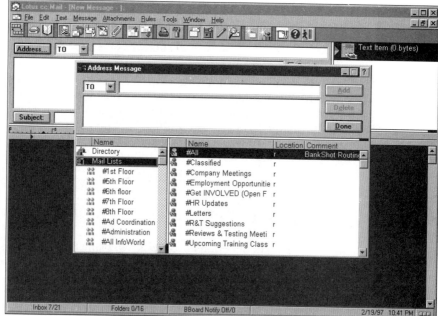

Figure 7-6:
The cc:Mail Address Message dialog box with Public Mailing Lists visible.

You may not have any public mailing lists — it depends on what your administrator has set up.

4. **Click the name of the Public Mailing List and then click Add to add the name to your address window.**

   Your message then goes to everyone on the list, so be sure that you really want everyone to see what you wrote. Accidentally sending messages to mailing lists can be quite embarrassing.

5. **To send to a private mailing list (assuming that you've already created one), repeat Steps 3 and 4, substituting Private Mailing List.**

6. Complete and send your message, or just cancel it.

Cancel by pressing Ctrl+F4, by pressing Escape, or by double-clicking in the top-left corner of the message window. Choose <u>C</u>lose Message and Discard Changes, and then click OK.

 Send by choosing <u>M</u>essage⇨<u>S</u>end, by pressing Ctrl+S, or by clicking on the Send icon.

One further note on mailing lists: In the New Address Book window, you can tell which addresses are mailing lists by the # sign in front of them. If the address doesn't have a # sign in front of it, the address is probably just an individual.

Creating a private mailing list

The most common, and probably most enjoyable, reason to create a private mailing list is to make sure that everyone you know gets every funny saying that makes it into your mailbox. Of course, you could also use these lists to do real work, but that wouldn't be half as much fun.

These steps describe the procedure for creating a private mailing list:

1. Choose <u>File</u>⇨<u>New</u>⇨<u>Private Mailing List</u>.

The Address Book window appears with the Private Mail Lists expanded. A cursor is blinking at the blank for a Private Mail List name, as shown in Figure 7-7.

2. Type a descriptive name for the Private Mailing List and press Enter.

You can use real words and spaces, so give your new list a good, descriptive name.

The Participants List dialog box then appears, as shown in Figure 7-8.

3. Select participants as if you were addressing a message. Click <u>A</u>dd after each participant.

Unfortunately, you can only add people who are in the cc:Mail directory. That means that you must manually include addresses of Internet friends each time that you send to the list.

 Alternatively, you could use the Drafts folder to hold a message that you have pre-addressed to everyone, Internet and local, to which you want to mail. See Chapter 12 for more information on the Drafts folder.

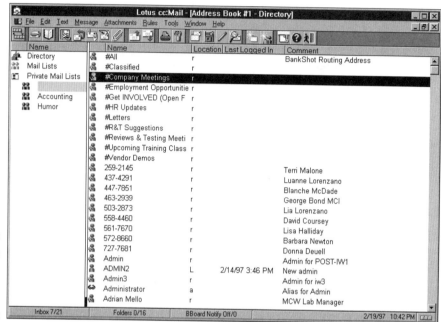

Figure 7-7:
Creating a
private
mailing list.

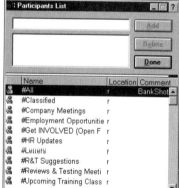

Figure 7-8:
The
Participants
List dialog
box.

4. Click Done when you've finished adding names.

The following are some additional notes about using private mailing lists:

 ✔ If you want to add names to a private mailing list after you create it, you can do so. Select Window⇨New Address Book Window, double-click the Private Mail Lists container to expand it, and drag addresses to the mail list that you want to add to. Alternatively, you could select Window⇨ New Address Book Window, double-click the Private Mail Lists container to expand it, and click to select a mailing list. Then choose

File➪New➪Mailing List Participants to bring the Participants dialog box back up.

✔ To delete a private mailing list, select Window➪New Address Book Window, double-click the Private Mail Lists container to expand it, and click to select a mailing list. Press Delete and then respond OK to the confirmation message. It's gone! Before you get extreme and delete your private mailing lists wholesale, remember that you can also delete individual members. Just double-click the name of the private mailing list in the left pane of the cc:Mail window to make sure that the correct list is shown on the right. Click the name that you want to delete, and press Delete (or choose Edit➪Delete) to remove the name from that private mailing list.

✔ Renaming an existing private mailing list requires that you select Window➪New Address Book Window, double-click the Private Mail Lists container to expand it, and click to select a mailing list. Select Edit➪Rename and type the new name. Press Enter when you're finished.

✔ By the way, you can fill your new private mailing list if you try to add more than 199 addresses to it. cc:Mail gives you an error message if you try to add more addresses than that.

Chapter 8
Preparing and Sending Messages

. . . .

In This Chapter

▶ Preparing a message

▶ Typing a message

▶ Sending a message

▶ Checking a message

. . . .

*I*t's Tuesday morning. Your boss calls to ask you what happened to that report you were supposed to have ready by last Friday afternoon. Hmmm. You personally delivered a copy of it to him. You even butted in line at the copy machine just to get the darned thing in on time. The boss must have lost it. Now what do you do?

Don't run! Don't scream! Don't blame the company dog for eating your report! All you have to do is use cc:Mail to get your boss a new copy. Using cc:Mail, you can create the mail message, add your comments (better wait 'til you cool off, though), log it to prove that you sent it, and request a return receipt to show that your boss received it. Pretty nifty, eh?

This chapter covers all the essentials of sending mail — preparing messages, getting the content in, checking for errors, and finally, sending it. Using this information, you not only look good, but you can help keep your boss on his or her toes.

Preparing a Message

When you want to send an original message, you need to start a new message. You can start a new message a number of different ways:

✔ Click the New Message button

✔ Press Ctrl+M

✔ Select <u>M</u>essage⇨New <u>M</u>essage

After you use one of these methods, you see the New Message screen, as shown in Figure 8-1.

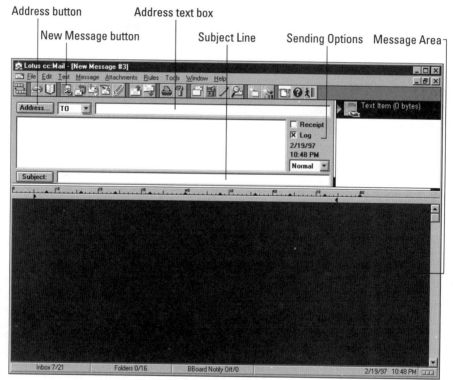

Address button   Address text box

New Message button   Subject Line   Sending Options Message Area

Figure 8-1:
The New
Message
screen.

You need to take care of a few things before diving into the message itself. The next few sections fill you in on addressing the message, selecting sending options, and filling in the subject line. Take care of these details, and you're well on your way to sending that message.

Addressing messages and selecting sending options

Addressing a cc:Mail message is pretty easy — even easier than writing an address on an envelope. From the New Message screen, use the following steps. If you need additional information about addressing messages, refer to Chapter 7.

1. Click the address button.

The Address Message dialog box appears, as shown in Figure 8-2.

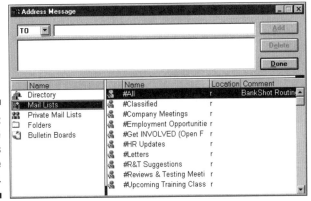

Figure 8-2:
The
Address
Message
dialog box.

2. Specify the sending option by clicking the arrow next to the Sending Option box.

cc:Mail automatically sends each message TO the addressee, unless you specify otherwise. You can send courtesy copies by selecting CC from the drop-down menu, or you can send blind courtesy copies by selecting BCC from the drop-down menu.

3. Select the recipient's address from the right pane of the dialog box and click Add.

You can also just double-click on the address itself.

4. Repeat Steps 2 and 3 until you have included all of the addresses that you want.

5. Click Done.

The New Message screen reappears with the address(es) filled in. Figure 8-3 shows an example of addresses with various sending options.

Filling in the subject line

The *subject line* is the place where you provide a tidbit about the topic of the message. It's important that you be descriptive in the subject line because this line is what gives your readers a clue about the content of the message.

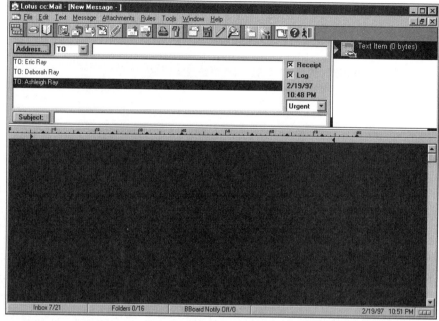

Figure 8-3:
A sample of addresses with various sending options selected.

You most likely sort and read your messages depending on what the message is about. That's why informative subject lines are so important. If the subject line does not accurately reflect what's in the message, readers may not even look at the message.

For example, suppose that you got a message with a subject line that reads "New Time." To you, that could mean that a meeting has been rescheduled, your golf game has been moved, you just got a reminder about resetting your clocks, or your flight will be departing three hours later than scheduled. Better subject lines are "Service meeting 2:30 Thursday," "Golf game 9:30 Saturday," "Set clocks back Wednesday night!," or "Flight to Dallas leaving 4:53 Friday." Use these more informative subject lines, and your readers can glean the gist of the message without even having to read the text.

To fill in the subject line, follow these instructions:

1. Click the Subject Line box.

2. Type a few descriptive words about the topic of the message.

3. Press Enter.

Your cursor then moves to the message area. Figure 8-4 shows an example of a completed subject line.

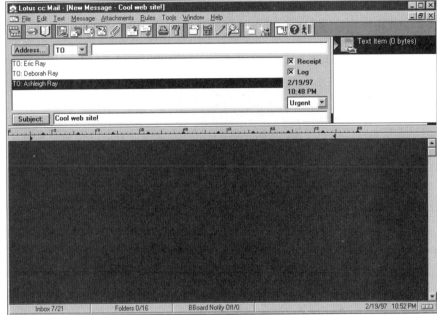

Figure 8-4:
The New
Message
screen with
the Subject
line
completed.

The following are some additional thoughts about preparing cc:Mail messages:

✔ cc:Mail allows you to store subject text that you use frequently. Simply click the Subject button after you type the subject text, and then click <u>A</u>dd to List. When you want to reuse the subject line in another message, click the Subject button, select the subject text, and then click OK.

✔ Don't make your subject lines too long. Take a look at Figure 8-5, which shows subject lines as they appear in the Inbox. Notice that longer subject lines are truncated and aren't as easily read.

Entering a Message

The meat of the message (in the Item-View pane) is called the message text. But right now, that blank message area is staring you in the face. You can even see your reflection in the monitor! Better get something written on that screen quickly.

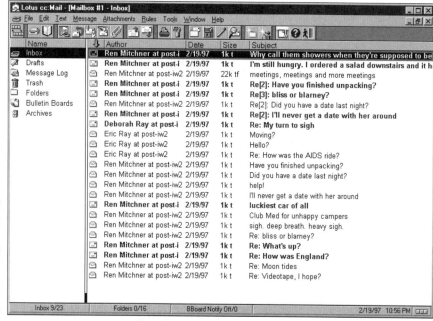

This section describes two methods of filling that big, blank message area:

- ✔ Typing text
- ✔ Importing text

When you're working in the cc:Mail text editor (inside the Item-View pane), you can use all of the standard Microsoft Windows editing and navigation keys to highlight text and move around within the e-mail message. Take a look at the appendix for a listing of all of the keys (and key combinations) that you can use in cc:Mail.

Typing text

One way to fill that message area is to — well, type some text. Simply click anywhere in the blank message area. The blinking cursor then appears in the upper-left portion of the message area. Type away!

Remember that cc:Mail is a Windows program, meaning that you can copy and paste text into your message. This is how you do that:

1. **Select the text that you want to copy from a word processing program, another e-mail message, or anywhere else.**

2. **Press Ctrl+C.**

3. Click where you want the text to appear.

4. Press Ctrl+V.

You can copy and paste (or cut and paste — Ctrl+X and then Ctrl+V) text within the same message, from other messages, or from other documents.

The following are some more tips on cut and copy and paste:

✔ To move and copy text, you can select Edit⇨Cut and Edit⇨Copy from the menu bar (or use the Ctrl+X and Ctrl+C keyboard shortcuts). The Cut command removes the selected text from its original location in the message text, and the Copy command makes a copy of it. Whenever you use either of these commands, the information is moved or copied to the Windows Clipboard.

✔ What is the Windows Clipboard? Well, the Clipboard acts like a storage buffer. You can cut or copy highlighted text to the Windows Clipboard and paste that text from the Clipboard to another location in the message (or even to other Windows programs if you feel inclined to). When you cut or copy text to the Clipboard, the new text replaces any text that was previously in the Clipboard.

✔ After positioning the cursor at the relevant point in the message, if you choose Edit⇨Paste from the menu bar (or use the Ctrl+V keyboard shortcut), the text that was in the Windows Clipboard is then pasted into the message where the cursor is located.

Importing text

Of course, if you've already prepared a text file (using Notepad or a comparable program), you can just insert that text.

These steps describe the process of inserting an existing text file into a mail message:

1. Start a new message by selecting Message⇨New Message, by pressing Ctrl+M, or by clicking on the New Message icon.

2. Address the message by clicking the Address button, selecting a name from the directory, and clicking Add.

3. Add something in the Subject line.

4. Click once in the message body to place the cursor.

5. Choose File⇨Import, select a file, and then click OK.

Search your hard disk until you find the file that you want to import. Remember that only plain text files (usually having an extension of TXT), not word processing documents, can be imported.

Seven tips of highly effective e-mailers

The following are seven tips about writing mail messages. Using these tips in your cc:Mail messages can help make your messages catchier, flashier, and possibly even more effective.

Tip #1: How to avoid flames

A *flame* is a nasty, rude, or obnoxious e-mail message sent with the intention of ticking off the recipient. Flames are uncool. Flaming is a bad habit to get into and is a definite no-no in business writing. To avoid getting flamed, try to keep your opinions to yourself and stick to the facts about things. If you don't, you may end up in a full-fledged *flame war*. If you happen to get flamed, just ignore it and go on about your business.

When you get that mail message that makes your blood boil, don't fire off a response telling the sender of the irritating message how you really feel. Get up, take a walk, get a glass of water, and do something (anything) other than respond right away. The reason for doing these things is that you never want an e-mail message to contain anything that you wouldn't want posted on the company bulletin board. Remember what you're doing: You're putting your feelings down electronically. And once you've sent that e-mail message, there's no way to get it back.

On the Internet, a subset of the mail culture exists that lives to flame other people. Flaming on the Net is sometimes considered fun; at other times, flaming is used by people who want to show knowledge of a particular subject.

Mailing an unwanted message to a large group of people is called *spamming* (derived from the favorite lunch item that keeps on giving). So if you want to avoid being flamed or (even worse) being called a spammer, use caution when sending your messages to a large group of people.

Tip #2: DON'T USE ALL CAPS

See how that looks like you're shouting? A good thing to remember is that in the e-mail world, if you capitalize everything you type, your action is called shouting, and shouting can be irritating to the people who read your messages on a regular basis; they assume that you didn't take the time to turn off Caps Lock.

Conversely, don't use all lowercase characters. It makes it look like you're working at home on your laptop and haven't decided whether to roll out of bed yet.

Tip #3: Grammar

Many people think that an e-mail message should have proper grammar and spelling and should be properly formatted. Other people think that an e-mail message is just an informal way of moving information from one place to another, and they wonder who cares about things like spelling. In many cases, the level of grammatical formality that is used when creating an e-mail message depends on the circumstances. If you're sending a message to your friend discussing that X-Files episode that you both saw last night, you really don't have to worry about spelling (unless you're trying to impress that special guy or gal) and formatting. If you're writing a message to the boss, though, you should at least have everything spelled correctly. Take a look at "Using the spell checker" later in this chapter for more about spell checking your document.

Use paragraphs. If you can't be bothered to stop your stream of consciousness to insert a couple of hard returns while writing, what makes you think that someone is going to take the time to read what you've written? Plenty of "white space" makes any document easier to read.

Be concise. Many people are now getting an extremely large number of e-mail messages. So think about the size of the e-mail that you're sending to your recipient. Is it two pages long when a half page can say the same thing? Some people say that they write long messages so that what they are trying to present comes out more clearly. But what we're working with here is an e-mail message, not a paper letter. So this practice of writing long messages may have just the opposite effect; people may skim your message to get the highlights and then move on. So think about how long your message is before clicking that send button.

Autograph your messages

cc:Mail doesn't let you use a "signature" or .sig file. If you want your name, e-mail address, and cute sayings to appear at the bottom of every message, you must type it all for every message or get creative.

You could create a new message with all of the closing information that you would like to use. Don't bother addressing the message or providing a subject — just insert the signature stuff. Choose Message⇨Save Draft to keep that message for posterity. Now, whenever you want to send a message and include a signature, just double-click on the Drafts Container to open it, and double-click your draft message to open it, in turn. Write your new message, address it, add a subject, and send it. cc:Mail will ask you if you want to delete the original draft message, say no (you want to keep using that draft message over and over again so you don't want to delete it). Just keep reusing the draft message as often as you want to keep putting your signature on those e-mails.

See Chapter 12 for more information about Drafts folders.

Tip #4: How to salute the addressee

In general, e-mail messages are more casual than other forms of business communication. One of the major differences between e-mail messages and business letters is in the message salutation. For instance, most business letters start with "Dear Mr. Crumpapple:" or possibly "Dear Ted:." In e-mail messages, you don't have to be so formal. You can just say, "Ted —" or "Ted," or even "Hi, Ted." I've even seen things like "Yo," "Hey," "Hi there," Howdy," and "What's happening?" appear as salutations, but I don't recommend those for business purposes.

Tip #5: How to sign the message

Just as the e-mail message salutation is pretty casual, so is the message closing. By all means, include your name somewhere at the bottom of the message, but including "Sincerely," "Yours truly," "Love," "XOXO," or "Best regards" probably isn't necessary.

Tip #6: How to express yourself

E-mail is pretty limited as far as expressing emotions. Though you can *say* something sarcastic and everyone who *hears* you probably recognizes the sarcasm, the tone and intonation that you use helps communicate the sarcastic intent. However, if you write the same thing, you may just sound rude or belligerent. As e-mail developed over the past few years, people started including silly little faces, created using various punctuation marks, to express being happy, sad, or indifferent, or to indicate that something you just wrote was intended as a joke. Though they aren't necessarily the epitome of professionalism, these smileys (called *emoticons*) can help convey emotions more effectively.

Samples of faces that you can include in your cc:Mail messages are as follows:

:>)	Happy, or text was meant as a joke
:)	Simply happy
:>(	Sad, irritated
:(	Just plain sad
:-I	Indifferent
;>)	Wink
:>0	Gasp!
8-)	Smiling, with glasses on
<8-)	Dunce cap, with glasses on

Tip #7: How to look cool

If you really want to look cool and seriously impede communication in your cc:Mail messages, use creative acronyms. Using these acronyms, which originated on the Internet, can help make you look like you know what you're doing.

The acronym digest

During your e-mail travels, you're bound to see a variety of acronyms that are used by a number of people in different situations. The following is a short guide to most of the common acronyms that are used in e-mail messages. Have fun. But remember: DGCA!

AA	Alcoholics Anonymous	**DTRT**	Do the right thing
AAA	Travel club	**EGADS**	Extremely good action, dumb story (refers to movies)
AAAAA	Travel club for alcoholics		
ADN	Any day now	**EOD**	End of discussion
AMOF	As a matter of fact	**EOL**	End of lecture
AFAIK	As far as I know	**EOT**	End of thread (that is, don't reply to this message)
AWGTHTGTTA?	Are we going to have to go through this again?		
		F2F	Face to face
B4N	Bye for now	**FAQ**	Frequently asked question
BBR	Burnt beyond repair	**FITB**	Fill in the blank
BIF	Basis in fact	**FUD**	Fear, uncertainty, and doubt
BL	Belly laughing!	**FWIW**	For what it's worth
BRS	Big red switch	**FYI**	For your information
BTA	But then again (in response to IOW)	**GAFIA**	Get away from it all
		GAL	Get a life
BTSOOM	Beats the [stuffing?] out of me	**GFR**	Grim file reaper (pervasive data destroyer)
BTW	By the way		
CMIIW	Correct me if I'm wrong	**GIGO**	Garbage in, garbage out
CU	See you	**GIWIST**	Gee, I wish I'd said that
CUL8R	See you later	**GMTA**	Great minds think alike
DGCA	Don't get carried away	**HAND**	Have a nice day
DIIK	Darned if I know		

(continued)

(continued)

HELP	Handling energetic little people (popular with moms everywhere)	**PTB**	Powers that be
		PTMM	Please tell me more!
HYEW	Hanging on your every word!	**RE**	Regarding
		RI	Romantic interest
IAC	In any case	**ROFL**	Rolling on floor laughing
IAE	In any event	**ROTM**	Right on the money
IANAL	I am not a lawyer	**RP**	Romantic partner
IBCNU	I'll be seeing you	**RSN**	Real soon now
IC	I see	**SGAL**	Sheesh! Get a life!!
IDTT	I'll drink to that!	**SIBU!HH**	Sure I believe you! Ha! Ha! (in disbelief)
IITYWIMI WHTKY	If I tell you what it means, I will have to kill you	**SOP**	Standard operating procedure
IMAO	In my arrogant opinion		
IME	In my experience	**TAFN**	That's all for now
IMHO	In my humble opinion	**TANJ**	There ain't no justice
IMNSHO	In my not so humble opinion	**TANSTAAFL**	There ain't no such thing as a free lunch
IOW	In other words	**TIA**	Thanks in advance
IWBNI	It would be nice if	**TLA**	Three-letter acronym
JIC	Just in case	**TNTL**	Trying not to laugh!
JTYWTK	Just thought you wanted to know	**TPTB**	The powers that be
		TTBOMK	To the best of my knowedge
KWIM	Know what I mean?	**TTFN**	Ta-ta for now
L8R	Later	**TYVM**	Thank you very much
LOL	Laughing out loud	**WFM**	Works for me
MEGO	My eyes glaze over	**WRT**	With regard to
NBIF	No basis in fact	**WYSIWYG**	What you see is what you get
NRN	No reply necessary		
OHDH	Old habits die hard	**WYGIWYPF**	What you get is what you pay for
OMG	Oh my gosh! (God!)		
OTOH	On the other hand	**YMMV**	Your mileage may vary
POV	Point of view		

The following are a couple more points on e-mail etiquette:

✔ There are certain things that should be stated face-to-face. Extremely good news and extremely bad news should usually not be stated in an e-mail message.

✔ There are times when a formal method of communication is more appropriate (that is, a paper letter with a paper envelope) than e-mail. For example, I wouldn't want to get the invitation to my best friend's wedding via e-mail. Actually, I wouldn't be surprised if he did that (but he's not a normal best friend).

✔ Again, thou shalt not spam.

✔ Not everyone equates you to Ralph Waldo Emerson. Just because you can send a message as fast as you type doesn't mean that people are going to read your message when they get it. So don't be disappointed when the President of the United States doesn't RSVP to your birthday party right away.

✔ Be aware: There is nothing stopping the person that you send a message to from forwarding your message to another 10, 100, or 1,000 people (either intentionally or accidentally).

Sending a Message

So just how does a message get from your computer to someone else's mailbox? You don't have to call anyone; you don't have to tie the message around your dog's neck with a note; you don't even have to put your computer in your regular mailbox. All you do is tell cc:Mail to send it, and there it goes!

After you've created your message, there's not much left to do. You can send the message in one of three ways:

✔ Click the Send button.

✔ Press Ctrl+S.

✔ Select Message⇨Send.

When you use one of these options, a notification box appears on your screen to tell you that cc:Mail is sending your message. That's all there is to it.

If you get pulled away from your desk before you can finish that crucial e-mail message and send it, you can store the message in the Drafts folder. See Chapter 12 for more information about Drafts folders.

There is no such thing as privacy or security when it comes to e-mail messages. Do I have your attention? (I'm almost shouting.) Good. At this point, you should be aware that anything you send as an e-mail message is not private or secure, especially if it's going to be sent over the Internet to its destination. You can make the e-mail that is on your computer somewhat private by managing access to your computer and the files that are on it. But if you want to get your message from one place to another, it usually crosses plenty of territory to get to its final resting place. Therefore, it could pass through thousands of networks before it finally gets to its destination. A message coming to you may or may not take a similar path. This means that potentially hundreds or thousands of eyes could see your messages without your knowledge. I don't mean to scare you; I just want you to remember this important fact when you're sending the company's confidential financial information on the new Whatchamahoo to the branch office in Oregon.

Exploring Sending Options

Just because you're using e-mail now and cutting the postal service out of some business doesn't mean that you have to use fancy options on sending your message. You can do anything except put a stamp on your message. cc:Mail offers several sending options, including Priority mail, requesting return receipts, and logging your outgoing messages.

Classifying a message as "Urgent"

Once in a while, you may need to scream to the person receiving your message, "This message is hot — read it now!" Well, instead of using up space in the subject line, you can just specify that the message is "Urgent." Yes, the message may arrive faster than normal depending on the situation, but the message is definitely marked "Urgent" on the reader's end. The recipient of this type of e-mail message sees an envelope icon that is red with a black exclamation point in the center.

You can specify urgency by using the priority drop-down box. To specify that you want the message classified as "Urgent," click the arrow and then select Urgent from the drop-down list. You can also specify that a message is of low priority by selecting Low from the drop-down list. Unless you specify otherwise, all messages are marked as "Normal" priority.

For those messages that leave your desk with no real urgency, you can select low priority. When recipients of this type of e-mail message receive such a message, they see an icon that is a gray envelope with a blue downward-pointing arrow at its center. A low-priority message may also get processed more slowly by the cc:Mail server.

What good is a low-priority message? A low-priority setting on a message can be useful if you are sending a long message and several short messages at the same time. If you use low priority for the long message and normal or urgent priority for the short messages, the short messages may go through the cc:Mail server first without being held up by the long one.

Getting a return receipt

Suppose that you're sending a message to someone who always seems to "lose" messages or claims that he didn't get one at all. Using the return receipt option, you get an e-mail message from the cc:Mail server letting you know that a message that you sent has been received and opened by its recipient. Simply check the Receipt box in the Message window, and cc:Mail sends you a message telling you when the reader received the message that you sent.

Beware, your recipient is probably going to notice the Returning Receipt message box and isn't likely to be pleased. Don't do this to your boss unless it's absolutely necessary.

If the Receipt option is enabled, it can be detrimental to the health of your Inbox because Receipt messages can clutter it up.

If you ever open an e-mail message and see a small dialog box flash on the screen with the message "Returning Receipt," you know that someone has sent you a message (usually important) with the Receipt option selected.

Receipts are not returned for e-mail recipients getting courtesy copies or blind courtesy copies, or for those messages that are sent to a folder or bulletin board.

Be aware that if you're sending return receipt messages to someone who isn't using cc:Mail or if your messages are going through the Internet to their destination, you may not get a return receipt. I hate when that happens!

Logging sent messages

Another cool way of verifying that you sent a message is to *log* it. When you log a message, cc:Mail makes a copy of the message and stores it in the Message Log folder. To save a copy of the message in the Message Log folder, select the Log check box in the message screen. Then, when you need to retrieve a logged message, double-click Message Log in your Inbox view.

Note that the cc:Mail administrator also has to enable the Message Log feature at the cc:Mail server.

See Chapter 12 for more information about the Message Log.

Finding Goofs Before You Send

Don't you hate it when you write something, give a copy to your boss, and then find out that there were loads of typos in it? Fortunately, cc:Mail offers you the full complement of spell checking and search and replace features. You should use these features after you draft a message but before you send it. The following sections give you the scoop on these nifty features.

Using the spell checker

The spell checker, as in other Windows programs, finds many typos and misspelled words that tend to creep into your messages. Be careful, though; the spell checker doesn't catch all of your mistakes. For example, errors in usage aren't caught (such as there versus their or to, too, and two), nor are floating letters (like "i" that should be "if").

You can access the spell checker in one of three ways:

- ✔ Click on the Spell Check icon.
- ✔ Press Ctrl+E.
- ✔ Select Tools⇨Spell Check.

After you access the spell checker, you see the Spell Check dialog box, as shown in Figure 8-6.

The following steps outline how to use the spell checker:

1. **Create a new message by clicking on the New Message icon, by selecting Message⇨New Message, or by pressing Ctrl+M.**

2. **Write or import your text.**

3. **Select Tools⇨Spell Check, press Ctrl+E, or click on the Spell Check icon.**

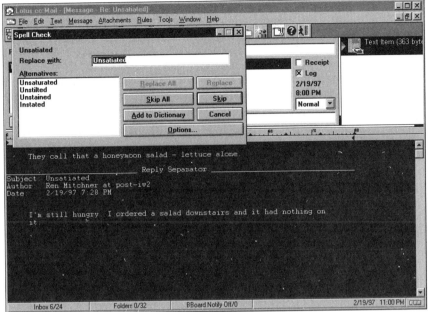

Figure 8-6:
The Spell
Check
dialog box.

4. As the spell checker finds alleged errors, you can choose what to do with each one.

Click a suggested word and click the Replace or Replace All buttons to fix a mistake throughout the message; click Skip or Skip All to disregard the word throughout the message; or click Add to Dictionary to include that word permanently in your cc:Mail dictionary (cool!). Choosing Options allows you to select which language and dialect is spell checked — American English, British English, or French or Canadian French; Brazilian, Portuguese, and Spanish are also options.

5. After the spell checker has checked every word, you see the cc:Edit Information dialog box with the message "Spell check is complete." Click OK to return to your message.

The following are a few additional thoughts about the spell check feature:

✔ The spell checker also roots through your document and stops at repeated repeated words. You then have the option to Skip the re-peated words if they're supposed to be there. To delete one of the words, press Delete and then press Enter.

✔ You can have the spell checker on all the time (checking the entire text of every outgoing new message, forwarded message, and message reply). This is done by choosing Tools⇨User Setup and pressing the down-arrow key once or clicking on the Prepare icon. After you've selected the Prepare icon, check out the section under the Defaults heading, select the Automatic Spell Check check box, and click OK (or press Enter). Click the Cancel button, or press Esc to exit the User Setup dialog box without turning on the spell-check-all-the-time feature.

✔ The cc:Mail spell checker is not foolproof and shouldn't be used in place of proofreading the message text. If a misspelled word in your message is not in its dictionary (and it doesn't have a word in the dictionary that seems similar to the misspelled word), it doesn't tell you that you've misspelled it. In some cases, the Spell Check dialog box doesn't have alternative spellings for a word, in which case you may have to pull out the old, paper-based dictionary and type the right spelling in the Replace with text box. Also, if you meant to type the word *football* in your message text and you typed the word *foot* instead, the spell checker considers both words to be spelled correctly.

✔ Because the spell checker cannot understand the context under which a message is created, you should proofread your messages before you send them (especially the important ones). This is just a word of caution (or the voice of experience — I'm not telling which).

Selecting and highlighting text

To make changes to a block of text within a cc:Mail message, to delete the block, or to replace it, you first need to select and highlight the text.

To select and highlight any text that you are working on, follow these instructions:

1. **Click and hold the left mouse button (right mouse button for you lefties) at the beginning of the selection of text that you want to highlight in the Message window.**

2. **Drag the mouse until you get to the end of the text that you want to highlight (you can go up or down the message text).**

3. **Release the mouse button (the selected text then appears as a different color than the text around it).**

4. **Perform the operation that you want on the highlighted text.**

   Click anywhere in the Item-View pane to deselect the highlighted text.

I strongly suggest that you review Appendix C to learn more about the various keystrokes that can ease your editing woes within cc:Mail.

The Delete and Backspace keys are your friends, not to mention Mr. Undo!

When you find yourself editing one of your messages, there are two keys that you may use more frequently than most of the others: the Delete key and the Backspace key.

Delete omits text characters to the right of the cursor (the cursor in a message is also known as the insertion point), but pressing Backspace deletes characters to the left of the cursor. If you want to delete a block of text, select the text before pressing either Delete or Backspace.

You can reverse the effects of a deletion by selecting Edit⇨Undo from the menu bar (or by pressing Ctrl+Z).

The Undo command only remembers the last delete that you did, so you must use it immediately to undo the effects of a delete. If you wait, you may not be able to use Undo.

The Undo command in cc:Mail is also very fickle. There are some things that the Undo command won't undo (like bringing back a deleted folder). So don't depend on the Undo command always being there to save you.

Using the Find & Replace feature

Another handy way to fix your problems is to use the Find & Replace feature. For example, suppose that you just drafted a three-screen message to your boss about the Thuzwoozit Product Specifications. Then you remember that the official name of the product is the Thuzwoozit III, and you need to change each reference in the document to reflect the official name, Thuzwoozit III Product Specifications. Using the Find & Replace feature, you can just tell cc:Mail to look for each occurrence and replace the existing text with whatever you want.

To use the Find & Replace feature, follow these instructions:

1. **Create a new message by clicking on the New Message icon, by selecting Message⇨New Message, or by pressing Ctrl+M.**

2. **Write or import your text.**

3. **Select Edit⇨Find/Replace.**

   The Replace dialog box appears, as shown in Figure 8-7.

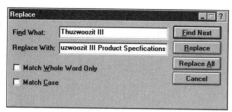

Figure 8-7:
The
Replace
dialog box.

4. In the Find What area, type the text that you want cc:Mail to replace.

5. Press Tab.

The cursor moves to the Replace With area.

6. In the Replace With area, type the text that you want cc:Mail to use as a replacement for the text in the Find What area.

7. Select Find Next, Replace, or Replace All.

If you select Find Next, cc:Mail stops at the next occurrence of the word that you want to replace. From there, you can, again, choose to Find Next, Replace, or Replace All.

If you select Replace, cc:Mail replaces only that instance of the text that's entered in the Find What area.

If you select Replace All, cc:Mail replaces all instances of the text that's entered in the Find What area.

8. When you're done finding and replacing, click OK.

cc:Mail returns you to your message window.

The following are some additional thoughts to ponder about the Find & Replace feature:

✔ You can specify that you want to find only instances of the whole word by selecting the Match Whole Word Only check box. For example, if you're searching for the word "in," cc:Mail stops and highlights the word "in" as it appears in words like *in*terchange, *in*tergalactic, and *in*formation. Using the Match Whole Word Only option, cc:Mail only stops at instances of the stand-alone word "in."

✔ You can specify that you want to find instances of a word that have a certain capitalization by selecting the Match Case check box. For example, you may be looking for the words *Market Street* as they appear, with initial capitalization. However, you may not want cc:Mail to also find instances of *market* or *street* that are not in capital letters. Checking the Match Case box, you can specify the instances of the words that you want to find.

Chapter 9

Sending Stuff with Your Messages

. . . .

In This Chapter

▶ Sending attachments

▶ Forwarding messages

. . . .

*A*ttachments. You mean those doohickeys that come with a vacuum cleaner? We get those with cc:Mail, too? And what's this stuff about forwards? cc:Mail has a basketball team?

Actually, an attachment is just a file (Word document, picture, spreadsheet, or sound file of the *X-Files* theme) that you include with a regular cc:Mail message. It's easy for you and the recipient (assuming that they're also on cc:Mail) to save and use whatever you attach.

Forwards, also hanging out in this chapter, are something else creative that you can do with messages — you receive a message and pass it on to someone else to read. Check out the following sections for the full story on both counts.

Sending Attachments

An *attachment* is a file from another program that is tacked onto an e-mail message. Instead of copying a file to a diskette and carrying or mailing it to the recipient, you just attach the file to your cc:Mail message and send the whole thing.

You may use attachments to share draft documents with others in your workgroup, to provide sample expense reports to your coworkers, or to make sure that all of your friends have the newest photo of your daughter. Whatever your use for attachments, they're easy to create and handy to use.

Sending an attachment

Back in the stone ages when you didn't have e-mail, you probably typed your document, paper-clipped any additional information that you wanted to send with it, and then stuck the whole thing in a big envelope. Using attachments with cc:Mail is very similar. You type your message, attach the message, and send the whole thing — message and attachment.

The following are the instructions, step by step, for attaching and sending an existing file that's currently on your hard disk.

1. **Start a new message by selecting Message⇨New Message, by pressing Ctrl+M, or by clicking on the New Message icon.**

2. **Address the message by clicking the Address button, selecting a name from the directory, and clicking Add.**

3. **Fill in the Subject line.**

4. **Type a brief description of the attachment in the text area of the message.**

   Technically, this description isn't completely necessary, but providing a little information such as "This is the Word 7.0 document that we discussed last week" helps your recipient know what to expect. Attachments generally arrive with a familiar-looking icon to clue the recipient in about the contents, but relying on the icons sometimes backfires.

5. **Choose Attachments⇨Files, press Ctrl+F, or click on the Attach icon.**

   You then see the Attach/Files dialog box, as shown in Figure 9-1.

6. **Search your disk until you've found the file that you want to attach. Click the file once to select it and then click Add.**

   You see the filename appear in the Attachments text box, so you know that it worked.

   Repeat Step 6 until you've attached all of the files that you want to attach. You can attach a maximum of 20 files to any message.

7. **Click OK to attach the files and return to your message.**

   You see icons for each of the files that you attached in the Attachments pane of your message, as shown in Figure 9-2.

8. **If you change your mind about an attachment after you've attached it to your message, click it once in the Attachment pane to highlight it and then press Delete.**

   This step deletes the attachment from the message but leaves the file untouched on your computer.

9. **Send your message by clicking on the Send icon, by pressing Ctrl+S, or by selecting Message⇨Send.**

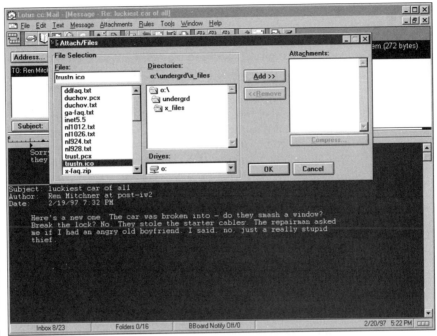

Figure 9-1:
The Attach/
Files dialog
box.

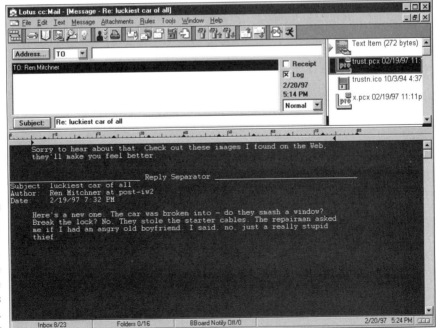

Figure 9-2:
Attached
files are
visible
in the
Attachments
pane.

The following are some additional comments about attachments:

✔ Even though cc:Mail can handle up to 20 attachments with any message, it's usually considered a good habit to keep the number of attachments down to around 5. For one thing, it's hard to scroll through 20 attachments in a single message. Second, it increases your chances that something can go wrong (you risk the chance that your message goes floating off into cyberspace) when you send your messages with a huge amount of attachments. So unless you find it really necessary to have more than 5 attachments, stick to Garza's Rule #112: It's better to get an e-mail message with 5 attachments then to get no message at all.

✔ If you work for a company that values its resources (and which company doesn't?), it probably has a policy about e-mail (and maybe even one just for attachments to e-mail messages). Check out your local e-mail policy to determine if you are limited to a certain number of attachments. This limitation is usually in place because many attachments that are sent by many employees can quickly devour hard drive space on your company's cc:Mail server.

✔ You may work for a company with a mixed computing environment (that is, one in which everyone is not yet running Windows). Before sending that 1-2-3 spreadsheet as an attachment, make sure that the people on the receiving end can use it on their computers. If you're not sure what kind of computer or operating system that the intended recipient is using, send him or her a message first to indicate what type of file you plan to send to make sure that the person can use it.

Sending an attachment with a twist

You can also attach files in more creative ways. More importantly, these ways, including sending a new document and dragging and dropping attachments, may make it a bit easier to get your work done.

The following are instructions for the different ways you can stick attachments to messages:

1. **Start a new message by selecting Message⇨New Message, by pressing Ctrl+M, or by clicking the New Message icon.**

2. **Address the message by clicking the Address button, selecting a name from the directory, and clicking Add.**

3. **Fill in the Subject line.**

What do you mean, you didn't get it?!

As much as we'd like to believe that attaching a file and sending it around the world is as easy as falling off a log, it just isn't so. Technically, sending it around the world actually is a snap. Receiving it, however, is another story. This sidebar explains where the problems lie and how to attempt to work around some of them.

Internet gateways, through which Internet e-mail messages pass, cannot handle anything except a plain text file. Binary files, like word processing documents, spreadsheets, pictures, sound files, or anything that has text and formatting, are not plain text files; therefore, they cannot go through Internet gateways in their original form.

The solution is to translate the binary files (which is what most attachments are composed of) into text-based representations as they pass from cc:Mail into the Internet, and then to translate them back into their original form when they're received on the other end. If a cc:Mail system is on both ends of this exchange, the translation generally works well. However, there are hundreds of different e-mail systems, many of which use different

systems and different rules to convert these transmitted text files back into usable binary versions.

In short, sometimes it works and sometimes it doesn't. Murphy's Law controls when it works and when it doesn't.

There are a few things that you can do to improve your chances of success:

- ✔ Use standard file extensions. For example, if you're attaching a word processing document, use DOC as the file extension. If it's a TIFF image, use a TIF extension. Don't use the extensions that only make sense to you, such as LTP for letter, personal.

- ✔ Try sending when not in a crisis. As soon as you determine that the transmission didn't work correctly, contact your cc:Mail administrator and ask for suggestions.

- ✔ Suggest that it would be much easier for everyone concerned if the person with whom you're corresponding used cc:Mail, too!

4. **Briefly describe the attachment in the text area of the message so that your recipient knows what's supposed to be there.**

5. **To create a new file and automatically attach it, choose Attachments⇨Run Applications.**

You then see the Attach New File dialog box, as shown in Figure 9-3.

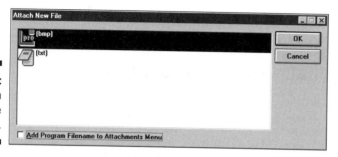

Figure 9-3:
The Attach
New File
dialog box.

6. **Select a file type to attach from the choices in the dialog box and click OK.**

   cc:Mail temporarily vanishes, only to be replaced by the application that you just selected. You can use the application to create a document (or file or picture). When you're finished, select File➪Exit to leave the application. When prompted, confirm that you want to save the document. The application then disappears, and cc:Mail returns; voilà, the new attachment that you just created is in the Attachments pane.

7. **If you want to attach a file by dragging and dropping it from your Windows File Manager (for Windows 3.1*x* users) or from the Windows Explorer (for Windows 95 users), open your file management tool and arrange it and cc:Mail so that you can see both the Attachments pane of your cc:Mail message and the file that you want to attach.**

8. **Drag the file from the File Manager or Explorer to the Attachments pane of the cc:Mail message.**

   Repeat Steps 5 and 6 *or* 7 and 8 until you've attached all of the files that you want to attach.

9. **Click OK to return to your message.**

   You then see icons for each of the files that you attached in the Attachments pane of your message, as shown in Figure 9-4.

   If you change your mind about an attachment, click the attachment once in the Attachment pane to highlight it and then press Delete. This step deletes the attachment from the message but leaves the file untouched on your computer.

 10. **Send your message by clicking on the Send icon, by pressing Ctrl+S, or by selecting Message➪Send.**

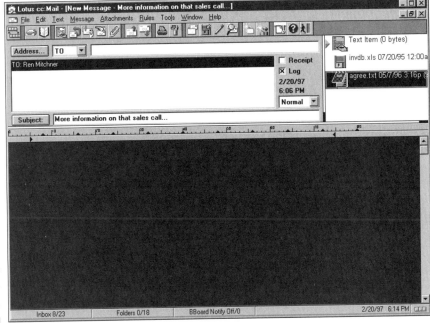

Figure 9-4:
The files
in the
Attachments
pane of
the new
message.

Read on for some additional hints about sending attachments:

- cc:Mail allows you to send up to 20 attachments, including the text "attachment" that holds your actual message. If you want to send more than that, you must use more than one message to carry all of the baggage.

- You can drag and drop attachments from the Attachments pane of one message into the Attachments pane of a different message. For example, if your boss attached an expense report to a message to you, you could drag that attachment into a second message that is addressed to someone in Accounting.

- If, for some reason, you want to attach a second text part to your message, you can do that by choosing Attachments⇨Text. Just double-click on the Text Item icons in the Attachment pane to open each of them so that you can add text.

- Finally, you can attach text or images from the Clipboard as well. Just copy the text or image from any program, switch to cc:Mail, and select Attachments⇨Clipboard to insert the clipboard contents as an attachment.

Forwarding Messages

A *forwarded message* is a message that you receive and forward to someone else. There's no limit to how often a message can be forwarded — just say the word, and cc:Mail forwards the message. What's more, you can add your own comments and additional information and then send the whole thing at once.

Forwarding messages is a great way of passing information along, with or without additional commentary.

For those forwarders in the audience, follow these steps:

1. **Double-click a message in your Inbox or another folder to open it.**

   You can also just select the message, without opening it, but that doesn't give you the option of adding comments to the message.

 2. **Select Message⇨Forward, click on the Forward icon, or press Ctrl+R.**

   You then see the Forward dialog box ask you if you want to Retain Forwarding History.

3. **Select or deselect the Retain Forwarding History check box and click OK.**

   If you deselect Retain Forwarding History, there is no imbedded information in the message to show that it was originally received by you and then forwarded. Retaining forwarding history clearly shows who sent the message to you and that you chose to forward it.

4. **Add or delete attachments to the message if you choose.**

   All attachments to the original message are retained in the forwarded message. If you want to delete one of the attachments, click the attachment once in the Attachment pane and press Delete.

 To add an attachment, choose Attachments⇨Files, click on the Attach icon, or press Ctrl+F, and select the file that you want to attach. If you want to attach files using other methods, refer to "Sending Attachments" earlier in this chapter.

5. **You can also add text to the message, either above or below the Forward Header.**

 6. **When you're finished, send the message by choosing Message⇨Send, by pressing Ctrl+S, or by clicking on the Send icon.**

The following are some additional comments about forwarding messages:

✔ You can set cc:Mail forwarding defaults by selecting Tools⇨User Setup. Choose Message in the left pane. Click to default to Include Forward Separator and Retain Forwarding History. Selecting these options determines the default setting in the Forward dialog box, but you can still choose to include (or not to include) the Forward separator line for each individual message.

✔ When forwarding a message, if you make any changes to a received message while you are reading it but before you click the Forward Message button (to forward the message), then the Forward separator line does not appear in the body of the message. As a result, the new recipients of the message do not know that the clever words of wisdom that you are passing along are actually not yours. This may be quite helpful if you like to mark up someone else's text before sending it on or if you like to make comments to a message directly in the body of the message.

✔ When you forward a message by clicking on the Forward Message button, the Forward separator line appears. You can cross that line any time you want to make comments in the original body of the message, or you can stay on your side of the line to show how you feel about the topic at hand. Jumping back and forth over the line can make the message pretty lively.

✔ Keep in mind that if you're going to change the original text of a message or add your comments in the body of someone else's original message, you may want to do your readers a favor by changing the color of your comments so that they can tell who wrote what. Refer to Chapter 10 for more information.

Chapter 10

Customizing Text Options

Cc:Mail doesn't look too bad right out of the box, but with a little creativity, you can apply your artistic talent to cc:Mail's appearance. This chapter focuses on some of the nifty tricks that cc:Mail lets you do to help you customize the appearance of your message — mostly for your benefit, but also for your readers, too. This chapter covers changing the fonts and font sizes that cc:Mail uses to display your messages as well as changing text colors and adjusting margins.

Changing Fonts

One of the neat features of cc:Mail is that it lets you customize the fonts that you see throughout the program. Though you could use this feature just to make sure that your new CD of Shareware Fonts for Fun doesn't go to waste, a better use is to make your cc:Mail window more readable or usable by selecting fonts (and font sizes) that you find easy to read.

Keep in mind two things as you're fiddling with the fonts. First, cc:Mail only lets you choose *monospaced fonts* for message windows and printed messages — that is, fonts that use an equal amount of space for each character. So, although you do get some variety in fonts, you don't get to choose from the really fancy ones all the time. Second, changing fonts only affects what *you* see, not what your readers see on their end. They will see the fonts (and font sizes) that they select, not the ones that you select.

Check out Figures 10-1 and 10-2 for examples of effectively changing fonts and sizes.

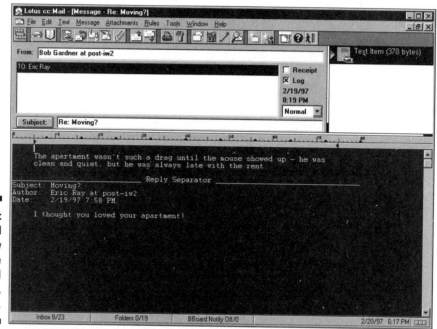

Figure 10-1:
A cc:Mail window using the standard font, style, and size.

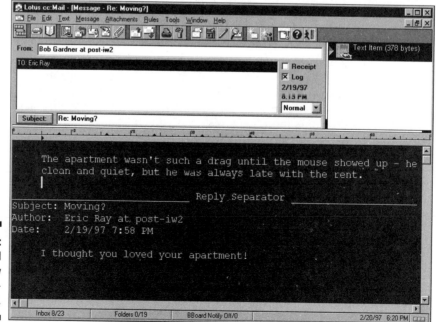

Figure 10-2:
A cc:Mail window with easy-to-read text.

These steps outline the process for changing your font settings:

1. **In cc:Mail, make a selection in the place that you want to change the font.**

   If you want to change the font in a message, double-click a message to select it.

2. **Select Text⇨Fonts.**

   You then see the User Setup dialog box with only Fonts as an option on the left, as shown in Figure 10-3.

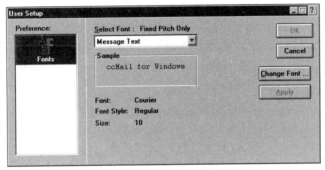

Figure 10-3:
The User
Setup
dialog box
is used to
change font
settings.

The Select Font area is where you can change the font. Under Select Font, you can choose each separately configurable area in which you can customize the fonts, including the Message Text, Container List, Printed Message, Attachments List, and Address/Message List.

3. **Click Change Font.**

   You then see the Font dialog box, as shown in Figure 10-4.

4. **Choose a Font, Font Style, and Size, and click OK to return to the User Setup dialog box.**

   When you make a selection to change the attribute of a font or change a font type, your change is reflected in the Sample box. This gives you an idea of what your change is going to look like when it's implemented.

5. **Choose Apply to immediately apply your change and remain in the dialog box so that you can explore other Select Font options.**

6. **If you want to escape from this plethora of font options without making font changes, just press Esc or click OK to implement all of your font selections, save your changes, and return to cc:Mail.**

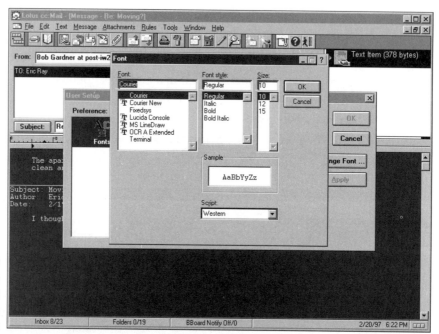

Figure 10-4:
The Font
dialog box.

An additional comment about changing fonts: You can change all of the different font settings in cc:Mail from one place without having to start by selecting an area in which you want to change the fonts. Select Tools⇨User Setup. Select Fonts in the left scrolling set of icons. Under Select Font, choose each separately configurable area in which you can customize the fonts, including Message Text, Container List, Printed Message, Attachments List, and Address/Message List. Select an area, and change the fonts all you want.

Changing Message Colors

Another cool thing you can do to customize your message is to change the message colors. You can change the text color, the message background color, or both. The changed text and background colors appear not only on your computer but also on your readers' computers, too. Changing message colors can make it easier to read messages or emphasize messages that are sent to other cc:Mail users.

Change your colors by following these steps:

1. **In cc:Mail, create a new message by selecting Message⇨New Message, by pressing Ctrl+M, or by clicking on the New Message icon.**

   You must have a message open to change text settings.

2. **Select Text⇨Colors, press Ctrl+H, or click the right mouse button.**

   You then see the Color Highlighting dialog box, as shown in Figure 10-5.

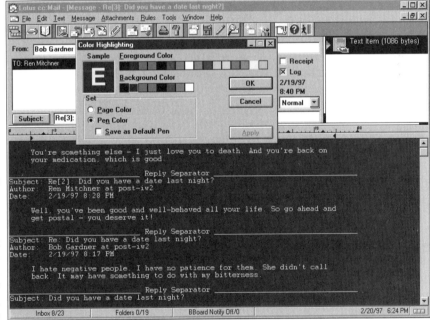

Figure 10-5:
The Color
Highlighting
dialog box
is used to
change
color
settings.

3. **Select Page Color to change the overall background color of the message, and then click the color of your choice from the Background Color row of samples.**

4. **Select Pen Color to change the colors of the text that you enter, and then select a Foreground Color and a Background Color.**

   Be nice! Strive for good contrast between the foreground color and background color. Some of us don't have great eyes anymore (as if we ever did) and can't stand to try to read lime green or yellow on white. Additionally, Christmas-like colors, such as red on green, look like just plain gray to people who are color-blind.

5. **If you want your Pen Color settings to apply to all of the text that you enter, click Save as Default Pen.**

   If you don't use Save as Default Pen, your color choices only apply to the text that you type in your current message.

6. **Click OK to return to your message.**

Read on for some additional notes about using colors to highlight text.

✔ You can also use color highlighting to emphasize specific words in your cc:Mail messages just as you would use boldface or italics to emphasize words in a letter or report. Highlight the text that you want to emphasize and select Text⇨Colors, press Ctrl+H, or click the right mouse button. Choose the colors that you want, and then click Apply. You may want to reselect the original colors that you were using, however, because after you click OK to leave the dialog box, everything that you type is in the color combination that you last selected.

✔ Remember, the colors that you select are only visible to other cc:Mail users in your cc:Mail directory. If you carefully emphasize text by using all kinds of creative color combinations and then send the message to a friend on the Internet, your friend doesn't see anything different about the colors of your message. Sorry, but that's just the way it works with e-mail to the Internet — you lose all of the fun stuff (except your colorful witticisms, of course).

Changing Margins and Tabs

cc:Mail lets you control the width of your message text as well as the tab stops. In this respect, it's fully as powerful as a 1906 Remington typewriter. Big deal, you say? Actually, adjusting the default margins and tabs can make your messages much easier to read, particularly for recipients outside your cc:Mail system, like Aunt Mabel on the Internet.

About margins

When you set a margin, you're really just adjusting the line length — making it longer (with small margins) or making it shorter (using big margins). Before you get too excited about changing margins, remember that most electronic mail systems hearken back to the old days of DOS and character-based terminals. Many potential readers of your e-mail message may still use those old terminals (horrors!), which can only display 80 characters of text on a line. If you change your margins and end up putting more than 80 characters on a line, your readers are going to be less than pleased. They see something like this:

```
Dear Stan,
I cannot tell you how happy I was to receive that Eskimo
          Joe's tee-shirt from you.
It is
without a doubt the nicest present I've ever gotten, at
          least in the past three days
or so.
By the way, the next time you are in town, please do drop
          in. We'll be happy to cook
some
hamburgers and cheese fries for you. We know how much you
like them.
```

Classy, huh? So keep those margins down! Generally, 60-character lines are a safe bet. So unless you have a good reason to change the default margins, it's probably a good idea to leave them alone.

About tabs

You can control the width of a tab stop. Every time that you press Tab, your cursor zips 8 characters across the screen; this uses up your real estate at a pretty good clip. Changing tab stops to 4 or 5 characters allows you to line up more things on the screen with tabs.

Use this next procedure for changing both margins and tab stops. (If you prefer to be a little more free-form with the margin settings, see "Using the Ruler" later in this chapter.)

1. **In cc:Mail, create a new message by selecting Message⇨New Message, by pressing Ctrl+M, or by clicking on the New Message icon.**

   You must have a message open to change text settings.

2. **Choose Text⇨Margins/Tabs.**

   You then see the Margins/Tabs dialog box, as shown in Figure 10-6.

3. **Enter the Left margin (in characters), press Tab, and enter the Right margin.**

   Try for a happy medium — lines that are too long may not fit on your reader's screen, but very short lines provide a newspaper-column effect that's also hard to read.

4. **To save these margins as default margins for all future messages (or until you change them again), click Save.**

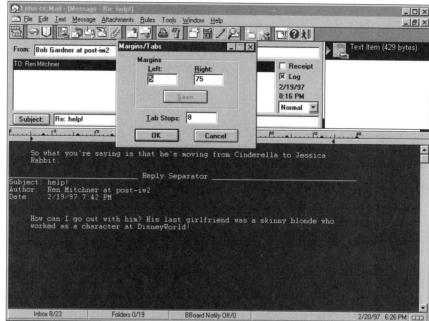

Figure 10-6:
The
Margins/
Tabs dialog
box.

5. To change the default tab length, type a new value in the <u>T</u>ab Stops text box.

6. Click OK.

Margins and tabs are usually best left at their default settings. Changing them without a good reason may get you questions asking why all of your messages look like they're spaced for a newspaper column. Also, when a message is sent to the Internet with fancy margin and tab settings, it all just gets hosed. Your nicely tabbed and margined document ends up looking like a ransom note without the glue.

Using the Ruler

The ruler is a standard cc:Mail feature that the administrator can use to rap your knuckles if you cause problems. Additional uses for the ruler include setting margins for individual messages and making it easier to see at a glance that your text lines up vertically.

Using the ruler to adjust margins sure beats any other uses for the ruler. Follow these steps to adjust margins:

1. **In cc:Mail, create a new message by selecting Message⇨New Message, by pressing Ctrl+M, or by clicking on the New Message icon.**

   You must have a message open to see the ruler.

2. **If the ruler isn't visible at the top of your message (between the message body and the address and subject area), select Text⇨Ruler.**

   You then see a blank message with a ruler, as shown in Figure 10-7.

3. **Select the text that you want your new margin settings to apply to.**

4. **Click and drag the left- or right-pointing triangles in the bottom half of the ruler to change the margins.**

   Unfortunately, you cannot save margin settings that you make with the ruler. You have to manually make the change in the Margins/Tabs dialog box and Save your changes for them to apply to future messages.

   If you decide that you don't like the change that you made, you can revert to the saved margin settings by pressing Ctrl+D or by selecting Text⇨Use Default Margins.

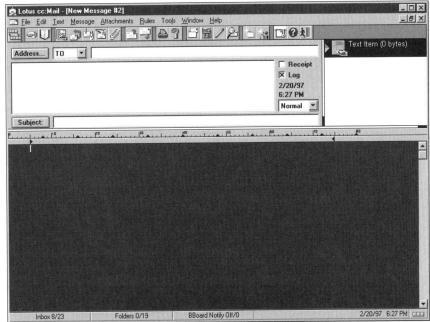

Figure 10-7:
A blank message with the ruler visible.

Chapter 11

Forms and What They're Good For

. . . .

. . . .

*F*orms — the bane of your existence or the only way of bringing a semblance of order to workplace? A big part of the answer to that question, of course, depends on what the forms are and how frequently you have to fill them out.

How frequently you interact with forms in cc:Mail depends primarily on your cc:Mail administrator or your form administrator. Your administrator may convert all of those paper forms that you currently use to cc:Mail forms, or he may more slowly migrate into them. Either way, this chapter prepares you to respond quickly, concisely, and in generally outstanding form.

About Forms

You know forms. They have blanks that are too small to write in, lots of boxes, vague threats if you fill in the form incorrectly, and all kinds of useless information that you must provide. Now you can use your computer to complete the forms and automatically send them to their destination.

For example, you could receive a travel expense form from the travel coordinator at your company, complete the form and send it along its predetermined route to your boss, for approval, and forward it to accounting so that the company reimburses you. Forms aren't ever going to be fun, but using cc:Mail to complete them sure beats having to wait for interoffice mail.

cc:Mail includes five standard sample forms, including a time card, travel expense reimbursement request, travel itinerary/preference, employee move notice, and computer hardware/software request, and they probably look very much like the forms that are currently in your office. See Figure 11-1 for a sample of the travel expense reimbursement request form.

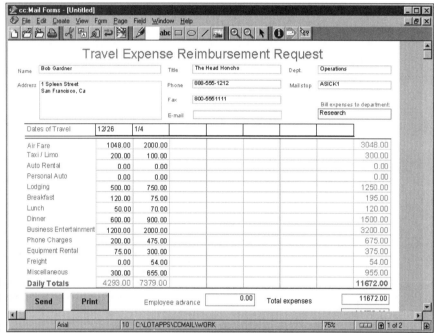

Figure 11-1:
The cc:Mail
Travel
Expense
Reimburse-
ment
Request
form.

How you use forms depends on your particular needs, the way that your office is organized, and the forms that your forms administrator sets up. You may attach blank forms to a cc:Mail message and send them to someone else to complete, or you could receive blank forms from someone else that you should complete and return or complete and forward.

Sending Forms

The following procedure shows you how to attach and fill in the sample Travel Expense Reimbursement Request form and send it to its recipient. You can use this procedure for sending any of the sample forms that cc:Mail provides.

1. **In cc:Mail, create a new message by selecting Message⇨New Message, by pressing Ctrl+M, or by clicking the New Message icon.**

2. **Address the message to your boss (or to yourself if you don't want to practice on your boss).**

3. **Add a subject about testing a form.**

4. **Choose Attachments⇨Forms to attach a form.**

   You then see the Attach/Forms dialog box, as shown in Figure 11-2.

Figure 11-2:
The Attach/
Forms
dialog box.

5. **Select the form that you want to attach, click Add, and then click OK or double-click the form that you want to attach, and then click OK.**

   You may have to look in a different directory on your hard drive for forms that your local administrator creates. Your administrator can tell you where to look.

6. **To fill in the form, click once on the Form icon in the Attachments pane to select it, and then choose Attachments⇨Launch Attachment.**

   You see the cc:Mail Forms application open, with the Travel Expense Reimbursement Request form visible.

7. **Complete this form as you would complete any form. When you're finished, proceed to the next step.**

8. **Choose File⇨Exit, and respond Yes when asked if you want to save your changes.**

   You are returned to cc:Mail. You can add a subject or text to the message if you like.

9. **Send your form by choosing Message⇨Send, by pressing Ctrl+S, or by clicking on the Send icon.**

Receiving and Resending Forms

The following procedure shows you how to receive a form, add or change information, and send the form to another recipient.

1. **In cc:Mail, double-click a message with the form attached.**

2. **To edit the information in the form, click once on the Form icon in the Attachments pane to select it, and then choose Attachments⇨Launch Attachment.**

   You see the cc:Mail Forms application open, with the form visible.

3. **Make any necessary changes to the form.**

4. **Choose File⇨Exit and respond Yes when asked if you want to Save Form before Closing.**

   You are returned to cc:Mail, and you see a Forward/Reply dialog box, as shown in Figure 11-3.

Figure 11-3: The Forward/Reply dialog box.

cc:Mail knows that you made modifications to the form and lets you omit your changes, Forward the form to another recipient, or Reply to return the form to the sender.

5. **Select Forward and click OK.**

   Depending on the form, of course, you should reply.

6. **cc:Mail asks you if you want to Retain Forwarding History. Select this check box (if it isn't already selected), and then click OK.**

   If you don't select Retain Forwarding History, there are no visible marks in the message to show that it was originally received by you and then forwarded. Retaining forwarding history clearly shows who sent the form to you and that you chose to forward it to someone else.

7. **Address the message by choosing Address, selecting an address from the Address Message dialog box, and clicking Add.**

8. Provide a Subject and message text if you like.

 9. Send your form by choosing Message⇨Send, by pressing Ctrl+S, or by clicking on the Send icon.

The following are a few additional notes about using forms in cc:Mail:

✔ If your forms administrator sets up automatic routing on a form, you will have less work to do! After you've launched the application and made changes to the form, just select Form⇨Send to Next Stop or Form⇨Send to Prior Stop.

✔ You cannot create a routing list, but you can choose the Form⇨Send/Route menu option in the cc:Mail Forms Application to send the form to a new recipient that you designate. In the Edit Route dialog box, select Address. Scroll through the Address List, and double-click on the addressee. Enter a Subject and a brief Message Text, if you choose, and then click Send.

✔ Saving a copy of forms that you send is probably a good idea. A copy of your own form would certainly help if someone else misplaces your reimbursement request. After you finish filling out the form in cc:Mail Forms, select File⇨Save, select a place on your hard drive to put the form, type a File name, and click OK.

✔ Form Routing lets the form designer establish a list of recipients for a form so that the form goes to the right people in the right order. Some forms, depending on the designer, have a predetermined routing list, perhaps even with special restrictions about who can change which fields. Other forms, like the sample forms that you get with cc:Mail, do not have an established routing list. Your cc:Mail administrator can tell you about routing the forms that you use.

Part IV
Bossing Your Mail Around

The 5th Wave   By Rich Tennant

"SO HOW'S THE NEW E-MAIL SYSTEM WORKING?"

In this part . . .

1 remember this one time when I was a kid, I had a bunch of friends over at my house. My mother came in and told me to clean up my room. "Awwww, Mom!" Well, being the crafty and resourceful young lad that I was, I stood up on my bed and directed all my friends to put things away. So there I was, getting my room cleaned without having to lift a finger. "Okay, put those socks in that hamper . . . and the baseball glove goes in the closet . . . and the stash of cookies goes under the pillow." Call me bossy if you want, but I got the job done quickly and easily.

Now that I'm a grown up (technically, that is), I still like to be crafty and resourceful. Take cc:Mail for example. You can direct messages to specific places, tell it to save messages, tell it to find messages you conveniently misplaced, and even direct it to do your dirty work for you. What's best is that you don't even have to stand on your bed to tell cc:Mail to do all of this. You just have to read this part.

Chapter 12

Using cc:Mail's Special Containers

*T*ake a look in the Container pane of your message window. (Go ahead — I'll wait.) Among other things, you should see three ready-to-use containers: Drafts, Message Log, and Trash, shown in Figure 12-1.

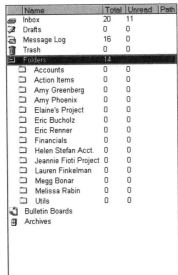

	Name	Total	Unread	Path
	Inbox	20	11	
	Drafts	0	0	
	Message Log	16	0	
	Trash	0	0	
	Folders	14		
	Accounts	0	0	
	Action Items	0	0	
	Amy Greenberg	0	0	
	Amy Phoenix	0	0	
	Elaine's Project	0	0	
	Eric Bucholz	0	0	
	Eric Renner	0	0	
	Financials	0	0	
	Helen Stefan Acct.	0	0	
	Jeannie Fioti Project	0	0	
	Lauren Finkelman	0	0	
	Megg Bonar	0	0	
	Melissa Rabin	0	0	
	Utils	0	0	
	Bulletin Boards			
	Archives			

Figure 12-1:
The
Container
pane.

Each of these containers gives you a ready-made place in which unfinished or form messages reside and copies of all your sent messages are kept, and a purgatory for your discarded messages to be kept, from whence they may be recalled or consigned to the old incinerator.

If you're using cc:Mail Mobile, you'll also see the Session Log container, which records information such as the time you connected and disconnected, number of messages sent and received, and whether any errors occurred during the session. For more information about the Session Log container, see Chapter 20.

Using the Drafts Container

Suppose you're working on some long-winded message to your boss explaining why you deserve a raise and a promotion. You're typing along . . . type-ity, type-ity, type-ity . . . and then you take a break and wander away from your computer. Then your buddy from the next cubicle over drops by to "show you something" and crashes your computer — everything's gone! You get back in time to see the computer rebooting. Aargh! You've just lost your long-winded message. Hours and hours of otherwise good work time down the tubes! Good thing you were just working on a message to your boss about that raise, huh?

You can avoid losing messages in progress by saving them in the Drafts container. The Drafts container is a special folder that holds messages you're working on but are not yet ready to send. By saving messages in the Drafts container, you can (sort of) prepare for system failures, revise messages at a later time, or complete messages that you were dragged away from by that emergency meeting. In the example, you could have used the Drafts folder just before you walked away from the computer. Then you could have really enjoyed the demo that crashed your computer.

Enabling the Drafts container

All this sounds good so far, but there's a catch — the Drafts container has to be enabled by both your cc:Mail administrator and you. So, your first step in using the Drafts container is to check with your administrator to find out whether the feature is enabled. Chances are that your cc:Mail administrator has enabled the Drafts feature because it is, after all, really handy. However, the Drafts feature may not be enabled because your draft messages (just like all the other messages) are stored on the cc:Mail server — in other words, they take up space. So, ask your administrator about the Drafts feature, and, as always, remember your pleases and thank-yous.

The second step in using the Drafts container is to make sure it's enabled on your own computer. After you've logged into cc:Mail (if necessary), do the following:

1. Go to Tools⇨User Setup.

The User Setup dialog box appears, shown in Figure 12-2.

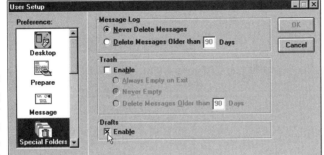

Figure 12-2:
The User
Setup
dialog box.

2. In the left pane, under Preference:, click to select the Special Folders icon.

You'll notice that the right side of the dialog box changes to show the Special Folders options.

3. Under Drafts, check the box next to Enable.

4. Click OK when you're done.

There. You've just enabled the Drafts container. Now all you have to do is *use* it. Read on.

Using the Drafts container

Suppose you've been working on that message to your boss about the big raise you want and then you're suddenly called away by the birthday party in the conference room. So far, your message reads

```
Dear Boss:

As you know, I've survived working at this company for a
very long time — longer than you, in fact. I've worked
nearly 8-hour days, used old, slow, and almost-wood-burning
computers, and lasted longer than any officemate I've had.
```

(continued)

(continued)

> Heck, I wasn't even fired after last year's big Arnold
> Account scandal. If it hadn't been for that unfortunate
> situation in the elevator with that big ex-client, I'd have
> even gotten a satisfactory evaluation last year. Therefore,
> I think you'll agree that I'm deserving of a long-overdue
> raise.
>
> Sincerely,
> (Your Name)

Hmmm. Perhaps you'll want to revise this later after the birthday party. All you have to do is save this message in the Drafts container, using one of two methods:

- ✔ Click the Save message to Drafts folder SmartIcon.
- ✔ Go to Message⇨Save Draft.

cc:Mail saves a copy of the message in the Drafts container.

Accessing and sending draft messages

Now, suppose you're ready to revise that message to your boss (you do want to, right?). To access the draft message, just double-click the Drafts container; the draft message appears in the message window (see Figure 12-3). If you have more than one draft message, you see all of them listed in the message window.

The message window provides you with essential information about your draft messages. For example, it shows who the message is to, shows the date you drafted the message, shows the size of the message, and shows the subject line of the message. All of this is particularly handy when you have more than one draft message. Otherwise, you'd have to root through each message to find the one you're looking for.

If you have a big bunch of unfinished drafts, you may use the cc:Mail search capabilities to find it. See Chapter 14 to see how to search for (and even find) specific messages.

After you've found the draft message you want to open, just double-click it, and the message opens. The opened draft message is just like a message you're drafting for the first time — you can change the text, add or delete people in the address box, change the subject line, request receipts and logs, and change the message priority.

Date message was drafted

Recipient's name   Message size   ┌ Subject line

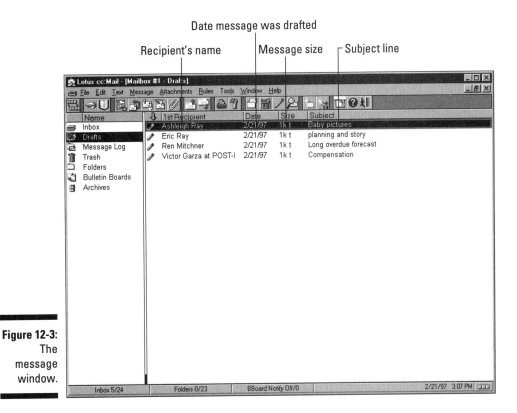

Figure 12-3:
The
message
window.

So, now the revised message to your boss probably looks something like

```
Dear Boss:

After careful consideration, I've decided that my working
conditions are simply stellar. Without a great boss like
you, I'd probably be working in a much less satisfying
profession and suffering from incipient burnout. As it is,
the only thing that could possibly increase my enjoyment
and pleasure at working for you would be a raise. Please?
I promise I won't talk to potential clients anymore.
Please?!?!

Sincerely,
(Your Name)
```

All you have to do is send it, using one of three methods:

- ✔ Click the Send Message SmartIcon.
- ✔ Go to Message⇨Send.
- ✔ Press Ctrl+S.

cc:Mail displays a dialog box that asks whether you want to delete the draft message.

- ✔ Choosing Yes deletes the message from the Drafts folder and sends the message.
- ✔ Choosing No leaves the message in the Drafts folder and sends the message.

After you've used one of these methods, there are two more steps you have to take:

1. **Hold your right hand up in the air.**

2. **Wave good-bye to your message.**

Some other uses for the Draft container include:

- ✔ Creating form letters to send out when people request information or ask common questions. Just write the generic message and save it as a draft. Send it on request.
- ✔ Creating a snazzy signature for your messages and reusing it without retyping. Check out the sidebar "Working around cc:Mail's eccentricities" in this chapter for more information.

Deleting draft messages

The Drafts container is kind of like an old landlord I had — she saved everything. She owned twelve houses around town, each piled high with 80 years' worth of stuff — like broken furniture, bloated canned goods, boxes of string pieces, just to name a few things.

Well, the cc:Mail Drafts container is similar to my old landlord; it won't throw out draft messages without your explicit OK. Even if you open a draft message and send it to someone, that draft message will still be in the Drafts container unless you say specifically to delete it.

To delete messages directly from the Drafts container, select a message and then use one of three methods:

✔ Click the Delete Message SmartIcon.

✔ Go to Message➪Delete Message.

✔ Press Ctrl+D.

Working around cc:Mail's eccentricities

If you've used other e-mail programs (or if you've been corresponding with people out on the Internet), you may be familiar with signature files (also called .sig files by those wanting to appear in-the-know). Simply put, a signature file is an informative or interesting or otherwise provocative bit of text at the bottom of a message that identifies you, the sender. For example, a basic signature file for Bill Clinton might look like:

```
Bill Clinton
president@whitehouse.gov
```

With a little embellishment, he could have

```
ᏁᏁᏁᏁᏁᏁᏁᏁᏁᏁᏁᏁᏁᏁᏁᏁᏁᏁᏁᏁᏁᏁᏁᏁᏁᏁᏁᏁᏁᏁᏁᏁᏁᏁᏁᏁ
Bill Clinton
president@whitehouse.gov

    "I'm in charge here because
    you said so!"
ᏁᏁᏁᏁᏁᏁᏁᏁᏁᏁᏁᏁᏁᏁᏁᏁᏁᏁᏁᏁᏁᏁᏁᏁᏁᏁᏁᏁᏁᏁᏁᏁᏁᏁᏁᏁ
```

Of course, that's a lot of typing and formatting to do for every message, not to mention the possibility of typos creeping into your e-mail address. Many other e-mail programs let you create a signature file that is automatically appended to the end of every message you create. cc:Mail doesn't, however (although it does offer other advantages).

With a little more effort, though, you can come fairly close to the same capability in cc:Mail. Here's the process, from the 20,000-foot view:

1. **Create a draft message, but don't put in an address or subject line.**

2. **In the body of the message, include your name, e-mail address, other contact information, and anything else you want to include.**

3. **Every time you send a new message, instead of clicking the new message icon or choosing Message➪New, just open your drafts folder.**

4. **Double-click to open the draft, then address and write the message just as with any other message.**

5. **Send it when you're done, and reply No when cc:Mail asks if you want to delete the draft message.**

As a rule, you want to keep your signature to four lines or less, if for no other reason than to avoid unnecessarily irritating people who see your message. Conventional wisdom (that is, a tradition that has origins in antiquity, overzealous followers, and not nearly the importance that people would like to believe) states that anything over four lines unnecessarily taxes computing resources, overloads the Internet, and contributes to global warming and whale extinction.

Of course, if your cc:Mail administrator will consent to upgrade you to cc:Mail 7 or 8, you'll be able to use stationery, which is a world better than this workaround. Check out Chapter 22 for details.

Going, going, gone

Occasionally, you may get a little delete-happy and delete messages you didn't intend to. Are they gone forever? Maybe not.

If you want to be able to retrieve deleted messages, you'll need to do two things. First, you need to determine whether your cc:Mail administrator has enabled the Trash container feature, which is just a folder that stores deleted messages. Second, you need to be sure that the Trash container feature is enabled on your computer (go to Tools⇨User

Setup⇨Special Folders, then check Enable under the Trash feature).

If your administrator has not enabled the Trash feature or if you have not enabled it on your computer, you can consider your messages unrecoverable, gone, poof, nada, no more, residents of that refuse bin in the sky, and forever lost. For more information about the Trash container, see "Using the Trash Container" later in this chapter.

Saving Your Butt (Using the Message Log Container)

The Message Log container is a special folder that keeps copies of messages you have sent. You can think of this container as a Cover-Your-Butt container because it often serves to help you cover your already-chewed-on behind in the event someone claims not to have received a message you sent.

For example, suppose you received a message from the departmental secretary informing you that you've been appointed Chief Picnic Planner for the annual company picnic (you know, the one where you do those ridiculous egg tosses, three-legged races, and volleyball games — all of which are bogus because it's your duty to let your boss's team win). So, you send a cc:Mail message back to the departmental secretary declining the responsibility:

```
Sorry!
I won't be able to plan the annual company picnic because
of current, recurrent, and ongoing hassles connected to the
current project. Also, I will be on vacation for the next
two weeks. And I have a severe grass and sweat allergy.
Sincerely,
(Your Name)
```

A few weeks later, you return to the office only to find your boss in an uproar because he — and only he — showed up at the company picnic. The department secretary pointed the finger at you for not planning the picnic. Lucky for you, you used cc:Mail's message log when you declined the generous appointment to Chief Picnic Planner. All you have to do is access the Message Log container and open a copy of the message that you sent to the department secretary, then forward it to your boss.

Logging outgoing messages is a cinch for either new messages or messages from the Drafts container. Take a look at Figure 12-4, which shows a New Message window.

Basically, you can instruct cc:Mail to log outgoing messages two different ways:

✔ You can manually place a check mark by the Log option in each outgoing message. (Warning, folks! This method is tedious, and Murphy's Law states that you'll forget to log your most important messages. Look it up!)

✔ You can set cc:Mail to automatically log all of your outgoing messages. (*Hint!* This is the preferred method of saving your butt! Logging 100 superfluous setting-a-place-and-time-for-lunch messages per each important communiqué is a small price to pay.)

Log box checked

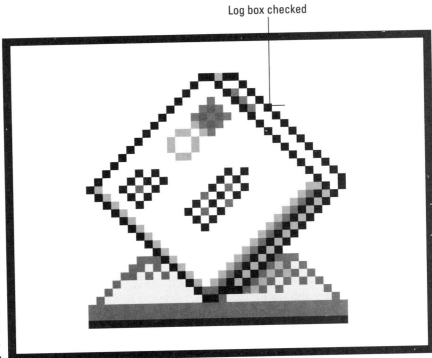

Figure 12-4:
The New Message window with logging enabled.

If you want cc:Mail to automatically log all your outgoing messages, just follow these quick steps:

1. Go to Tools⇨User Setup.

The User Setup dialog box appears, as shown in Figure 12-5.

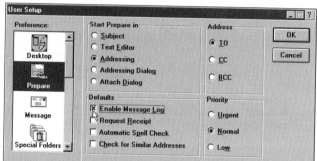

Figure 12-5:
The User
Setup
dialog box.

2. Under Preference:, click the Prepare icon.

You'll notice that the right side of the dialog box changes to show the preparation and default options.

3. Under Defaults, check the box next to Enable Message Log.

4. Click OK when you're done.

After enabling the message log option, you have a record of all messages that you send from this point forward. Sorry, there's no way to do it retroactively.

After a message is logged in the Message Log container, it remains there until you delete it or move it. To delete messages from the message log, you can use one of three methods (and yes, the methods for deleting messages from the message log are just like the methods for deleting from any other container):

   ✔ Click the Delete Message SmartIcon.

   ✔ Go to Message⇨Delete Message.

   ✔ Press Ctrl+D.

If you happen to be sending a message that you really don't want to log, you can disable the log option by unchecking Log in the message window.

If you've decided to use the message log to help prevent confusion and misunderstandings, you'll find that the container ends up with a lot of messages very quickly. With a combination of custom folders (like one for communications with your boss) and rules (to automatically file messages in the custom folders), you'll cover your butt and have time for a long lunch. See Chapter 13 (for custom folders) and 16 (for rules) to get moving.

Using the Trash Container

After you've been using cc:Mail for a while, you're likely to end up with piles and piles of messages — in your Inbox, Message Log, and Drafts containers, not to mention the messages you've stored in folders you've created. At some point, you'll probably want to get rid of messages that you no longer want or need. cc:Mail's Trash container makes it easy and safe for you to discard messages.

Think of the Trash container as being similar to trash cans in your office. When you're done with a piece of paper, message, or file, you just toss it into the trash can. Then a few times a week, someone comes by and empties the trash. The Trash container works the same way: You move messages you want to discard into the Trash container, then the container gets emptied every so often.

Actually, depending on the options you choose, you can have a trash can like the one in the office (emptied automagically on a schedule) or like the one at home (emptied sporadically, if at all). Just check out the next few sections, which tell you how to enable the Trash container and set its options.

Enabling the Trash container

Like other cc:Mail containers, the Trash container must be enabled by both your cc:Mail administrator and you. Check with your administrator to find out whether you can use the Trash container — as always, say please and thank you, and provide donuts if you have to. If you do have the Trash container feature, you'll also need to enable it on your computer. Here's the scoop:

1. **Go to Tools⇨User Setup.**

   The User Setup dialog box appears, as shown in Figure 12-6.

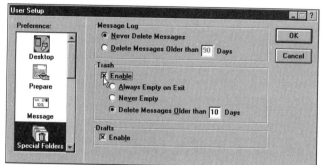

Figure 12-6:
The User
Setup
dialog box.

2. **In the left pane, under Preference:, click the Special Folders icon.**

   You'll notice that the right side of the dialog box changes to show the Special Folders options.

3. **Under Trash, check the box next to Enable.**

4. **Choose how often you want the trash to be emptied.**

   - Always Empty on Exit — Sets the Trash container to be emptied every time you exit cc:Mail.

   - Never Empty — Sets the Trash container so that it will only be emptied manually (you'll have to go to Tools⇨Empty Trash).

   - Delete Messages Older than 90 Days — Lets you set the Trash container to be emptied however often you want (click the text field and type in a new number).

5. **Click OK when you're done.**

Realistically, you won't have the foggiest idea what 90-day-old messages may lurk in your trash container, so you may as well set the number to something like 7 or 10 days. That's long enough to cover almost any accidental deletion without storing too many bazillion messages almost forever. Otherwise, cc:Mail will be getting rid of the trashed messages about the office Thanksgiving bash just as you're getting valentines from your sweetie in the Inbox.

Putting messages in the Trash container (Deleting messages)

After you have the Trash container enabled, you can move messages from any container to the Trash container using one of four methods, after you've selected a disposable message (not the one officially notifying you of your raise):

✔ Click the Delete Message SmartIcon.

✔ Go to Message⇨Delete Message.

✔ Press Ctrl+D.

✔ Click (and hold) on a message and drag it to the Trash container.

You can use the Shift and Ctrl keys to help you move several messages at one time. To move several sequential messages: Select the first message in the series, press (and hold) the Shift key, then select the last message in the series. To move several nonsequential messages: Press (and hold) the Ctrl key, then choose the individual messages that you want to move.

If you're really into deleting messages, you may take advantage of the Read Message SmartIcons set — it's got the standard trash can icon, in addition to a trash can with an upward-pointing arrow (delete and move to previous message) and a trash can with a downward-pointing arrow (delete and move to next message). Either way, the messages head for that trash can in the container Pane. All that's lacking now is a trash can with Oscar the Grouch in it (for delete, give up on the adult world, and go watch "Sesame Street").

Emptying the Trash container

Depending on how you set your options (see "Enabling the Trash container" earlier in this chapter), cc:Mail either empties the Trash container for you, or you have to empty it manually.

Why would you want to empty your Trash container? Really, it's not like the old messages will grow legs and walk out of the trash can on their own. Rather, it's because all your messages (except archives) are stored on the cc:Mail server — in other words, they take up space and slow things down (albeit only slightly). So, if for no other reason, emptying your Trash container will make your cc:Mail administrator jump around ecstatically — or at least look up from the monitor.

If you've set your Trash container options so that cc:Mail empties the trash for you, then you basically don't have to do anything. For example, if you choose the Always Empty on Exit option, then cc:Mail empties your trash each time you exit cc:Mail. This is the option for those who have never realized moments too late that they locked their keys in the car. Or if you choose the Delete Messages Older than 90 Days option, then cc:Mail will toss messages — you guessed it — older than 90 days (or however many days you specified).

Keep in mind that if you choose the Ne_v_er Empty option, you have to empty your Trash container manually by going to Tools⇨Empty _T_rash. If you never empty the trash, your cc:Mail administrator will eventually start to nag you about wasting space on the server, just as your mom used to nag you about the stench coming from the old pizza boxes under your bed.

Chapter 13

Managing Mail Your Own Way

So you've decided that your cc:Mail Inbox with 348 messages is a little out of control? In other words, you're pretty convinced that cc:Mail is managing your workflow and process just like your cats have you trained to feed and water them on schedule. Hmmm . . .

Organization is the key to reclaiming control of your life! You can file your messages away — safe and sound, but out of your face — and go back to visit them whenever you want. That way, your Inbox remains a place for the incoming messages rather than a storage site for all sorts of miscellaneous stuff that has no better home. This chapter will give you the tools you need to regain control over those piles of mail.

(Sorry, no guidance here on training those felines. If I knew how to take control of my life back from cats, I'd have written about that, too . . . move over, Lucy, you're blocking my monitor . . .)

Using Folders

Although cc:Mail has some pretty useful built-in containers, you'll probably find the need to create your own little filing system that will help you manage your messages. One really good way to manage your messages is to create your own folders. For example, you may want to create folders to file your messages according to the projects they relate to (like Anderson Account, Widget X, or Projects from Hell 1–57). Or you may want to create folders to file messages according to who sent you the message (like Susan K, Mom, The Boss, or The Beav).

Creating folders

However you choose to organize your messages (beyond the provided containers), you need to create these folders before you can store messages in them. Creating a folder in cc:Mail is just like creating a folder you'd use in your file drawer — you'd get a folder, put a name on it, then stick it in the file drawer. With cc:Mail folders, you create the folder, name it, and then let cc:Mail file it (alphabetically, of course) for you. Here are the few quick steps to create folders:

1. Go to File⇨New⇨Folder.

You'll see the Folder container in the Container pane expand and create a new folder. Oohhh!

2. Type in a folder name at the blinking cursor.

Figure 13-1 shows the new folder (naming in progress).

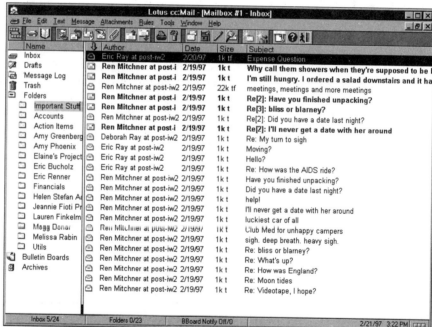

Figure 13-1: Typing in the name of a new folder.

3. Press Enter.

There. You've just created a new folder, complete with a name. Aahhh!

Each time you create a new folder, the new folder appears in alphabetical order under the Folders Container.

There are no real limits to the number of folders you can have, although I usually find it most useful to keep the number of folders to about the number that will fit on a screen. Ninety seven folders with 2 messages each doesn't help my efficiency much.

After you've used folders for a while, you start to wish that you could put folders within folders. That is, have a taxes folder, then folders within the taxes folder for 1998, 1999, Audits, Loopholes, and so on. Sorry! Not in cc:Mail 6 you don't. However, if you can prevail upon your administrator to upgrade you to cc:Mail 7 and refer to Part VI of this book, you'll get to experience the (not insignificant) joys of nested folders.

Moving messages to folders

Once you've created folders, you can move your messages to them by using one of two methods:

- ✔ Click (and hold) the message you want to move and drag it to the appropriate folder. You'll have to expand the Folder container (by double-clicking it) so that the target folder is showing before you move a message.

- ✔ Go to Message➪Store (or click the Store Message SmartIcon, or press Ctrl+T) and use the Store dialog box, shown in Figure 13-2.

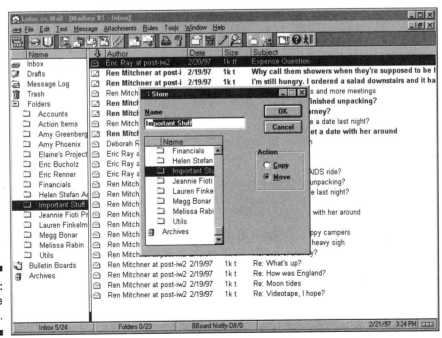

Figure 13-2:
The Store
dialog box.

The Store dialog box lets you choose a folder two different ways.

- Type in the name of the folder (actually, typing just the first few letters of the folder name selects the folder) in the text area and click OK.
- Click a folder name in the Name list and then click OK.

Also, notice that you have the option to either copy or move the message to a folder. If you copy a message, you end up with the message in the original container as well as in the folder to which you copied the message. If you move a message (which is the default), you end up with the message only in the folder to which you moved it.

Accessing and deleting messages in folders

You've probably guessed it by now, but you can access and delete messages from folders you create. (Totally exciting, right?) Let's say you're looking for a message that your boss sent you praising you for all your hard work (it *could* happen). Accessing messages? There's nothing to it. It's really just about like reading messages from your Inbox. Here's the process, in double time:

1. **Double-click the Folders container to expand it.**

   This step allows you to see the folder names.

2. **Double-click the folder (Messages from Boss, perhaps?) that contains the message you want to see.**

   As Figure 13-3 shows, this opens the folder up so that you can see the list of messages.

3. **Double-click the message to open it.**

   Voilà!

Now suppose you want to delete the message from a folder.

- To delete a message (when the message isn't open): Open the folder, select the message you want to delete, and click the Delete SmartIcon (or go to Message⇨Delete Message, or press DEL).
- To delete an open message (one that you've been reading): Click the Delete SmartIcon (or go to Message⇨Delete Message).

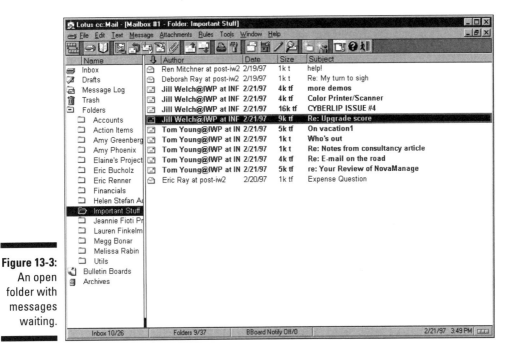

Figure 13-3:
An open
folder with
messages
waiting.

Using Archives

An archive is a folder that holds messages that you want to keep but that
you don't need ready access to. Archives are sort of like storage boxes that
you keep out in your garage; you can stuff things in them and keep them out
of your way, but they're incredibly inconvenient for taking things out of or
reorganizing.

For example, suppose you kept a box of old jeans out in the garage (you
know, the jeans that you've outgrown but are sure you'll one day fit into
again). Then one day, you finally admit that you'll never fit into most of them
and that you should toss all but the largest in the box. You'll probably never
go out and root through the jeans because it's (a) easier to let them sit out
there or (b) easier to throw out the whole box than to fish around for one
stinky pair. Archives work about the same way. You'll keep them just in case,
but you'll probably never use them or reorganize them.

So why keep archives if they're so much hassle? Well, archives do have an
advantage over regular folders — they're kept on your local computer
rather than on the cc:Mail server. Remember that regular folders are kept on

the cc:Mail server, and your cc:Mail Administrator has probably allotted you a certain amount of space on the server. Think of it as having a certain-size mailbox in which you can receive and keep mail. If the mailbox gets full, you can't put anything more into it. Because you keep archived messages on your local computer, you're not limited by allotted space, only by your hard disk size (or the number of floppy disks you're willing to keep).

Creating archives

To create an archive folder, just use these quick steps:

1. **Go to File⇨New⇨Archive.**

   The Create Archive dialog box appears, shown in Figure 13-4.

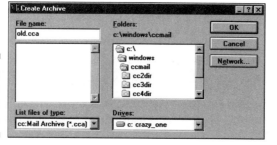

Figure 13-4: The Create Archive dialog box.

2. **Choose a Drive (probably a local one, but you could also choose a network drive).**

3. **Choose a Folder (probably where you'd store your personal-type files).**

4. **Choose a File name (be descriptive, particularly if you plan to keep more than one archive).**

   Even if you're using Windows 95, cc:Mail expects filenames to be no more than eight characters long. The .cca that cc:Mail volunteers at the end of the name has to stay there as well. So the instructions above should really read as follows: Be as descriptive as you can with only eight characters and no spaces to work with. Bssmsg98, for example.

5. **Click OK when you're done.**

   You now see a new folder under Archives in the Container pane.

Deleting messages from an archive

Deleting messages from an archive is a big pain in the butt, an even bigger pain than scrounging around in that box of old jeans in your garage. You can't just select a message you want to delete and hit the Delete key. You have to find messages you want to keep, then throw out the rest.

For example, suppose you want to throw out all but one pair of jeans from that box in the garage. You have to go out in the garage, find the box, find the stinkin' pair of jeans you want to save, take it out of the box, put it into another box or container, then throw out the rest (pant, pant . . . so to speak).

With archived messages, you have to go to the archive, find the folder, find the message(s) you want to keep, create a second (empty) archive, move the messages you want to keep, then throw out the old archive. Cripes! Hopefully, you don't want to go through all that, but if you do, here's how:

1. **Create a new archive (go to File⇨New⇨Archive).**

2. **Go to the Archive folder from which you want to delete messages.**

3. **Select the message or messages you want to *keep*.**

    Remember you can use the Shift or Ctrl keys while clicking to select multiple messages.

 4. **Go to Message⇨Store, press Ctrl+T, or click the Store Message SmartIcon.**

    The Store dialog box appears.

5. **Select the new archive name from the list or type the name in the text area.**

    Technically, you could also select a regular folder if you want to move the messages from an archive to a folder.

6. **Click OK.**

7. **Click the archive folder containing messages you want to delete.**

8. **Press the Delete key or go to Edit⇨Delete.**

    The Delete dialog box appears, shown in Figure 13-5, confirming that you want to delete the archive.

Figure 13-5:
The Delete
dialog box.

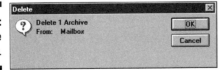

9. **Click OK if you're ready to delete the archive from cc:Mail; click Cancel if you don't want to delete it.**

Now a warning dialog box appears to ask if you want to delete the archive file from the disk, as shown in Figure 13-6.

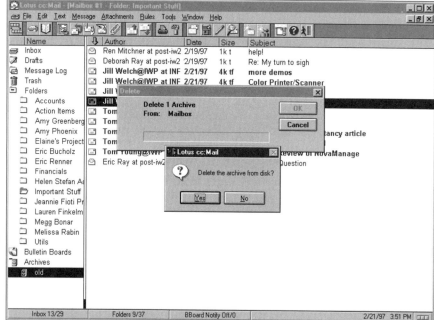

Figure 13-6:
The Delete
from Disk
warning.

10. **Choose Yes to irrevocably delete the archive.**

If you choose No, the archive is removed from your list in cc:Mail but the file remains on your disk in case you need it later.

Saving Messages as Files

Suppose you received a message from your boss that actually has some usable information in it. You could retype the information or copy and paste it into WordPro or Word, but — gads! — why would you do all that work if you don't have to? cc:Mail lets you save messages as files so that you can *use* the information or take it home on a floppy disk, rather than just staring at it as a mail message.

You don't have to read this because you don't maintain your stinkin' jeans, either

If you're not pretty interested in managing your messages with archives, you may stop reading here. I'm presenting a tried-and-true cc:Mail archive-management tip for soon-to-be power users.

Let's say that you keep absolutely every message you ever send or receive. (You think your butt is in dire need of coverage.) You store all messages to or from individuals in folders by their name. Of course, over the course of a year, that ends up as a lot of messages — say 20 people at 2 messages each per day, plus assorted other messages. That's 5,000-plus messages in a year. What you can do is archive the messages onto floppies and file them away.

1. **First thing on January 1, create a boss archive on your hard drive.**

   You're creating it on your hard disk because it's faster and easier. If an archive happens to be too big for a floppy disk, it'll still fit on the hard drive.

2. **Move all the messages from your Boss folder to the boss archive.**

3. **Delete the folder from cc:Mail but reply No when asked if cc:Mail should delete the archive from disk.**

Deleting the archive from cc:Mail but leaving it on the hard disk may not be as strange as it sounds. You don't need to keep the archive from last year in the list in cc:Mail — it's not like you'd refer to it each day — but you would probably want the security of keeping it somewhere that's accessible.

To move the archives onto floppies, just use your File Manager (for Windows 3.1*x* users) or Windows Explorer (for Windows 95 users) to seek out the files on your hard disk and copy them to floppy disks. If they don't fit, leave them on the hard drive and ask the local guru to zip them for you, or enlist the help of your system administrator.

See *Windows 3.1 For Dummies* or *Windows 95 For Dummies*, both by Andy Rathbone, for more information about file management in Windows.

Later on, when your boss pings you about something that she'd said you weren't going to be responsible for, you can haul that archive out:

1. **Put the boss archive floppy disk in your disk drive (if necessary).**

2. **Create a new archive and browse to the archive in your A drive or on your hard drive to restore the archive to cc:Mail.**

   The New Archive dialog box has a browse button that makes it a snap to cruise around your computer and find the archive in question.

3. **Forward the message back to the boss.**

4. **Delete the archive again, and again don't delete it from the disk.**

   Pretty slick, huh?

Seriously, keeping archives on floppy disk can be good insurance for a variety of possible but unfortunate circumstances. If you get canned for poor performance, you probably won't be able to access your cc:Mail account to print out the accolades you've received over the past couple of years. However, if you have the archive on a disk at home, you can restore the archive on the cc:Mail system in your lawyer's office and you're back in business.

You can also save attachments as files, but that's a whole different ballgame. Check out Chapter 6 for more information.

1. **Open the message you want to save as a file.**

2. **Go to File⇨Save As.**

   The Save As dialog box appears, shown in Figure 13-7.

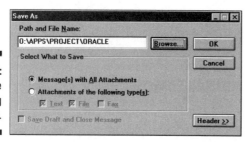

Figure 13-7:
The Save
As dialog
box.

3. **Type in a Path and File Name (or click Browse and choose a path and filename from the File Name and Location dialog box; click OK to exit this dialog box).**

   In the Save As dialog box, you can choose to include the message header information in the file by clicking Header and then choosing:

   - None — includes no part of the message header.

   - Partial — gives you options to include information about the author, subject, date/time, recipients, and priority.

   - Full — includes all information from the message header. You can also choose to include the Forwarding History.

4. **Click OK when you're done.**

5. **Use your File Manager (for Windows 3.1x) or Windows Explorer (for Windows 95) to look for the message under the filename you saved it as.**

Chapter 14

Locating That Darned File

· ·

In This Chapter

▶ Using Quick Search

▶ Using the Search window

▶ Doing advanced searches

· ·

Some things you lose, and you don't have much control over it. Like, this one time I lost my cat (hey, it's not my fault the neighbors had better scraps in their trash can!). Other things you lose, and it's your own dumb fault. Like, I once lost my car keys and found them under my pillow. And yet other things you lose, and they take you forever to find because there's so much junk to wade through. Like the time I lost my car in the San Francisco airport parking garage and had to wander around on all the different levels searching and searching until I found it.

You'll find that even the best of message filing systems break down occasionally, and you'll need help finding containers, folders, messages, or addresses. For example, your filing system might become so big that it becomes cumbersome to use. Or you'll misplace a message or two that you really do need. On a really bad day, you might even feel that you're playing hide-and-go-seek with your messages.

Fortunately, cc:Mail's find features, including Quick Search and the Search dialog box, can help you find just about any address, container, name, text quip, or message you seem to have misplaced. (Hey, it's not your fault that messages lurk in the wrong folders, right?)

Doing a Quickie Search

Quick Search is a great way to quickly find containers or addresses, particularly when you have many of them in your cc:Mail window. For those of you who do have long lists of containers or addresses, you probably find yourself scrolling and scrolling just to get to the one you're looking for. Thanks to cc:Mail's Quick Search, now there's an easier way.

Quick Search is one of cc:Mail's very practical features, letting you simply start typing the container name or address, and — whooosh! — you're swept away to the very container or address you're looking for. Miraculous? I think not! The next two sections show you how to use Quick Search to whisk yourself away to containers and addresses.

Using Quick Search to find containers

Take, for example, Figure 14-1, which shows a Container pane with a huge list of containers.

You could scroll up and down through the Container pane to find folders, but that quickly becomes tedious (not to mention time-consuming). All you have to do is use Quick Search, like this:

1. Click somewhere in the Container pane.

2. Type the first few letters of the container you want to access.

For example, if you want to access a container called Elaine's Projects, type **e** (or possibly **el** or **ela**, depending on what e-word containers you have). The Quick Search dialog box, shown in Figure 14-2, pops up on your screen.

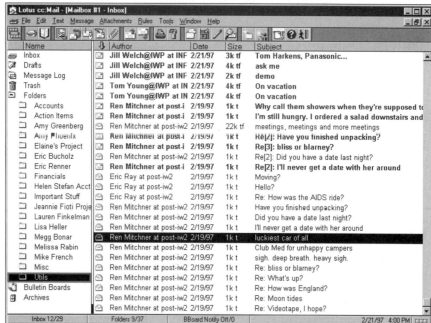

Figure 14-1:
A Container pane loaded with containers.

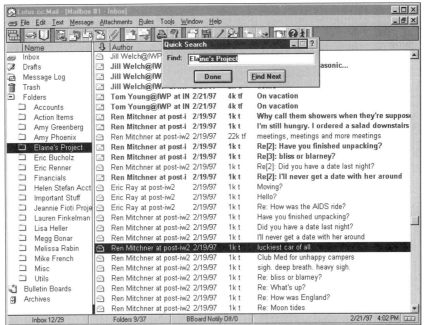

Figure 14-2:
The Quick
Search
dialog box.

Notice that the Elaine's Projects container is highlighted in the Container pane, indicating that it is selected and ready for you to open.

3. **Click Done or press Enter when you've found the container you're looking for.**

Some additional notes about using Quick Search to find a container:

✔ You can use the Find Next button in the Quick Search dialog box to find the next containers that use those specific initial letters. This way, you can quickly find containers named Trash, Tragic Project, Trapped at this Job, or Tranquility.

✔ If you're having problems finding a specific message, not a folder, you'll need to check out the full-blown mongo search options described later in this chapter.

Using Quick Search to find addresses

The same process used for finding folders or containers applies to finding addresses in your address window. Take a look at Figure 14-3, which shows an address book window.

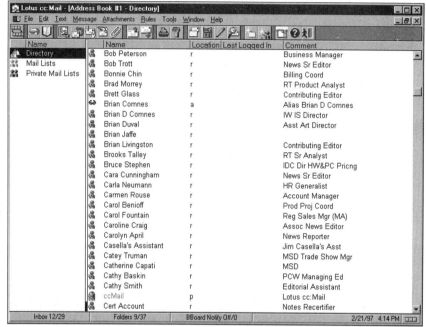

Figure 14-3:
An address
book
window
full of
addresses.

Again, you could scroll through the list, but doing that over and over takes time and effort. Instead, try using Quick Search, like this:

1. Choose Window⇨New Address Book Window.

The address book window appears, as shown in Figure 14-3.

2. Type the first few letters of the addressee's name.

You'll have to keep in mind the address conventions your cc:Mail administrator set up. For example, if cc:Mail addresses are listed First name Last name, then you type the first letters of the first name. On the other hand, if cc:Mail addresses are listed Last name, First name, then you type the first few letters of the last name.

3. Voilà!

While this process isn't terribly impressive in the address book window (unless you're just checking the spelling of someone's name), it works exactly the same when you're addressing a message as well.

You can also use Quick Search in the Address Message dialog box to find folders, private mail lists, or public mail lists in the Container pane. Just click somewhere in the dialog box's container pane and type a few letters as always. This is particularly handy if you're addressing a message to a mailing list (for public distribution) or to a folder (to file it away).

Doing the Search Window Thing

Suppose you remember seeing a cc:Mail message announcing the new Work Overtime for Discounted Cafeteria Food policy. Now, because you're working scads of overtime anyway, you decide to try to use the discounted food policy. Hmmm. Darn it. Where'd that message go?

Fortunate for you, cc:Mail's Search window can help you locate that important message quickly and easily. The Search window is designed to help you search for messages (or addresses) by entering keywords, dates, or names from the text or address.

Take the discounted cafeteria food message as an example. Let's say the cc:Mail message looked something like Figure 14-4.

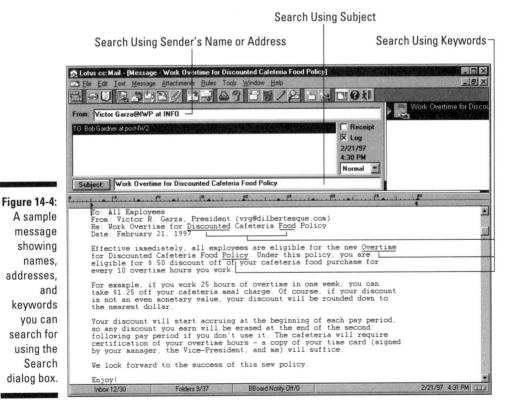

Search Using Subject

Search Using Sender's Name or Address

Search Using Keywords

Figure 14-4:
A sample message showing names, addresses, and keywords you can search for using the Search dialog box.

As you can see from Figure 14-4, you can use names, addresses, and keywords from a message to help you search for it. All you have to do is use the Search window, accessed by using one of these methods:

✔ Clicking the Search for Messages or Addresses SmartIcon

✔ Going to Tools⇨Search

✔ Pressing Ctrl+Q

The Search window, shown in Figure 14-5, appears on your screen.

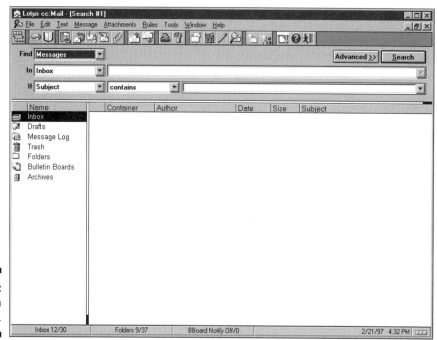

Figure 14-5:
The Search
window.

Getting acquainted with the Search window

For your reading enjoyment, the next few paragraphs dissect the fascinating world of Search window parts.

✔ Find — This drop-down list lets you choose to search through messages or through addresses.

✔ In — This drop-down list lets you select a specific container to search through, or, if you choose All, to search through all the containers (which could take a while). If you choose a container that has folders in it, you can also specify which folder you want to look in by using the drop-down list to the right of the In drop-down list.

✔ If <blank><blank><blank> — These drop-down lists let you select which part of a message (such as the message subject, age, or size) you want to search through. You can also tell cc:Mail specific words or phrases to look for (contains, is) or not look for (does not contain, is not) using the text areas to the right of the If drop-down list.

As you're filling in the blanks, just read the line to yourself — for example, "If Subject contains cafeteria" or "If Author is John."

✔ Container pane — This area of the dialog box shows which container(s) the message (or whatever) was found in. For example, if a message was found in the Trash container, the Trash container is highlighted when the search is complete.

✔ Window pane — This area of the dialog box lists the search results.

Using the Search window: A sample search

Using the Search window varies from search to search, just as the search for your car keys depends on where you think you'll find them and when you think you lost them. If you think you lost the message in a folder, you look in the folders only. If you really have no idea, you select All and look through everything.

The following steps walk you through a sample search, looking for the Work Overtime for Discounted Cafeteria Food policy message.

1. **Go to the Search window (click the Search SmartIcon, go to Tools⇨Search, or press Ctrl+Q).**

2. **Use the Find drop-down list to choose to search Messages or Addresses.**

   In this case, we'll search by message.

3. **Use the In drop-down list to narrow the search to a particular container.**

   In this case, we'll choose to search All containers (because we don't know which container it's in, right?). Because All really does mean all, there won't be anything to choose in the other In drop-down list.

4. **Use the If drop-down list to choose the part of messages you want to search.**

   In this example, we'll choose Text because we're pretty sure we know some keywords to search for.

5. **In the next drop-down list, choose "contains" because you want any message with this specific word in it.**

6. **In the third field, fill in "cafeteria" because that's the word you choose to search for.**

   In this example, we could also enter words like *Discount, Food, Overtime,* or *Policy*.

7. **Click <u>S</u>earch or press Enter.**

The resulting messages (at least with this little sample search on my computer) yielded the results shown in Figure 14-6.

Notice in Figure 14-6 that the resulting messages appear in the Window pane, and the Trash container is highlighted in the Container pane. Also notice that the number of results is listed toward the top of the Search window.

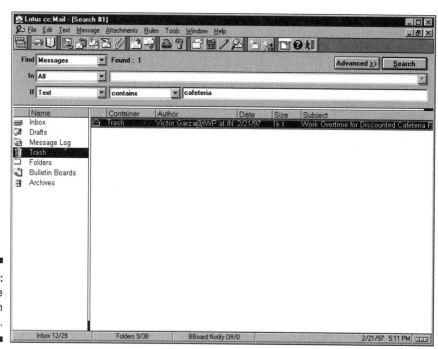

Figure 14-6:
Sample
Search
Results.

See, that was pretty intuitive. Here are some additional thoughts about using the Search window:

> ✔ If your search doesn't yield any results, you'll see a dialog box that says No Matches Were Found. Just click OK or press Enter to get rid of this pesky box.
>
> ✔ If your search didn't turn up the message you were looking for, try broadening the search criteria using the Find, In, and If drop-down menus to cast a wider net.

Using the Advanced Search Feature

If you're of a particularly technical bent or just can't resist anything that says "Advanced," you might try out the advanced search feature in the Search window. However, unless you have a pretty serious searching problem and know exactly what you're looking for, you're unlikely to have notably better results with an advanced search than with a basic search.

Realistically, the advanced search will only be truly useful to you if you know that you're looking for specific combinations, such as *Cafeteria* in the subject and *discount* in the text and a send date of 12/31. Here's the process:

1. **Go to the Search window (click the Search SmartIcon, go to Tools⇨Search, or press Ctrl+Q).**

2. **Click Advanced≥>.**

   This brings up the Advanced (instead of basic) Search window, as shown in Figure 14-7.

3. **Use the Find drop-down list to choose Messages or Addresses.**

   In this case, we'll search by message because we're looking for that darn cafeteria note again.

4. **Click In to specify the container in which to search.**

   In the Find Messages dialog box, select a container from Find Messages in. If you've selected Folder or Archive, you can also select the specific folder or archive in the right drop down list.

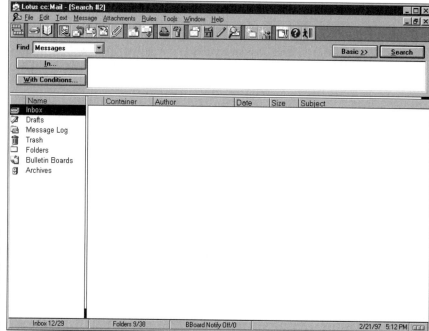

5. Click Add to add the container to the list.

You can continue selecting containers and adding them to the list. If you make a mistake and add one by accident, you can select it and click Delete, or select it and click Replace to replace it with a more appropriate container. Because the search progresses through the list in order, you might consider clicking Insert to put the more likely locations at the top of the list.

6. When you're finished adding containers, click OK.

7. Click With Conditions to specify the criteria for the search.

The Conditions dialog box (Figure 14-8) lets you specify which characteristics the messages should have.

Just as in the basic search, you can specify conditions such as "Subject contains cafeteria" or "Date is 12/31/97," but here, you can add criteria in combinations. For example, you might require both a subject containing *cafeteria* and a date of 12/31/97.

8. Click Add to add a condition to the list.

As with the containers, you can add, delete, replace, or insert other conditions.

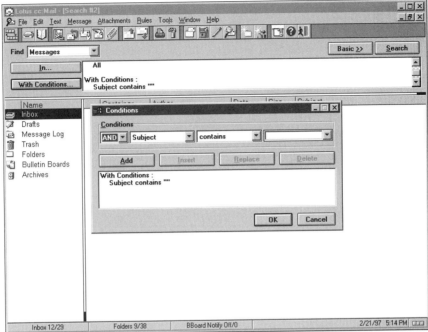

Figure 14-8:
The
Conditions
dialog box.

Additionally, for each condition, you can choose AND or OR to require specific combinations of conditions. For example, you could search for a specific subject OR a specific date, or for a certain author AND subject.

9. **Click OK when you're finished.**

10. **Now, click Search to find that message.**

Advanced searching is slower and more painful, but much more specific. You decide if it's worth it.

/

Chapter 15

Customizing cc:Mail

. . . .

In This Chapter

▶ Giving your cc:Mail desktop a makeover

▶ Changing your password

▶ Changing confirmations and notifications

▶ Changing the sort order of messages

▶ Changing the SmartIcons palette

. . . .

*W*hen you shop for a new car, you have all sorts of options to consider. For example, you could buy the lime green station wagon with the roof rack, spiffy wheels, fold-down backseat, almost-authentic wood grain on the sides, and — don't forget — the neon sign that flashes "I'm a geek." Or you could buy the red sports car with hot wheels, leather seats, a stick shift, power locks, and the supermodel in the passenger seat (okay, you have to get the supermodel separately). Chances are, though, you're going to opt for something in the middle, buying options that you not only like but are also likely to use.

cc:Mail comes with a pretty standard set of options and functions that you can use without having to change a thing on your desktop. But cc:Mail also comes with some nifty options that let you customize your desktop. These options don't necessarily cost extra, but they will take you a few minutes to set up. In a sense, you can upgrade your cc:Mail model from a standard four-door sedan to a peppy all-terrain vehicle with cruise control, power windows, remote door locks, and an antitheft device.

This chapter outlines different ways you can customize cc:Mail to better meet your needs. In particular, this chapter covers customizing user setup (changing your desktop, setting a new password, and changing message confirmations and notifications), changing the sort order of messages, and changing the SmartIcons palettes.

Other customization options for cc:Mail are covered in different (and more appropriate) parts of the book. For example, customization options specific to cc:Mail Mobile are covered in Part V.

Customizing User Setup

cc:Mail allows you to customize your user setup in several ways that can help you more efficiently send, receive, and read messages. For example, you can change certain aspects of your desktop, such as to display (or not display) certain menus and toolbars. cc:Mail also lets you change your password, which can help further protect message privacy. And, as a bonus (I'm sure), cc:Mail even lets you change your message confirmation and notification settings.

To make all these changes, you need to use the User Setup dialog box, accessed by using one of two methods:

- ✔ Click the User Setup SmartIcon.
- ✔ Go to Tools⇨User Setup.

Take a look at the User Setup dialog box, shown in Figure 15-1.

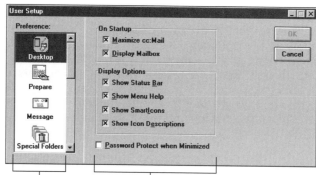

Figure 15-1:
The User
Setup
dialog box.

User Setup Categories — User Setup Options

You use this dialog box just as you've used other dialog boxes — by scrolling through selections, turning on options by checking the check boxes, and turning off options by unchecking the check boxes.

The next sections provide instructions for changing your desktop, changing your password, and changing your confirmation and notification options.

Changing your desktop

Your desktop is simply your cc:Mail workspace, where you have your message windows, menu bar, toolbars, and so on. By default, your cc:Mail desktop opens displaying your mailbox, the status bar, and SmartIcons (with descriptions available). Using the User Setup dialog box, you can pick and choose which ones of these features you want to display. Just follow these quick steps:

1. **Go to the User Setup dialog box (Click the User Setup SmartIcon or go to <u>T</u>ools⇨<u>U</u>ser Setup).**

2. **In the Preference: area, click Desktop once (if it's not already highlighted).**

3. **Select the desktop options you want (check to select; uncheck to deselect).**

    - <u>M</u>aximize cc:Mail — Maximizes cc:Mail on startup.

    - <u>D</u>isplay Mailbox — Displays your mailbox on startup. If you deselect this option, cc:Mail opens without the mailbox window, showing only the toolbars and menu bar items you select. (Of course, if you later open the mailbox window, it cannot be closed. Figure that.)

    - Show Status <u>B</u>ar — Displays the status bar at the bottom of your screen.

    - <u>S</u>how Menu Help — Provides a brief description of open menus in the title bar.

    - Show SmartIcons — Displays the SmartIcons palette. If you choose not to display the palette, you'll need to complete commands by using the menu bar or keyboard shortcuts.

    - Show Icon D<u>e</u>scriptions — Displays balloons with descriptions of the icons when you hover your mouse over the icon.

    - <u>P</u>assword Protect when Minimized — Provides added security when you're away from your desk. Choosing this option will require you (or other users) to enter a password before cc:Mail can be restored.

4. **Click OK when you're done.**

Changing your password

Until now, you've probably been using a password that your cc:Mail administrator set up for you. More than likely, your password is pretty boring — like the word *password,* or your name. Or it might reflect whatever your administrator was thinking about at the time — like lasagna, spousemad, or hungry.

Using the assigned password is okay, but there are some compelling reasons to change your password.

✔ Your password should be a collection of letters and numbers that is unique to you. You certainly don't want other people accessing your mailbox, so it's a good idea to make one up that's significant to you.

✔ Your password should never be a real word — not one from any dictionary. The closer it is to a real word, the easier it is for others to figure out.

✔ Your password should be changed occasionally. If you change your password every so often, the chances of someone figuring out your password and using it are minimized. If nothing else, you'll keep password-pickers on their toes.

✔ Your password should be changed if you've had to let other people access your cc:Mail account. For example, suppose you're sick for a week straight and you need to let your officemate check your mail for you. If you've told anyone your password, you should change it as soon as possible to reduce security problems. (Of course, if you can get your administrator to upgrade your cc:Mail account to cc:Mail Version 8, you won't have any reason to give out your password — see Chapter 22 for details.)

With that said, here's how to change your password:

1. **Go to the User Setup dialog box (Click the User Setup SmartIcon or go to Tools⇨User Setup).**

2. **In the Preference: area, click once on the Password icon.**

3. **Type in your Old Password in the space provided.**

   You'll notice that your password is represented with asterisks (in case anyone's looking over your shoulder).

4. **Type in your New Password in the space provided.**

5. **Type in your New Password Again (just to verify that you typed it right the first time).**

6. **Click OK when you're done.**

Changing message confirmations

cc:Mail gives you a slew of message confirmation options, each of which basically just gives you a dialog box asking you if you're sure you want to complete the command. For example, if you tell cc:Mail to delete a folder, you'll see the Delete dialog box, as shown in Figure 15-2.

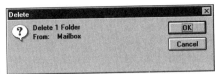

Figure 15-2:
The Delete
dialog box.

To confirm that you want to delete the folder(s), you click OK. Of course, if you've changed your mind about deleting the folder or if you goofed and accidentally tried to delete the folder, you can always click Cancel. (Whew, right?)

Here's the rundown on changing the default message confirmations:

1. **Go to the User Setup dialog box (Click the User Setup SmartIcon or go to Tools⇨User Setup).**

2. **In the Preference: area, click the Confirmation icon once.**

3. **Select the confirmation options you want (check to select; uncheck to deselect).**

   - Confirm to C**o**py — Confirms that you want to copy messages (or entire folders) to another folder or container.

   - Confirm to Mo**v**e — Confirms that you want to move messages (or entire folders) to another folder or container.

   - Confirm to Delete a **F**older — Confirms that you want to delete a folder.

   - Confirm to Delete an **A**rchive — Confirms that you want to delete an archive.

   - Confirm to Delete a Mailing **L**ist — Confirms that you want to delete a mailing list.

   - Confirm to Delete a **M**essage — Confirms that you want to delete a message. (I can't believe you're still reading these!)

   - Confirm to Delete an A**d**dress — Confirms that you want to delete an address. (Don't you get the point by now?)

   - Confirm to **S**end a Message — Confirms that you want to send a message.

   - Confirm to **C**ancel a Message — Confirms that you want to cancel a message.

   - Confirm to **E**xit cc:Mail — Confirms that you want to exit cc:Mail.

4. **Click OK when you're done.**

Changing message notifications

Have you ever been driving in your car and wondered where that turning signal noise comes from? Ding-tic. Ding-tic. Ding-tic. On top of that, the ding-tic is accompanied by little flashing lights to tell you that your turning signal is on. Actually, if you think about it, the ding-tic and flashing lights are probably only present to help those people who drive down the highway for miles and miles with their signal on. But the rest of us know that the only thing that will help those folks is a megaphone and banners flying in front of them.

Anyway, cc:Mail has a feature — much like the turning signal ding-tic and flashing lights — that notifies you whenever you get new mail. Using the User Setup dialog box, you can set cc:Mail to notify you of new mail with a dialog box, flashing window, or a tone (that doesn't sound like ding-tic). You can also set how often you want cc:Mail to check for new mail and where you want it to check, and set it to display in the Status Bar the number of messages you've read and not read.

By default, cc:Mail will notify you of new mail every six minutes with a dialog box and a tone. If you want to change this default, just use these steps:

1. **Go to the User Setup dialog box (click the User Setup SmartIcon or go to Tools⇨User Setup).**

2. **In the Preference: area, click the Notify icon once.**

   The User Setup dialog box now looks like Figure 15-3.

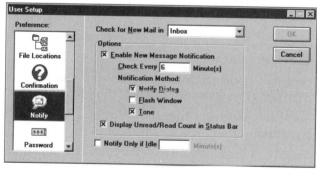

Figure 15-3: The User Setup dialog box showing Notify options.

3. **Select the notification options you want (check to select; uncheck to deselect).**

   • Check for New Mail in — Lets you choose to check for new mail in your Inbox, folders, or Bulletin Boards.

   • Enable New Message Notification — Turns the message notification feature on or off.

- Check every 6 Minute(s) — Lets you specify how often cc:Mail should check for messages. Just double-click the text area and change the number. Then click outside the text area or press Enter.

- Notify Dialog — Sets cc:Mail to notify you via dialog box that you have new messages.

- Flash Window — Blinks the cc:Mail title bar when you get mail.

- Tone — Sets cc:Mail to notify you via tone that you have new messages.

- Display Unread/Read Count in Status Bar — Provides the option to see (or not see) how many unread and read messages you have waiting for you in the active folder.

- Notify Only if Idle ## Minutes — Tells cc:Mail to notify you of new messages when it has been idle for a specified number of minutes. Click the text area and type in the number of minutes. Then click outside the text area or press Enter.

4. Click OK when you're done.

Changing the Sort Order of Messages

By default, cc:Mail sorts your incoming mail by putting the newest messages at the top of the message window. This is probably pretty handy for most of you because you don't have to do any scrolling to see the new messages as they come in. However, if, for example, you also use other e-mail software that drops new messages at the bottom of the list (such as an America Online account or an Internet service provider's software), you might want to change the sort order of your cc:Mail messages so that you're not constantly having to remember where your new messages are. Or you might like seeing a progression of messages as they come in and want your newest messages at the bottom.

Whatever the reason, you can change the sort order of messages quickly and easily using the Ascending/Descending button in the Mailbox window, shown in Figure 15-4.

To change the sort order of messages, click the Ascending/Descending button once. Whichever order you choose, that order will carry over to all your containers and folders. For example, if you set the order to descending while you're in the Inbox, your messages will be presented in descending order in the Drafts container, the Message Log container, the Trash container, and so on. Not to worry, though; you can change it back just by clicking the Ascending/Descending button again.

Ascending/Descending button

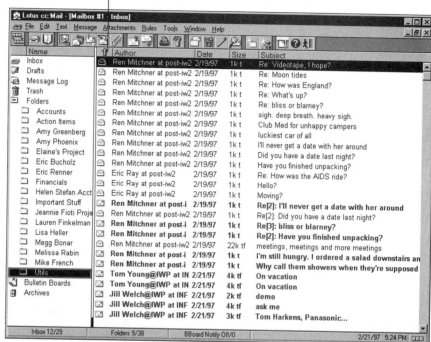

Figure 15-4:
The
Ascending/
Descending
button in
the Mailbox
window.

Customizing SmartIcons Palettes

 Certainly by now you've used the SmartIcons palettes (a.k.a. sets) a few times. Perhaps you've even tried scrolling through the different SmartIcons sets by clicking the Change to Next SmartIcons Set button. Huh, you say? Well, each time you click this button, a new SmartIcons palette appears, giving you a new selection of SmartIcons. Cool, eh?

Generally, cc:Mail will present the appropriate SmartIcons for any task. For example, cc:Mail presents a different set of SmartIcons when you're reading a message than it does when you're writing a message.

However, it's fairly unlikely that cc:Mail will guess all of your needs accurately. Chances are, you regularly use only some of the SmartIcons but others go completely unused. Well, you can customize these SmartIcons palettes to eliminate the unnecessary and add the useful by using the SmartIcons dialog box, accessed by going to Tools➪SmartIcons.

The following sections will help you get acquainted with the SmartIcons dialog box and show you how to customize your SmartIcons palettes.

Getting acquainted with the SmartIcons dialog box

The SmartIcons dialog box, shown in Figure 15-5, lets you choose a palette you want to modify, then add or delete SmartIcons from the palette, and then save the new set. You can even delete entire palettes, change the SmartIcons size, and change where the SmartIcons palette appears in the cc:Mail window.

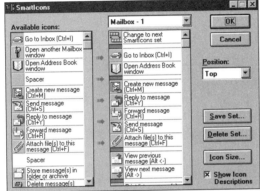

Figure 15-5:
The
SmartIcons
dialog box.

✔ Palette selection drop-down list — Lets you choose a specific palette to modify. When you select a palette in this list, the SmartIcons in that palette are shown below the drop-down list.

✔ Available icons list — Provides a list of SmartIcons that are available for you to add to a selected palette using the drag-and-drop technique.

✔ Position drop-down list — Lets you select where you want the SmartIcons palette to appear on your cc:Mail window. By default, the palette appears under the menu bar, but you can also choose to have it appear at the left, right, or bottom of the window.

✔ Save Set button — Lets you save a new or modified SmartIcons palette using the Save Set of SmartIcons dialog box, shown in Figure 15-6. In this dialog box, you can name the palette, choose a filename for the palette, and select where the palette should be saved.

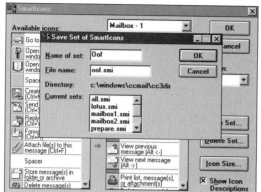

Figure 15-6:
The Save
Set of
SmartIcons
dialog box.

✔ Delete Set button — Lets you delete SmartIcons palettes using the Delete Sets dialog box, shown in Figure 15-7. In this dialog box, you choose which sets you want to delete and click OK to delete it.

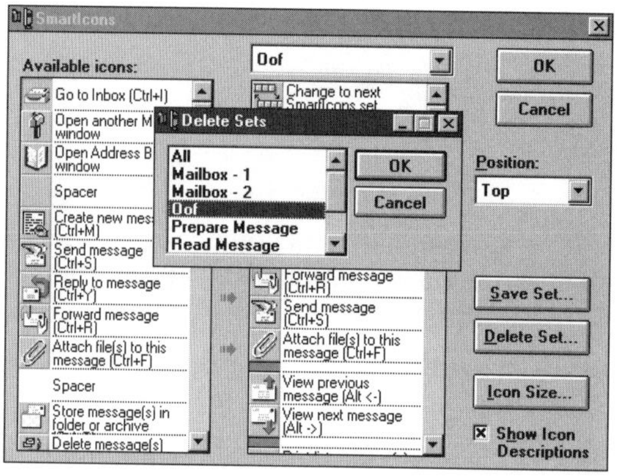

Figure 15-7:
The Delete
Sets dialog
box.

✔ Icon Size button — Lets you choose the SmartIcons size using the Icon Size dialog box, shown in Figure 15-8. Just select either Medium or Large and click OK.

✔ Show Icon Descriptions — Gives you the option to display (which is the default) or not to display SmartIcon descriptions when you hover your mouse over a SmartIcon.

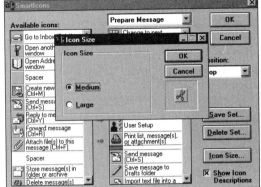

Figure 15-8:
The Icon
Size dialog
box.

Customizing a SmartIcons palette

Suppose you've been using the Read Message palette quite a bit and have decided that you want to customize it to better suit your needs. As is, the Read Message palette looks like Figure 15-9.

Figure 15-9:
The Read
Message
SmartIcons
palette.

Here's what you want to change (we're just supposing here):

✔ You want to delete the Open Address Book and the Launch Associated Application SmartIcons. (This applies only to this particular SmartIcons palette.)

✔ You want to add the Create New Message SmartIcon to the palette. (This also applies only to this SmartIcons palette.)

✔ You want to move the entire palette so that it appears on the right side of the window. (This applies to all SmartIcons palettes.)

✔ You want to make the SmartIcons bigger so that you can still see them if you're sitting across the room. (This, too, applies to all SmartIcons palettes.)

The following steps tell you how to make these changes using the SmartIcons dialog box.

1. **Go to the SmartIcons dialog box (go to Tools⇨SmartIcons).**

2. **Choose the Read Message palette from the palette selection drop-down list, as shown in Figure 15-10.**

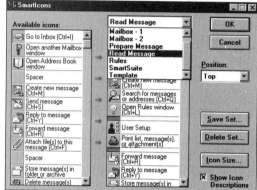

Figure 15-10:
The palette selection drop-down list.

3. **Scroll down in the SmartIcons list and look for the two SmartIcons you want to delete.**

   In this example, we'll get rid of the Open Address Book and the Launch Associated Application SmartIcons.

4. **Click (and hold) the Open Address Book SmartIcon and drag it out of the scroll box.**

5. **Click (and hold) the Launch Associated Application SmartIcon and drag it out of the scroll box.**

   There. That took care of deleting the SmartIcons you didn't want in the palette.

6. **Scroll through the Available icons list at the left of the dialog box and find the Create New Message SmartIcon.**

7. **Click (and hold) and drag the Create New Message SmartIcon onto the list of icons in the Read Message palette.**

   The SmartIcon appears wherever in the list you drop it, so you may need to scroll up or down in the Read Message list before you drag the new SmartIcon onto the list. Remember, if you accidentally drop the icon in the wrong place, you can just drag it out and try again. Now, onward to moving SmartIcons palettes to the right side of the window.

8. **Click the down-arrow under <u>P</u>osition: and select Right from the drop-down list.**

   There. That took care of moving the palettes to the right side of the window. Now, on to making the SmartIcons bigger.

9. **Click the <u>I</u>con Size button, which gives you the Icon Size dialog box.**

10. **Select <u>L</u>arge and click OK.**

    There. Now even my blind cat can read those darned SmartIcons. Hmmm. Now you have to save your changes.

11. **Click <u>S</u>ave Set.**

    You now see the Save Set of SmartIcons dialog box, in which you can choose a new name or keep the same name. Click OK when you're done.

12. **Click OK to exit the SmartIcons dialog box.**

Now your Read Message palette should look something like Figure 15-11.

Always remember to save your changes to SmartIcons palettes (click the <u>S</u>ave Set button) before exiting the SmartIcons dialog box.

Modified SmartIcons palette

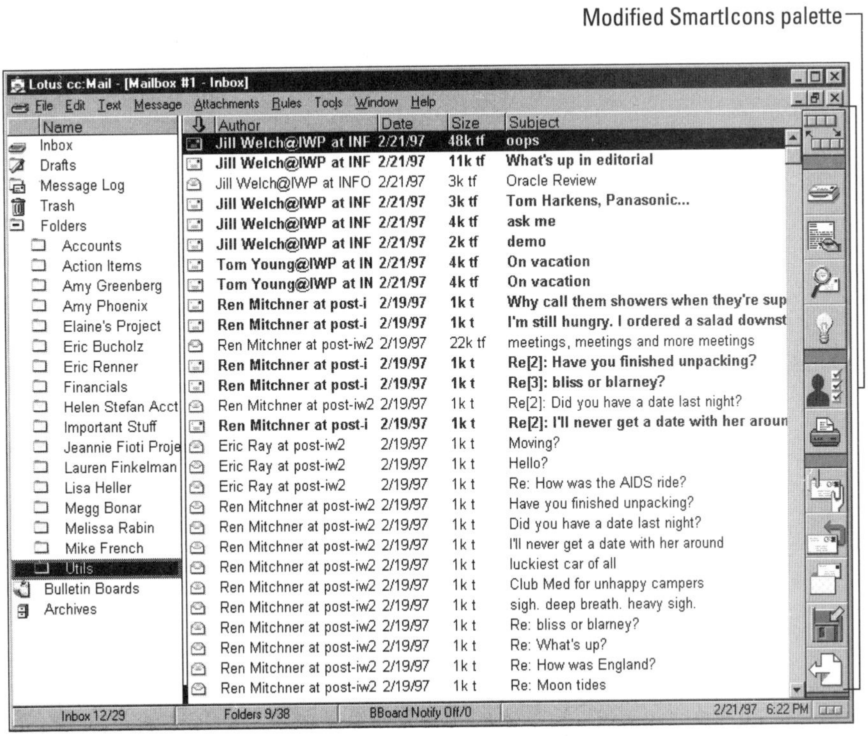

Figure 15-11:
The modified Read Message SmartIcons palette.

Chapter 16

Making Up Rules As You Go Along

. . . .

In This Chapter

▶ Figuring out what a rule is

▶ Getting familiar with cool rule tools

▶ Using existing rules

▶ Modifying existing rules

▶ Making up your own rules

. . . .

*R*ules come in all kinds. There's rules you follow because you have to; there's rules you follow because you want to. And let's not forget those rules you follow because Mom said so (nag, nag, nag, nag, nag).

cc:Mail comes with its own kind of rules — ones that are designed to process your mail automatically. You can use cc:Mail rules for a variety of purposes:

✔ You can automatically file incoming messages. For example, you can use rules to automatically file all messages from your boss in a designated Boss folder.

✔ You can automatically notify people when you log in or log out. For example, you can use rules to send a message to your boss telling him that you've logged in or logged out of the system. (It's a subtle way to inform your boss that you come in early and leave late.)

✔ You can automatically forward messages to people, without having to read the message. For example, you can use rules to forward all messages with the words *golf* and *Saturday* in the subject line to your golf buddies.

✔ You can automatically delete unwanted messages. For example, you can use rules to automatically delete all incoming messages from your boss, though I wouldn't recommend it. However, deleting all incoming messages from that coworker who's always trying to pawn work off on you might not be a bad plan.

cc:Mail comes with a variety of existing rules that you can use as they are or modify to fit your needs. Or better yet, you can also create your own set of rules. Now that's really bossing cc:Mail around! Each of these rules runs on a specific schedule — when you start cc:Mail, exit cc:Mail, or do any number of other things.

This chapter tells you all you want to know about using existing rules, modifying existing rules, and making up your own rules.

Getting Acquainted with Cool Rule Tools

When using existing rules, modifying rules, or creating your own rules, you'll be using two tools: the Rules menu and the Rules List window. The following sections provide you with an overview of these tools, which should help acquaint you with using rules to make your life easier.

The Rules menu

The first big rule tool is the Rules menu, located on the menu bar, shown in Figure 16-1.

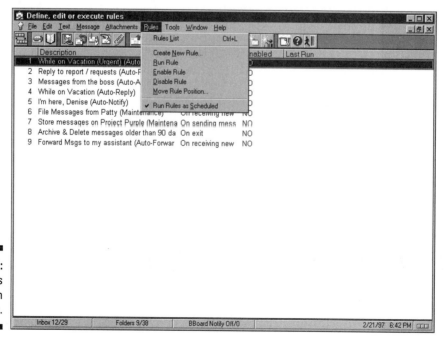

Figure 16-1:
The Rules
drop-down
menu.

✔ Rules List — Brings up the Rules List window.

✔ Create New Rule — Brings up a blank Rules Editor dialog box for you to fill in.

✔ Run Rule — Runs a rule selected in the Rules List window.

✔ Enable Rule — Enables a rule selected in the Rules List window.

✔ Disable Rule — Disables a rule selected in the Rules List window.

✔ Move Rule Position — Moves a selected rule to a new location in the Rules List window, and thereby a new position in the order of execution. The rules execute from the top of the box down.

✔ Run Rules as Scheduled — Runs rules as scheduled. Duh! Unchecking this is very much like disabling every rule.

The Rules menu is primarily used to access dialog boxes and windows that provide you with Rules options and settings. Most frequently, you'll use the Rules menu to access the Rules List window, discussed in the following section.

The Rules List window

The biggest tool you'll use when using, modifying, or creating new rules is the Rules List window, accessed using one of three methods:

✔ Clicking the Open Rules Window SmartIcon.

✔ Going to Rules⇨Rules List.

✔ Pressing Ctrl+L.

The Rules List window, shown in Figure 16-2, provides you with information about existing rules and provides access to the Rule Editor dialog box (which you'll use later in this chapter to create and modify rules).

In addition to providing a list of rules (obviously!), the Rules List window tells you when (and if) the rules are scheduled to run, if the rules are enabled or not, and when the rule ran last. Double-clicking a rule brings up the Rule Editor, which is where your bossing really starts.

Getting Started with Rules

Before you get too carried away having cc:Mail do your filing and sorting for you, you might consider enabling the notification and confirmation features so that you're notified every time cc:Mail takes care of business for you.

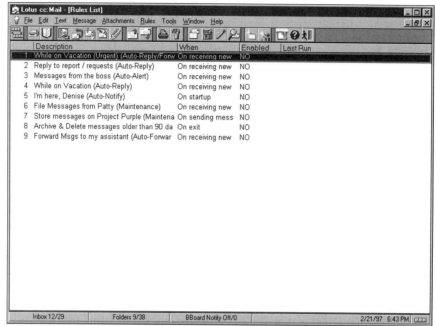

Figure 16-2:
The Rules
List
window.

For example, if you set cc:Mail to file all messages from your boss in a Boss folder, you'll probably want to be notified when cc:Mail does this for you, at least until you're used to it. Otherwise, your Boss folder could get pretty fat before you even realize messages have been coming in.

To enable the rules notification and confirmation options, use these quick steps:

1. **Go to Tools⇨User Setup (or press Alt+L).**

2. **Scroll down under Preferences: and click the Rules icon.**

3. **You'll see the rules options in the right side of the dialog box.**

4. **Enable all of the rules options by checking all the options, as shown in Figure 16-3.**

5. **Click OK when you're done.**

After you've been using rules for a while, you might decide that you don't want or need notification every time any of your rules run, although you might still want to be notified when you get messages from your boss. No problem — you can handle notification through the actual rules as well. Read on!

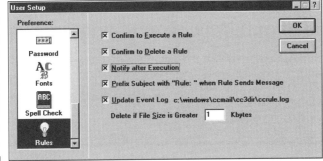

Figure 16-3:
The User
Setup
dialog box,
showing
enabled
rules
options.

Using Existing Rules

cc:Mail comes with a pretty good stock of existing rules that are readily available for you to modify and use.

How do you know which rule you want to use? Well, you can get more information about a rule's function by double-clicking it. You'll see the Rule Editor dialog box, which gives you a few details about the rule. For more information about the Rule Editor dialog box, see the section "Modifying Existing Rules" later in this chapter.

To enable one of the existing rules, use these steps:

1. **Click once on a rule you want to enable.**

   Although most of the stock rules won't do you any good without being modified, some can still be useful, like Archive and Delete Messages older than 90 days.

 2. **Click the Enable Rule(s) SmartIcon (or go to Rules⇨Enable Rule).**

   Notice in the Enabled column that the status changed from No to Yes. This indicates that the rule is enabled.

If you set a rule to Manual, you won't have the option to enable or not enable it. Manually running rules is no more difficult than selecting the rule and choosing Rules⇨Run Rule. Of course, if you're going to run the rule manually, you might as well just do it yourself.

Modifying Existing Rules

After you've fished around a little in the Rules List dialog box, you're likely to find a rule that's close to what you need — but not exactly. First of all, the rule's title is not likely to mean anything to you. For example, the rule called

---

A kind of quick fix on enabling rules

Enabling, running . . . yeah, whatever. It's just a bunch of jargon. Here's the skinny: Rules don't do anything until they run. Rules can only run when they're enabled. Enabled rules run on a schedule. When you do something that triggers a rule (like receive a message from your boss), the rule runs. Until then, it doesn't.

Manual rules run whenever you tell them to, enabled or not.

"I'm here, Denise." Just who is Denise, anyway?! Second of all, the rule might not do exactly what you want it to do. For example, if you want cc:Mail to notify you when messages from your boss come in, you'll need to modify the Messages from the Boss rule to include your boss's name (unless, of course, your boss's name is Patty Roberts). You'll probably find other reasons to modify existing rules, but those reasons are the biggies.

To modify existing rules, you'll need to use the Rule Editor dialog box.

1. **Choose a rule you want to modify.**

2. **Double-click the rule.**

   The rule will appear in the Rule Editor dialog box. The Rule Editor showing the "I'm Here, Denise" rule is shown in Figure 16-4.

   • <u>D</u>escription — Provides the name of the rule and a brief description of what the rule does.

   • <u>W</u>hen to Run — Provides a drop-down list of when the rule will run (for example, on exit, when a new message appears in your inbox, when you start cc:Mail, and so on).

Figure 16-4:
The Rule Editor dialog box, ready to edit the "I'm Here, Denise" rule.

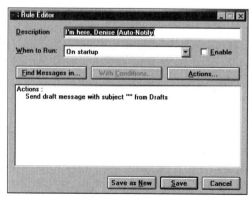

- <u>E</u>nable — Selecting this box enables the rule to run.

- <u>F</u>ind Messages in — Clicking this button accesses the Find Messages dialog box (shown in Figure 16-5), which allows you to specify where the rule should look for messages.

Figure 16-5:
The Find
Messages
dialog box.

- With <u>C</u>onditions — Clicking this button accesses the Conditions dialog box (shown in Figure 16-6), which lets you specify conditions that determine whether the rule applies to the message in question. That is, if the message doesn't meet the condition "from my boss," the rule won't tell me I got a message from the boss.

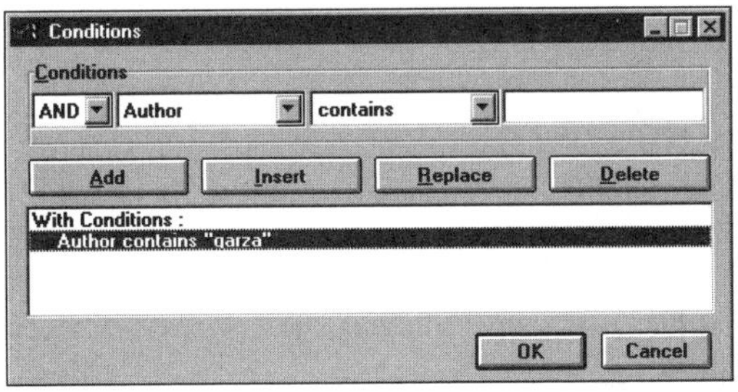

Figure 16-6:
The
Conditions
dialog box.

- <u>A</u>ctions — Clicking this button accesses the Actions dialog box, which lets you determine what action the rule should perform (send a message, beep at you, store a message, or even all of the above).

- Save as <u>N</u>ew — Saves the rule under a new name (so that your newly modified rule doesn't mess up the existing rule).

- Save — Saves changes you made to an existing (or already created) rule. Use this with caution, particularly if you're modifying an existing rule, because you don't want to break a previously functional rule.

- Cancel — Cancels whatever Rule Editor actions you've done (but not saved).

3. **Back to "I'm here, Denise." Change the description to the name of someone that *you* want to notify of your presence.**

4. **Leave When to Run set to On startup.**

If you're telling someone that you've arrived, running the rule on startup is logical. Running another rule on exit would be useful to announce that you've left. Keep in mind, however, that if you exit cc:Mail and restart it during the day, the rule will run again and Denise or whoever will be notified again.

Because you're running the rule on startup, it isn't dependent on finding messages, receiving messages, or any other conditions. You start cc:Mail, the rule runs.

5. **Click Actions to specify what happens when the rule runs.**

You'll see the Actions dialog box, as shown in Figure 16-7.

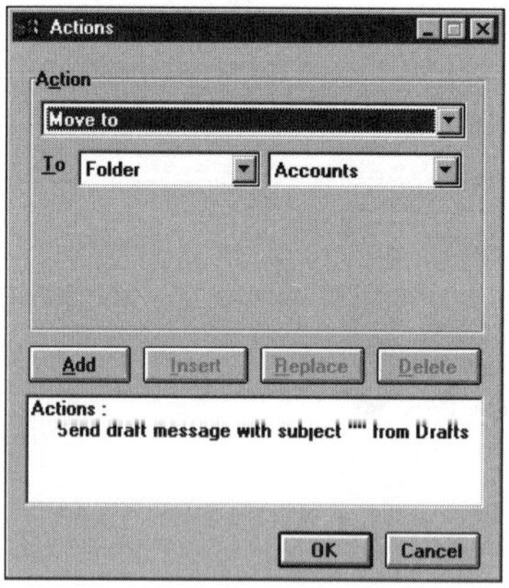

Figure 16-7:
The Actions
dialog box.

The rule currently sends a specific message (with no subject) from the Drafts folder. This message in the Drafts folder is already addressed to Denise. If you set up a draft message (to yourself, just for testing purposes), you can select it in the From: line of the Actions dialog box.

After you complete the instructions about where cc:Mail is to find the message to send, click Add to add the action to the list of actions to be taken. You'll probably want to click the other action once (to select it) and click Delete.

If you want to have multiple actions, you can. Just keep filling out the top part of the dialog box and clicking Add.

Creating Your Own Rules

Creating your own rules is perhaps easier than modifying rules because you don't have to get rid of stuff you don't want and tweak the rest to meet your needs — you just create it how you want it, and that's that.

Although cc:Mail provides a pretty good selection of ready-to-use rules, you'll probably find occasion to make up your own (if for no other reason than the fact that it's probably easier than modifying an existing one). For example, you might want to create rules to send automated responses to requests for information, or to file messages in the appropriate folders.

The following example illustrates a rule that files messages with specific subjects in an existing folder. Modify these somewhat interesting steps to create your very own rules:

1. Go to Rules⇨Create New Rule.

A blank Rule Editor dialog box appears, as shown in Figure 16-8.

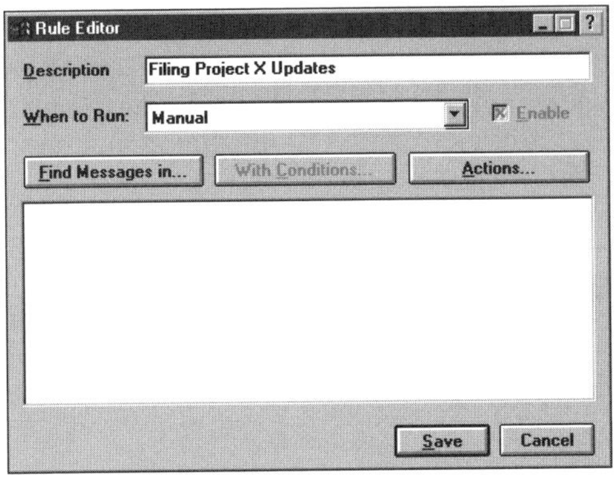

Figure 16-8:
The Rule Editor dialog box, ready for you to concoct a new rule.

2. Provide a Description of your new rule.

I'm calling this rule Filing Project X Updates.

3. In When to Run, choose the scheduling option of your choice.

Because I'm creating the rule to file away new messages about Project X, I want the rule to run every time I get a new message. As soon as I get new messages in the Inbox, the rule will run, and I won't even have to see the message until it's in the proper folder.

4. Click With Conditions to bring up the Conditions dialog box.

5. Complete the blanks to Add the Conditions that identify which messages should trigger a response from the rule, and then click OK.

I've noticed that all regular reports about Project X have the subject "Project X Status Report," so I'll use that as the only condition necessary. If the subject alone weren't enough to identify these reports, I might also add conditions like the sender's name, or certain text within the message. My Conditions dialog box looks like Figure 16-9.

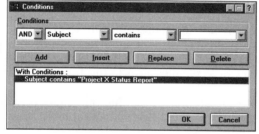

Figure 16-9:
My
Conditions
dialog box.

6. Click Actions to bring up the Actions dialog box, in which you instruct cc:Mail about what it should do.

7. Complete the blanks in the Actions dialog box and click Add to add the action to your new rule.

I want to move all reports about Project X to the Project X folder, so I choose Move to, Folder, and Project X (which is an existing folder I have in cc:Mail), and then I click Add. The Actions dialog box now looks like Figure 16-10.

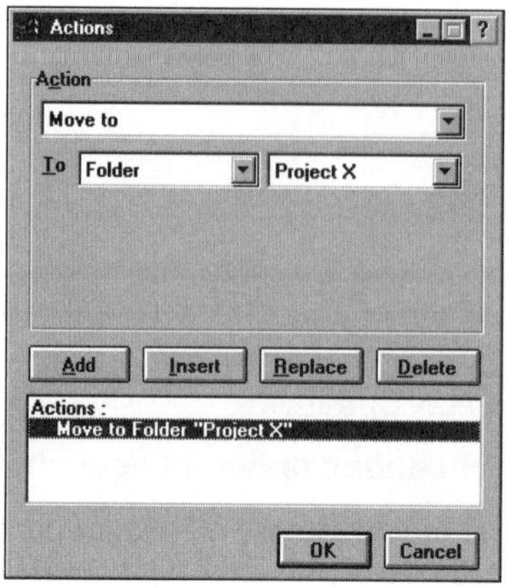

Figure 16-10:
My Actions
dialog box
for my
new rule.

If I'm afraid I won't notice when I get the update, I can add an additional action to alert me with the text "You just got the Project X Status Report."

8. **Verify that Enable is checked and then save the new rule.**

That's all there is to it. To test the rule out, I could send myself a rule with Project X Status Report as the subject line and see if it works right.

Here are a few additional rules about creating new rules:

✔ If you're working on a rule that will send messages or notices, you should probably construct the rule in two phases. First, create the rule and conditions. Instead of actually sending messages, just flash the window or create an alert message. That way, if your conditions weren't exactly right, you won't be sending out erroneous messages. Second, after you're sure that all the conditions are right, change the action to send the message or notification you choose.

✔ Be careful to identify messages as specifically as possible. If you can provide more information and still accurately identify messages, you should do so. In the preceding example, I could have just used "Project X" in the subject and cc:Mail would still have accurately filed all the project messages away. However, cc:Mail would also have filed away a message from the company president with a subject like "Why are you letting Project X go down the tubes?" That one probably shouldn't be filed anywhere except in the Urgent bin.

✔ Give some thought to the order of your rules. It's not unlikely that a message arriving in your Inbox might trigger more than one rule. You should have the most important rules at the top of your rules list so that they'll execute first. (Go to the Rules List window and use the Move Rule Position option.) For example, if your boss sends you a message with a subject "Send me the latest Project X Status Report" and your very first rule advises you that you got a message from your boss, you're in like Flynn. However, if your first rule files the Project X reports, the message will no longer be in your Inbox by the time the boss message rule executes, so you won't be notified about the message. Whoops!

Part V
Remotely Accessing Mail

"Oh, Scarecrow! Without the database in your laptop, how will we ever find anything in Oz?"

"*O*n *In this part . . .*
n the road again. I can't wait to get on the road
again."

If you're a road warrior — jetting about the world with a
laptop — or a telecommuter who would rather sleep late
and drink an extra cup of coffee instead of fighting traffic,
cc:Mail Mobile can have you e-mailing to your heart's
content from wherever you happen to be.

This part introduces you to cc:Mail Mobile and some of the
ways to use it most effectively. Not only does cc:Mail
Mobile let you take to the road and communicate just as
easily as if you were in the office, but you can also configure
cc:Mail Mobile to send and receive messages on schedule,
to reject unwanted messages (before you have to see
them), and to work hand in hand with your cc:Mail LAN
connection.

By the way, if you've ever tried sending e-mail from your
hotel room, you're already aware that the number of
things that can go wrong is incredible. Don't get discour-
aged if things don't go just right the first time. If I had a
quarter for every modem, communications, or configuration problem that came up while working on this part, I'd
be richer than Bill Gates. (Actually, if I had a quarter for
every grain of sand in the world, I wouldn't be as rich as
Bill Gates, but you get the idea.) You're in good hands: A
troubleshooting guide is at the end of this part.

Chapter 17

Installing and Running cc:Mail Mobile

• •

In This Chapter

▶ A brief introduction to cc:Mail Mobile

▶ Installing cc:Mail Mobile

▶ Using cc:Mail Mobile for the first time

• •

*P*ack your bags! It's time to hit the road with cc:Mail Mobile. cc:Mail Mobile brings all of the power and capabilities of the regular cc:Mail program to business travelers and telecommuters alike. Best of all, you don't have to learn new procedures or commands — all of those tidbits of "how to use cc:Mail" that you've socked away still apply to cc:Mail Mobile. You just have to acquaint yourself with a few additional features and you're on your way (so to speak).

What Is cc:Mail Mobile?

It's 6 p.m. on Monday night. You're on a business trip and sitting in your hotel room, recovering from a hard day of meetings. Whoops! You just remembered that you should have moved the Thistlebottom report from under the Wimplefeathers report on your desk so that your boss could find it for his 2 p.m. meeting tomorrow. Additionally, you have about five pages of additional information that need to be added so that Ms. Thistlebottom is satisfied.

You could call and leave voice mail for your boss explaining the situation, try to find a functional fax machine, or just polish up that report and mail the whole thing to your boss as though you had planned it all along.

cc:Mail Mobile lets you work from anywhere in the world, just as though you were right there in the office. Want to send or read e-mail? No problem. Need to send an attachment? No problem. Don't have time to wait for the status reports to download? No problem there either — just filter them out.

There are a couple of differences between cc:Mail and cc:Mail Mobile that you must get accustomed to, but that's what the next sections are for.

Viva la Difference!

So, just exactly what are the differences between cc:Mail and cc:Mail Mobile? The differences are in the way that cc:Mail Mobile connects to your home post office (where your mail hangs out and waits for you to pick it up) and, to a much lesser degree, how it looks. You work in cc:Mail Mobile in the same way that you do with cc:Mail, just with a couple of extra steps. Sorry, there are really no shortcuts on the extra steps. You just gotta do them!

Differences in how it works

The biggest difference between cc:Mail Mobile and cc:Mail is in the connection to the post office. When you're using cc:Mail, you are on your office network and have a permanent (mostly) connection through that cable in the back of your computer. You can check your mail, receive messages, and send messages at any time, and the messages just jaunt over to the post office and send themselves.

With cc:Mail Mobile, the connection to the post office isn't assumed to be permanent. You use cc:Mail Mobile most frequently with a modem and telephone line, but you could also be connecting with a regular network, with different dial-up connections, or even with a wireless modem. Therefore, cc:Mail Mobile requires you to tell it how to connect to the post office. Additionally, you must tell cc:Mail Mobile when to connect, when to send messages, and when to receive messages.

Before you start writing letters to complain about all this extra work, keep in mind that you only have to tell cc:Mail Mobile this information once for each place that you connect from, and it then remembers that information. The momentary pain of configuring cc:Mail Mobile to connect from each location is more than offset by the ease with which you connect thereafter.

Differences in how it looks

cc:Mail and cc:Mail Mobile not only work about the same way, but they also look very similar. Take a look at Figures 17-1 and 17-2, the cc:Mail and cc:Mail Mobile windows, respectively. The cc:Mail window probably looks familiar. However, as you can see, cc:Mail Mobile window has those funky things that hang from the ceiling over a baby's bed. No, wait; they took that feature out. Ahem. cc:Mail Mobile has a couple of extra containers that are hanging out in the container pane (at the left side of the Inbox window), a new menu bar item (Mobile), and some new SmartIcons. Additionally, a separate application, called cc:Mail Background, handles the connections to the post office. That's it for the visible differences.

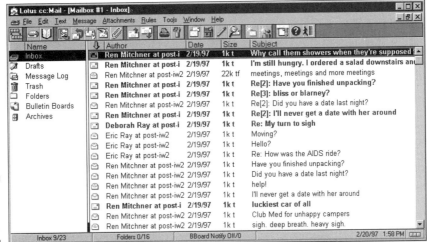

Figure 17-1:
The cc:Mail window.

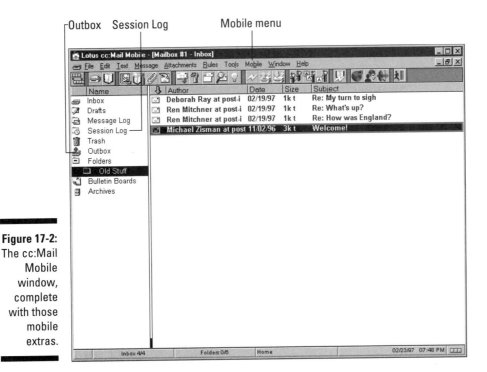

Figure 17-2:
The cc:Mail Mobile window, complete with those mobile extras.

Installing cc:Mail Mobile

cc:Mail Mobile lets you send and receive e-mail from anywhere you happen to be — your home, the branch office, or Nebraska. Though being able to work everywhere is a mixed blessing at best, at least you're no longer cabled to your office network. As soon as you have cc:Mail Mobile set up and operational, you're free. Free! Well, relatively speaking.

Onward to installing and setting up cc:Mail Mobile!

With any kind of luck, your installation procedure consists of calling your cc:Mail administrator, delivering your laptop, and picking it up the next day with cc:Mail Mobile completely set up and configured. Of course, if you have that kind of luck, you've also won the lottery three times and can afford to hire your own personal cc:Mail administrator.

Realistically speaking, you probably have a CD or a pile of diskettes and are told to get yourself set up and call with problems. Darn. This chapter carries you through your initial installation and first login to cc:Mail Mobile.

For those of us who get a CD or set of diskettes for cc:Mail Mobile from our system administrator, along with a whispered "Good luck," here's the procedure:

1. **Get ready!**

   Turn on your computer.

2. **Get set!**

   If you're a Windows 95 user, Windows appears on your screen. If you're still using Windows 3.1*x,* do whatever you usually do to start Windows.

3. **Go (from the diskettes)!**

   Insert Disk 1 in the disk drive.

   If you use Windows 3.1*x,* select File⇨Run from the Program Manager. Enter **a:\install** in the text box and click OK.

   If you use Windows 95, choose the Start menu and then select Run. Enter **a:\install** in the text box and click OK.

4. **Go (from CD)!**

   Put the cc:Mail 6 CD in the CD-ROM drive. (As opposed, I suppose, to putting it in the stereo.)

   If you use Windows 3.1*x,* select File⇨Run from the Program Manager. Enter **d:\winmail\r6mobile\install** in the text box and click OK. If your CD drive uses some other drive letter than D, substitute that drive letter at the beginning of the command.

If you use Windows 95, choose the Start menu and then select <u>R</u>un. Enter **d:\winmail\r6mobile\install** in the text box and click OK. If your CD drive uses some other letter, substitute that letter at the beginning of the command.

After a few seconds of disk or CD activity, a screen like Figure 17-3 appears.

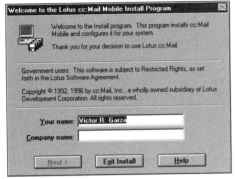

Figure 17-3:
Welcome to
the cc:Mail
Mobile
Install
Program.

5. **Provide the requested information and click <u>N</u>ext.**

6. **cc:Mail Mobile asks you again to verify that you didn't commit a typo. Just click <u>Y</u>es and proceed.**

7. **Click <u>N</u>ext to accept cc:Mail Mobile's suggested directory.**

   Unless you're sure you know what you're doing and have some really good reason to do so, just accept cc:Mail Mobile's suggestions on the cc:Mail Mobile directory, as shown in Figure 17-4.

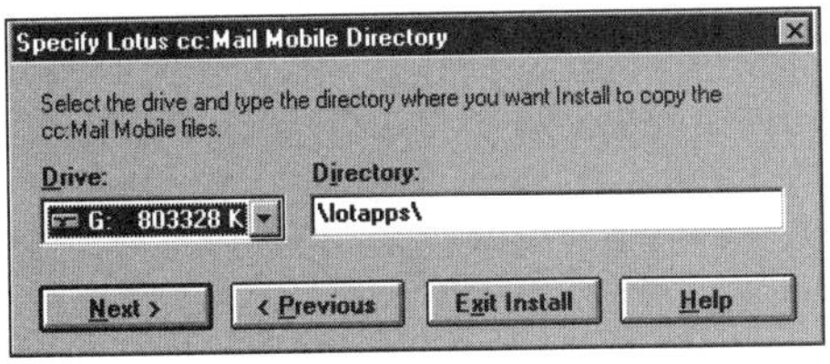

Figure 17-4:
The Specify
cc:Mail
Mobile
Directory
dialog box.

8. **Click <u>N</u>ext to accept cc:Mail Mobile's suggested directory for Shared Tools.**

9. **Select the cc:Mail Mobile Applications that you want to install by checking the boxes in front of the items. Click <u>N</u>ext to proceed when you're done.**

See Figure 17-5 for a status check.

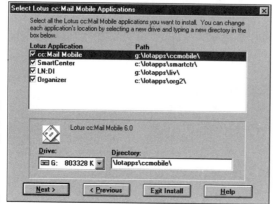

Figure 17-5:
The Select
cc:Mobile
Applications
dialog box.

- You certainly want to install the Mobile option, but the remaining applications are optional, depending on the space that you have and if you want to have something else to tinker with on your computer.

- SmartCenter is a different way of organizing and running the programs on your hard disk. Install it if you like, but it doesn't provide any new capabilities. You end up with these strange virtual file drawers at the top of your screen and programs in them. Maybe it works for some people, but an additional layer of complexity is the last thing that I want on my computer.

- LN:DI is image and fax viewing software. This is probably a good choice if you have the space for it. If you don't, you may not be able to view some attachments, like that picture of your new nephew that your brother e-mailed to you.

- Organizer is the Lotus personal information manager software. It's very good software and works well with your trusty Day-Timer. If you can spare the space, go for it. If your time management system is as good as it gets, however, Organizer is expendable.

10. **Choose either Default features — Automatic Install or Minimum features — Automatic Install in the Install Options dialog box (Figure 17-6). Click Next to continue.**

If you have ample disk space (right, like anyone does!), choose the Default features option. If disk space is pretty tight, go for Minimum features.

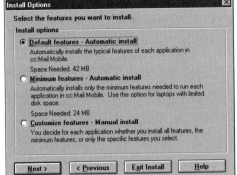

Figure 17-6:
The Install
Options
dialog box.

The third choice, Customize Features, is recommended only if you really want to take extra time to tinker with your computer or really care about the particulars. This option isn't recommended for busy people.

11. **If you selected LN:DI image viewing software, you see another dialog box with more choices. Choices, choices, choices. Just take the suggestions and click Next.**

12. **In the Select Program Group dialog box, select the program group that you want to find cc:Mail Mobile in. The default choice is, as usual, just fine. Click Next to continue.**

Aren't you glad you selected the automatic install so that you don't have to make any decisions?

13. **Click Yes! Stop asking questions and begin copying files to your hard disk.**

On the other hand, maybe you just spent ten minutes answering inane questions because you like to. In that case, answer No, don't install the files. I want to go back through these questions again.

14. **Wait and feed the computer diskettes if you need to.**

15. **Click the OK buttons that appear in the next two dialog boxes.**

These two small dialog boxes are here to let you know that changes have to be made to your autoexec.bat file (here I go again with that cryptic DOS stuff) so that cc:Mail Mobile can operate properly. Just click away and be happy that you don't have to make the changes manually.

16. **After you see the Install Complete dialog box, click Done to gracefully accept the congratulations from the install program and get on with your day.**

17. **Complete the registration dialog boxes, clicking Next to move to the next one in the sequence, or just click Exit if you're tired of this process.**

    Sometimes your system administrator may specifically want you to register and sometimes not. Just ask, and if you aren't sure, choose Exit. You get another chance in two weeks.

If you have a CD drive on the computer on which you are installing cc:Mail, by all means install from the cc:Mail CD. The diskette install takes 17 diskettes and can drive you up a tree.

Using cc:Mail Mobile for the First Time

The toughest thing about using cc:Mail Mobile is getting it set up to work with your modem and to connect to the post office. Worst of all, you can't even send a panicked e-mail message for help until you don't need help anymore. The first connect time is the worst.

Don't worry though; it's not all that difficult. The first time that you run cc:Mail Mobile, you must provide all kinds of information. Grin and bear it, and rejoice in the knowledge that you don't have to do it much more.

Unless you're pretty confident that you have all of the information that you need and that you expect everything to go swimmingly, you should run cc:Mail Mobile for the first time when your network or system administrator (a) is not on vacation, (b) *is* taking calls, and (c) has the time and inclination to help you. A donation of donuts the first thing in the morning does wonders for quick success with cc:Mail Mobile later in the day.

Here's the procedure for making your first connection, assuming that cc:Mail Mobile is already installed on your system:

1. **Start cc:Mail Mobile.**

   If you're a Windows 3.1*x* user, your Lotus cc:Mail Mobile 6.0 icon is probably in the Lotus Applications program group. Double-click on the icon, or select it and press Enter.

   If you're a Windows 95 user, choose the Start menu and then select Programs⇨Lotus Applications⇨Lotus cc:Mail Mobile 6.0.

Neither rain, nor snow, nor dark of night . . .

You've doubtlessly noticed countless references throughout this book to system administrators, cc:Mail administrators, network administrators, or other administrative types. We're not just being deliberately vague — here's why I keep passing the buck and exactly what it's all about.

The "person in charge" of cc:Mail at your company or institution may have any number of different titles but is generally responsible for keeping the whole shooting match running well. Additionally, particularly when it comes to cc:Mail Mobile, that techie type is probably the only one who knows exactly how to set up all of the options and knows the most likely problems that you can expect to encounter.

Although this book can point you in general directions for identifying potential problems and working through them on your own, there are many cases in which deferring to the system administrator is the only, or at least far and away the fastest, solution.

Here are a few gentle suggestions for working with your system administrator.

Be nice. Your cc:Mail administrator is probably overworked and underpaid and has a lot to do. Making your life difficult isn't a priority unless you're too obnoxious.

Try to work out your first mobile connection when it isn't a crisis. The computers know when you're in a hurry and respond accordingly. Additionally, that sign that floats around most offices about "Lack of planning on your part doesn't constitute an emergency on my part" probably originated in an administrator's office.

Be prepared. Have as much information as you can when you first contact the cc:Mail administrator and, if possible, be sitting in front of the computer on which you will be using cc:Mail Mobile. If you need technical support to sound like you know what you're talking about, bring your grade-schooler to work with you in case you get in over your head.

Be sure to ask the administrator for the correct post office name, the post office phone number, how your name is listed in the post office directory, and any other important information about the primary connection to the post office. If you find that you're having a problem connecting to your Post Office or otherwise find yourself in a situation where you're at your wit's end, it's time to call in the big guns. Pick up the phone and give your administrator a call.

Patiently wait for the Lotus cc:Mail Login - Mobile Mode dialog box, shown in Figure 17-7, to appear.

2. Type your Log-in Name in the text box that is provided.

You must type your Log-in Name just as it appears in the cc:Mail directory (you may need to get this from your administrator). cc:Mail isn't able to tell that "Joanna S. Doe" is the same as the "Doe, Joanna S." in the directory.

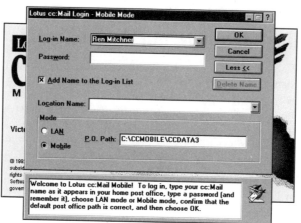

Figure 17-7:
The Lotus
cc:Mail
Login -
Mobile
Mode
dialog box
awaits your
command.

3. Type your Password.

And remember it. You should use the same password that you use in the office.

Keep in mind that if someone guesses your password, that person then has access to all of your e-mail. Yes, you use a notebook computer and you're the only one that uses it, but what happens when the computer gets stolen from the x-ray machine at the airport? Aha!

Make your passwords at least six characters long, and make sure that they aren't words in any dictionary.

4. Make sure to select the Add Name to the Log-in List check box.

You want to make sure that cc:Mail Mobile keeps all of this information that you're about to add for the next time that you use it, so add that name.

5. The drop-down list for Location Name is empty because you haven't yet set up a location. However, you're about to do so.

6. Under Mode, make sure that Mobile is checked and a P.O. Path is automatically entered by cc:Mail.

Unless you have a specific reason to change the P.O. Path, don't. cc:Mail likes doing things its way, and you need to pick your battles. This isn't one of them.

If a network installation of cc:Mail is already on your system, the information for connecting to that post office is already entered. But if you want to connect remotely (which is why you're using this program in the first place), you must tell the program what post office to connect to and all kinds of other neat things about your connection method.

7. Click OK.

You are confronted with the "No post office was found. Would you like to create a new one?" dialog box.

8. Choose OK to create a new post office.

No bricks are required. This new post office is now on your own computer and handles your mobile mailing needs.

Note that this new post office resides on your own computer, while the home post office that you connect to and send mail through is located somewhere on your company network. If you're in the office or using LAN mode, you share the post office on a network drive with everyone else.

9. Type the PO Name in the top text box of the Home Post Office Setup dialog box.

The Home Post Office Setup dialog box, as shown in Figure 17-8, is where you enter the basic connection information about your mobile setup.

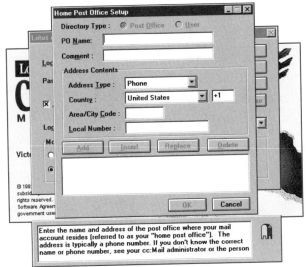

Figure 17-8:
The Home
Post Office
Setup
dialog box.

Your system administrator must provide the name of the post office — guessing doesn't get you there.

10. Add a Comment or description if you like.

11. In the Address Contents area, fill in the blanks.

Generally, your first Mobile connection has an Address Type of Phone, which is the default choice. Select the Country from the drop-down list and then enter the Area/City Code and Local Number.

If you don't already know the phone number, call your cc:Mail administrator and ask for it (don't forget to ask how he liked the donuts that you got for him).

If your mobile connection is something other than Phone, refer to Chapter 18 for more information about configuring locations in cc:Mail Mobile.

12. Click Add to complete the connection type (if you make a mistake, click the Delete button and complete the phone number section again), and then click OK to finish your Home Post Office Setup configuration (for now).

You then see the Edit Communication Method dialog box, as shown in Figure 17-9.

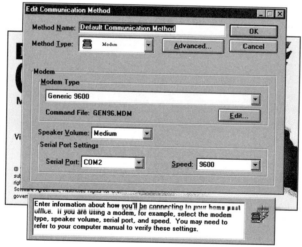

Figure 17-9:
The Edit Communication Method dialog box.

13. Enter a descriptive name in the Method Name text box.

If you're at home, "Home" is a good choice. Likewise, if you're at a branch office, "Branch Office" would be optimal.

Steer clear of "Location1" or "First Call Location." Those aren't going to do you much good down the road. For that matter, don't type in "Down the Road" either.

14. Leave Method Type set to Modem, the default setting.

If you want to configure a different type of connection, refer to Chapter 18. Your first mobile connection will most likely use a Modem connection.

15. Select your Modem Type from the drop-down list. When in doubt, the generic choices are usually acceptable.

16. Select the correct Serial Port from the drop-down list, and select the correct Port Speed.

Your Serial Port is probably COM1 or COM2. If you know that your modem uses a particular port, select that port.

Unfortunately, cc:Mail Mobile doesn't automatically detect your modem or its characteristics, so if you don't know what port your modem is connected to or the proper port speed, call your cc:Mail administrator, your neighborhood PC guru, or your teenager or check your computer's documentation.

17. Click OK to complete the setup.

That's it! You're set up and ready to go! You don't actually get verification that you did everything right until you connect for the first time. See Chapter 19 for the specific procedure.

Chapter 18

Setting Up and Configuring cc:Mail Mobile

. . . .

In This Chapter

▶ Setting up locations

▶ Selecting locations

▶ Editing the Home Post Office Configuration

▶ Using Mobile Setup

. . . .

*I*t's a wonder that anyone really uses any software. All of the really painful stuff comes right at the beginning, before you even know if it's worth it. After you're comfortable with the program and have grown to love it, there's no hassle. Sigh. The mysteries of life continue.

cc:Mail Mobile unfortunately stands as an example of these mysteries, particularly when it comes to configuring locations. cc:Mail Mobile lets you set up different locations, also called *configuration files,* to make it easy to connect to your home post office. If you spend a lot of time traveling, this feature alone can save you a remarkable amount of time. These locations are kind of a pain at first, but after they're done, you're ready to go.

This chapter explains how to set up and configure cc:Mail Mobile to correctly connect to the post office from each location that you use, in addition to describing the procedures for adding connection methods and customizing your cc:Mail Mobile setup.

Consider that, depending on where you are and what you're doing, you want to call into the post office from your home, a branch office, a hotel, or your mother-in-law's house (on vacation). If you're dialing in from home, you probably need to dial *70 (to disable call waiting — if you have it — and wait for the second dial tone). If you're calling from a branch office, you may have to dial 9 to get an outside line. And if you're calling from a hotel room, you may need to dial an 8, and then you probably need to enter your telephone credit card number.

Each of these places can be defined as a location for cc:Mail Mobile. You tell cc:Mail Mobile about each place from which you connect to your home post office, and it remembers all the trivials about what to dial when or about how to make a connection from that location.

Setting Up a Location

The following is the procedure that you use to set up a new location. Using these steps allows you to choose your location and then have all that extraneous dialing business take place automatically:

1. **Start cc:Mail Mobile and log in.**

2. **Choose Mobile⇨Locations.**

Take a minute for orientation. The default location is Office — as shown at the top of the Locations dialog box in Figure 18-1. The Telephone icon at the left is highlighted, so the remainder of the dialog box provides information about the Telephone Dialing Rules.

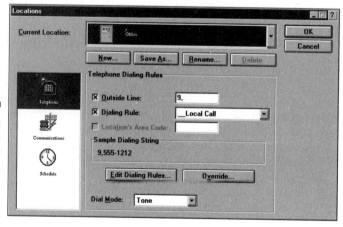

Figure 18-1:
The Locations dialog box, ready and waiting.

Click on the Communications icon at the left of the dialog box, and you see the (probably short) List of the Communications Methods that you've set up, along with options for changing them.

Select Schedule at the left, and you can set a schedule for when cc:Mail Mobile should send and retrieve mail.

Keep in mind that all of these settings apply to the Office location, because that is the one selected at the top of the dialog box. If you change locations or add a location, you can reset all of these preferences. For example, you may want to send and retrieve mail hourly from the branch office but only on startup and exit from a hotel.

Click the down arrow at the right of the Current Location dialog box to see the other two predefined locations, Home and Hotel, complete with fancy graphics.

3. Click New to set up a new location profile for your Branch Office.

4. Enter a name in the New Location dialog box, select an appropriate icon for the location, and click OK.

Branch Office seems to merit the cowboy boot icon — it's in Oklahoma.

5. Select the Telephone icon and set the Telephone Dialing Rules for the branch office.

- Keep your eyes on the Sample Dialing String — the changes in configuration show up immediately there, so you can see if the number to be dialed is correct.

- Hypothetically, you have to enter 9 to reach an outside line, so select the Outside Line check box and enter **9,** (that's the number nine followed by a comma) in the text box. The comma tells cc:Mail Mobile to wait for a second (so that the dial tone can return) before continuing to dial.

- Under Dialing Rule, select Long Distance Domestic (the option to choose if you're dialing regular long distance or to an 800 number).

- Location's Area Code, referring to where the branch office is located, is not an available option because the call is long distance.

- The button marked Edit Dialing Rules takes you to another dialog box in which you can add to or customize the list of Dialing Rules. The listed options include those for entering calling card numbers from the major long-distance carriers, but you're free to add a dialing rule for El Discounto Long Distance Co.

- Override just lets you temporarily replace the number to dial for your home post office. If, for example, the main phone line is having problems and your office has arranged a temporary substitute number, you can set up the temporary number here, rather than reset the Directory entry.

• Finally, the dialing instructions also include a Dial Mode list box indicating whether the dialing is to be done via a tone telephone line, a pulse telephone line, or manually. The manual option allows you to manually dial a number every time that you want to make a connection rather than let cc:Mail Mobile automatically do it for you. I don't think that I could ever find a use for this one, but hey, your mileage may vary.

6. Select the Communications icon.

In the List of Communications Methods, you see all of the different methods that you've set up for your home post office. Click each of the methods, and click the button in the lower left to Enable or Disable them.

You may have to consult with your system administrator about some of the options, particularly if you have quite a few different communications methods available and some of them work in combination with others.

7. Select the Schedule icon.

Click On Startup, On Exit, or On Sending Message to determine when cc:Mail Mobile is to connect to the home post office to send a message.

Selecting both On Startup and On Exit is pretty sensible — you get all of the new messages since your last mail session on startup, and you send all of your new messages at the end of the session. If you send a lot of mail, connecting to the home post office for each message could get to be a pain (I wouldn't recommend clicking this one unless you really don't send or receive that much e-mail).

Click Enable schedule and select the Frequency and Time that you want cc:Mail Mobile to send and retrieve messages. For example, cc:Mail Mobile can, at your command, call hourly, daily, or weekly at a specified time.

A few additional notes about setting up locations follow:

✔ If you're a power user (or power user in training), you may want to know about other configuration options that are available. In the Locations dialog box, select Communications and then the method that you want to edit. Choose Edit to bring up the Edit Communication Method dialog box. By clicking the Advanced button, you can specify a script to be executed when a connection is established. The cc:Mail mobile program does not, however, provide prewritten scripts, so you're stuck writing one or bribing your local cc:Mail guru.

✔ If you click the Edit button in the Modem window (of the Edit Communication Method dialog box), you can manually edit the modem configuration file. I strongly recommend that you refrain from proving this fact unless you are confident that you know what you're doing and know whom to call when your modem stops working.

Selecting a Location

After you've set up the locations that you need, changing locations is a breeze. Here's the procedure:

1. **Read the signs in the airport so that you know where you are.**

2. **Fire up the computer, Windows, and cc:Mail Mobile, in that order.**

3. **Select Mobile⇨Locations.**

4. **Click the arrow at the right of the Current Location drop-down list and select your current location.**

5. **Look on with glee as the proper configuration appears (not that you really see much of anything change).**

6. **Click OK.**

Editing Your Home Post Office Setup

After you're up and functional with cc:Mail Mobile, or possibly earlier, you may need to edit your home Post Office setup. Perhaps the phone number changed, or maybe your company started offering additional connection methods. You can edit any part of your Home Post Office configuration as well as configure cc:Mail Mobile to take advantage of as many different connection methods as you'd like.

Adding connection methods is one of the most likely changes that you make to your Home Post Office Setup. Many other changes would fit in the "if it ain't broke, don't fix it" category.

One good example of needing to add a connection method would be if your company starts distributing dial-up accounts so that you can dial into your company's toll-free number and surf the Internet — oops, I mean, work — from your hotel room when you're traveling on business. Your surf-the-Internet connection provides a TCP/IP link to your company. You may be able to take advantage of this TCP/IP link for your cc:Mail Mobile communications as well so that you can do everything you need with one call, rather than having to break your Internet connection and reconnect with cc:Mail Mobile.

Additionally, if you have a somewhat unstable network that crashes a lot, you can use mobile mode in the office. You still need to connect to the post office to send or receive messages, but if you're using the network protocol (probably NetWare or TCP/IP) and schedule frequent connections to transfer mail, you probably won't notice the difference.

You can change the dialing commands, communications methods, and scheduling for any of the locations, and you can save the location under the current name or save it as a new location.

Here's the procedure for changing the communication methods that you have at your disposal.

1. **Start cc:Mail Mobile.**

2. **Select Mobile⇨Mobile Setup.**

   The Mobile Setup dialog box offers a number of different options, but the only ones that you need right now are the post office–related ones at the top.

3. **Click Edit Address to customize the connection methods for cc:Mail Mobile.**

   The Home Post Office Setup dialog box appears with the main connection method highlighted, as shown in Figure 18-2. When you selected your modem and communications port during the setup procedure, you created the default communications method. This dialog box offers you the opportunity to create other communications methods for connecting via other means.

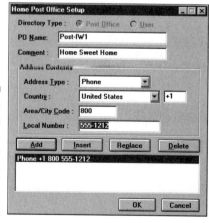

Figure 18-2:
The Home Post Office Setup dialog box, ready for editing.

An additional connection method may be used to connect with an alternate phone number or with a network connection if the modem isn't configured properly. In most cases, the only additional connection that you may use would be a second phone number; however, other methods are available if your cc:Mail administrator sets them up at your home post office.

4. **To add a new address, select the Address Type from the drop-down list.**

   Fill in the blanks with the information that you obtained from your system administrator. The blanks that you see depend on the Address Type that you selected.

5. **Click Add to add the address to the bottom of the list, Insert to add the address at the highlighted address, or Replace to replace the existing address with the new one.**

6. **To delete an address, click once on the address to select it and then click Delete.**

7. **Click OK.**

The following are some additional notes about alternative addresses, connection types, and connection methods.

✔ If you can use additional connection methods, collect all of the pertinent information from your system administrator, who has surely prepared a handout with all of the information that you need neatly summarized on one page. Or you can just call and ask what you need to know for an additional connection method.

✔ If you want to request a communication method by name, cc:Mail Mobile supports the following communication methods: Phone, Wireless, NetWare, TCP/IP, X.25, ISDN, PBX, Direct, and Directory Entry. Your system administrator can tell you which, if any, are appropriate choices for your situation and how to configure them.

Customizing Mobile Setup

You can change the home post office address and customize many (noncritical) things about the way cc:Mail Mobile makes connections, and you do most of it from Mobile Setup. You may need to enable additional information to facilitate troubleshooting or possibly to make sure that your password doesn't show up on the screen.

The procedure for special customization is as follows:

1. **Start cc:Mail Mobile.**

2. **Select Mobile⇨Mobile Setup and configure to your heart's content.**

   The Mobile Setup dialog box, as shown in Figure 18-3, offers a field where you enter the Calling Card Number that is to be used if your location is set up to use a calling card. The dialog box also allows you to specify the number of retries that should be attempted if your call does not go through and the appropriate period of time between calling attempts.

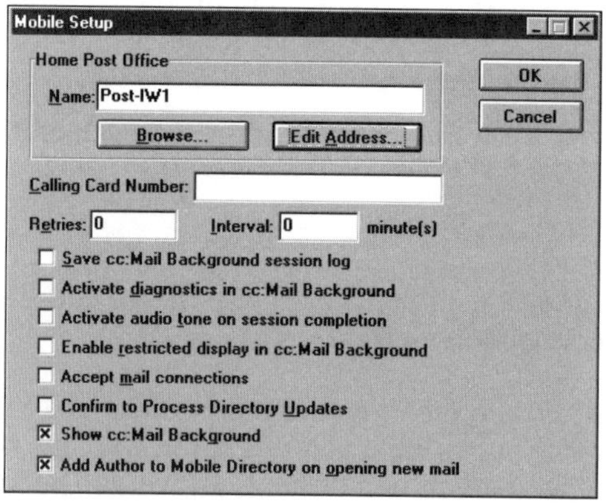

Figure 18-3:
The Mobile
Setup
dialog box.

Mobile Setup

Home Post Office

Name: Post-IW1

[Browse...] [Edit Address...]

Calling Card Number:

Retries: 0   Interval: 0   minute(s)

☐ Save cc:Mail Background session log
☐ Activate diagnostics in cc:Mail Background
☐ Activate audio tone on session completion
☐ Enable restricted display in cc:Mail Background
☐ Accept mail connections
☐ Confirm to Process Directory Updates
☒ Show cc:Mail Background
☒ Add Author to Mobile Directory on opening new mail

[OK] [Cancel]

Additionally, the Mobile Setup dialog box allows you to specify the following options:

- Save cc:Mail Background session log. (*Session logs* store information about connections that can be useful in troubleshooting failed sessions.)

- Activate diagnostics in cc:Mail Background. (This option causes additional information about connections — for example, modem strings and packet logs — to be displayed for troubleshooting purposes.)

- Activate audio tone on session completion. (This option causes the computer to emit a tone to let you know that the cc:Mail session has completed the task that you assigned it — for example, Send/Receive Mail.)

- Enable restricted display in cc:Mail Background. (This option prevents the cc:Mail Background screen, which pops up when you make a connection to the home post office, from displaying potentially sensitive information — for example, post office names and addresses.)

- Accept mail connections. (This option allows the program to receive incoming calls from other users of cc:Mail Mobile. This is a great feature for advanced users. You don't even need a cc:Mail post office to exchange mail with other cc:Mail users!)

- Confirm to Process Directory Updates. (The usual procedure is for directory updates from the home post office to be processed automatically after the connection is finished. This option allows you to defer that processing.)

3. **When you've clicked on everything that needs a click, you're done. Click OK.**

Chapter 19

Using cc:Mail Mobile

In This Chapter

▶ Using Directory Updates

▶ Making connections

▶ Filtering out messages

▶ Using Docking mode

*A*fter your cc:Mail Mobile software is all set up and you've configured the locations and other things, you're ready to use it. This chapter assumes that you're already familiar with cc:Mail activities like sending and reading mail, and it takes you through the main differences between using cc:Mail in LAN and Mobile modes.

Using Directory Updates

A cc:Mail directory is that list of addresses from which you choose who is to receive your e-mail messages. When you're using cc:Mail on a local-area network (LAN) connection, you always see the complete cc:Mail directory. However, in Mobile mode, you have to work a little to get and maintain your directory. (Why is it that preventive maintenance always get your finger-nails dirty?)

See Chapter 7 for more information about the cc:Mail directory and about addressing messages.

Sending messages is much easier if the recipient is listed in your cc:Mail Mobile directory, which is simply a listing of people and post offices along with their addresses. This list is maintained at the home post office by the cc:Mail administrator. Unfortunately, your cc:Mail Mobile directory starts out almost empty, even if the cc:Mail directory from your LAN connection is chock-full of addresses.

Before you can do any addressing the easy way, you have to get all of those addresses into your copy of cc:Mail Mobile. There are four basic ways to do so:

✔ **Automatic directory updates** are the easiest way to get your cc:Mail Mobile directory set up. Pick up the phone, and ask your administrator to send you an automatic directory update that contains the home post office's entire mail directory. So when you next make a call to the home post office, all of the names and addresses are automatically added to your mobile directory.

In addition, whenever the administrator issues a directory update message to all users, the names and addresses that are contained in the update are automatically added to your mobile directory when you receive the update message.

Processing automatic directory updates can take several minutes or even hours if the directory has a large number of entries or if your computer is fairly slow. If you're in a hurry, you have to take preventive action *before* you get the directory update. Choose Mobile⇨Mobile Setup, and check the box for Confirm to Process Directory Updates.

If you check this box, you can make the decision when you get the directory update as to whether or not the update is processed. It's usually a good idea to process updates as soon as you get them, but if you're really in a hurry, you can postpone this processing.

✔ **Manually adding addresses** is fine if you only have a few addresses to add. To manually add a person to your directory, select Mobile⇨New Directory Entry. The Directory Entry dialog box lets you specify whether the new entry is a post office or a user and provides fields in which to enter the name of the user or post office and a comment. The address type of Directory Entry is already filled in. You can select the user's home post office from a lookup list that appears when you click the Browse button.

✔ **Copying addresses from received messages** can be easy if you choose Mobile⇨Mobile Setup and check the box for Add Author to Mobile Directory on opening new mail.

If you already have messages that include other *recipients* who aren't in your directory, the easiest way to add them is to drag the names to the Address Book window. Select Window⇨New Address Book Window to open your directory listing. Next, open the message with the recipients' names. Choose Window⇨Tile Horizontal to tile the windows so that you can see them both. Finally, highlight the names that you want to copy, click and hold the mouse button and drag the names to the Directory window.

✔ **Importing a directory file** from the home post office is an option that you exercise only if your administrator sends you the directory in a file instead of as a directory update message. This procedure involves activating an import command from the DOS command line (not fun).

If you get something from your administrator that claims to be an Automatic Directory Update but nothing seems to happen when you open it, you may have gotten the directory as a file. The best choice is to ask the administrator to resend the directory so that you can enjoy an automatic update of your own.

Connecting to the Post Office

cc:Mail Mobile's procedures for sending and receiving mail in Mobile mode differ somewhat from the process in LAN mode. In LAN mode, you're always connected to the post office, whereas in Mobile mode, you have to tell the computer to connect to transfer mail.

Though the basics of creating messages, entering text or attaching files, and reading mail remain the same, your processes now have a couple of differences that show up in the communications with the home post office (a.k.a. the rest of the world).

When you're working in LAN mode, everything that you send proceeds directly to the home post office, without stopping and without passing Go! or collecting $200. Similarly, messages that are sent to you appear in your Inbox shortly after they are sent, without a holdup.

In Mobile mode, messages are passed back and forth between your mobile client and the home post office only sporadically — whenever you connect to send or receive mail. All outgoing messages are created off-line and are transferred in batches when you call the home post office, at which time any new messages for you are retrieved by your cc:Mail Mobile client.

This process also helps reduce phone bills, because you don't stay connected to the home post office while you're composing your message — you're only connected long enough to send the completed messages and download the new ones.

Fortunately, cc:Mail Mobile's procedures for sending and receiving mail are simple to follow and even have some advantages over being on the network. You can't even accidentally forget to connect to your home post office and transfer your outgoing messages, because cc:Mail warns you that you have waiting unsent mail. Now that's thoughtful!

This section walks you through the process of receiving and sending messages from your cc:Mail Mobile connection.

Receiving messages

If you configured cc:Mail Mobile to send and receive messages on startup and on exit, you can probably take care of most transfer obligations right there. After you've connected to your post office, the messages are transferred automatically; you just look for them in your Inbox (press Ctrl+I or double-click on the Inbox).

You may not have set cc:Mail to send and retrieve messages on startup and on exit, or you may want to check mail only periodically. The procedure to retrieve and read your mail, in case you feel that need to check for new mail in the middle of your cc:Mail Mobile session, is as follows:

1. **Select Mobile⇨Send/Receive Mail or Mobile⇨Receive Only.**

   If you've sent messages and have them hanging out in the Outbox, you probably want the Send/Receive Mail option. Otherwise, Receive Only is just fine.

2. **Wait.**

   Transferring messages over a telephone connection is generally considerably slower than over a regular LAN connection. Unless you have an unlimited phone budget and lots of patience, you may consider filtering out unwanted messages without waiting for them to download.

3. **If you have set up Filtering and have new mail waiting for you, you may have to explicitly accept your messages by clicking the Accept button.**

   See "Filtering Messages" later in this chapter for details.

   After all of your messages have been transferred to your computer (or rejected, if you filter your mail), cc:Mail Mobile disconnects from the post office.

4. **Double-click on your Inbox icon in the Container Pane, select Window⇨Go to Inbox, or press Ctrl+I to see your new messages, if you have any.**

   Read your messages at your convenience. Because they are all now on your computer, you don't have to be tied to the telephone or a specific location. You could even take your computer to the beach and read your mail there. (This is not recommended for owners of desktop computers or if you're likely to get sand kicked in your face for being a geek.)

Sending mail — an introduction to the Outbox

In principle, sending messages from cc:Mail Mobile is almost the same as sending messages from cc:Mail in LAN mode. The basic procedures of creating a new message, addressing it, typing the message or attaching a file, and clicking the Send button are just the same. The devil, or angel, in this case is in the details.

Because cc:Mail Mobile doesn't maintain a full-time connection to the post office when connected in Mobile mode, your messages are not sent immediately. As soon as you click Send, the message dives into the Outbox, in which it lurks until cc:Mail Mobile connects to the home post office to send mail.

Sending messages from cc:Mail Mobile is also pretty straightforward. The messages that you send take a brief pit stop in the Outbox. The procedure for sending messages from your cc:Mail Mobile session is as follows:

1. **Create a message by selecting <u>M</u>essage⇨New <u>M</u>essage or by pressing Ctrl+M or by clicking the New Message button.**

   This procedure presupposes that you have something to say and someone to say it to. If nothing else, send the mail to yourself.

2. **Address your message by choosing <u>M</u>essage⇨<u>A</u>ddress or pressing Ctrl+A.**

   If you haven't received a directory update from your cc:Mail administrator, you may not have any addresses in your address dialog box from which to choose. If that's the case, you must enter the address.

   Of course, if you haven't received a directory update yet, your first message should be to your cc:Mail administrator asking for one of those fancy Automatic Directory Updates to populate your directory.

3. **Type an appropriate subject and write your message.**

   If you're writing to the administrator, be nice!

4. **Send your message by clicking the Send Message button or by choosing <u>M</u>essage⇨<u>S</u>end or pressing Ctrl+S.**

   If your cc:Mail configuration calls for Confirmation on Send, click OK to send the message.

   See Chapter 8 for information about Send options.

   You can double-click the Outbox in the Container pane to see the limbo state of your message. See, it's right there! To send it, you have to connect to your post office.

If you were a LAN user or connected in LAN mode, that message wouldn't have stopped in your Outbox, and it would be on its way by now.

5. Select Mobile➪Send/Receive Mail or Mobile➪Send Only.

If you suspect that you will be getting lots of messages and don't want to wait for them all to download, choose the Send Only option. Otherwise, pick Send/Receive mail.

6. Wait.

After the message disappears from the Outbox, it's gone and you're done.

Here are a couple of additional notes about sending and receiving mail in cc:Mail Mobile.

✔ cc:Mail Mobile's Outbox feature gives you a second chance in case you fired off an e-mail message without spell-checking it or, worse yet, without tact-checking it. You can just root around in your Outbox, double-click to bring up the message, and continue writing or editing it. When you're ready to resend it, select Message➪Send or press Ctrl+S. You then get the choice of discarding your original draft or keeping it in addition to the newer message that you just finished editing.

✔ If you like getting e-mail frequently and appreciate that message that tells you how many messages you haven't yet read, you can select Mobile➪Receive Only at any time during your session to catch up. On the other hand, choosing Mobile➪Locations and selecting Schedule lets you schedule mail retrieval automatically at any time. Click OK when you're finished.

✔ Although the default connection option is to automatically send and receive all mail, you can tell the program to send messages without receiving any or to receive messages without sending any. To exercise either option, select Mobile➪Send Only or Mobile➪Receive Only.

Filtering Messages

Filtering messages allows you to choose, sight unseen, which messages should and should not be downloaded. You would want to do this because transferring messages over a telephone connection is generally considerably slower than over a regular LAN connection. Unless you have an unlimited phone budget and lots of patience, you may consider filtering unwanted messages without waiting for them to download. To make sure that you only download select messages, you can set up cc:Mail Mobile to filter, or screen, messages from the home post office.

This section tells you how to set up filtering for your cc:Mail Mobile connection and how to retrieve messages after filtering is activated.

Setting up filtering

If you're already in cc:Mail Mobile, follow this procedure to filter your incoming mail:

1. Select Mobile⇨Filters.

You see the Filters dialog box, as shown in Figure 19-1.

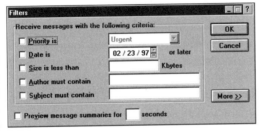

Figure 19-1:
The Filters
dialog box.

2. Select the filtering criteria that you want to apply.

The Filters dialog box includes five check boxes that determine the criteria that are used to accept messages. Messages are downloaded if:

- The priority is Urgent, or Urgent or Normal (depending on the drop-down list selection that you choose).
- The date is on or after a specified date.
- The size of the message is less than a specified size.
- The Author field contains a specific set of characters.
- The Subject field contains a specific set of characters.

You can activate any or all of these filter criteria by placing a check mark in the box.

At the bottom of the Filters dialog box is a check box for Preview message summaries. If you select this box, you can preview message summaries for a specified number of seconds, 10 by default, before the messages are downloaded.

If you activate this feature, cc:Mail Mobile displays the author, date, size, and subject of each message, as well as the titles of any attached objects, when you connect to the home post office. You can then click any of three buttons: Accept Message, Reject Message, or Stop. The Stop button causes the message to be rejected and the connection to be terminated.

If you don't select one of these three buttons within the amount of time that you specified in the Filters dialog box, the message is automatically accepted.

The Preview message summaries feature is especially handy if you are making a long-distance call. By screening messages, you can decide not to take the time — and spend the money — to download messages that clearly aren't urgent or that have large files attached to them.

3. Click More to set up specialized Rules on Mail download.

Figure 19-2 shows the Filters dialog box with Rules on Mail download visible.

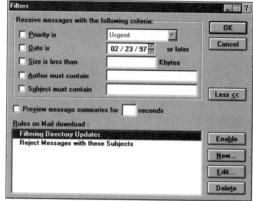

Figure 19-2:
The Filters dialog box with Rules on Mail download visible.

You can establish all kinds of rules within cc:Mail. cc:Mail rules tell the program what to do with messages based on the subject, priority, sender, and a number of other characteristics. See Chapter 16 for more information about using Rules.

- If you want to establish a rule for downloading your mail, for example, to reject anything from the joker who sends out regular pictures of his dog, choose New.

- Type a Description of the rule, and make sure that Enable is checked.

- Choose With Conditions, select Author, choose contains, and then type the joker's name. Choose Add, and then click OK.

- Click Actions, select Reject from the drop-down list, click Add, and then click OK.

- Click Save to keep your new rule.

You no longer get any messages from a person with that name. Cool, huh? Don't get too carried away, though — you not only don't get garbage, but you also don't get anything meaningful from that person.

4. Click OK.

You're done. Just retrieve your mail to see the results of your efforts.

Retrieving messages with message summary previews

After you set up Filtering, if you select Preview message summaries, you have a little extra task when you download your mail. You must manually accept or reject each message. If you don't respond to the message box within 10 seconds (or the number of seconds that you specified in the Filters dialog box), the message is automatically downloaded. The procedure, in case you feel that you need to check for mail in the middle of your cc:Mail Mobile session, is as follows:

1. Select Mobile⇨Send/Receive Mail or Mobile⇨Receive Only.

2. Wait.

3. Choose Accept Message, Reject Message, or Stop from the Message Summary dialog box.

Repeat Steps 2 and 3 for every message that you received.

4. Head for the Inbox (press Ctrl+I), or click on the Inbox icon.

That's it! You're done!

Using Docking Mode

You can use cc:Mail Mobile to connect to post offices both remotely via modem and locally over the network. Most significantly, you can do both at once and make sure that all of your important messages are safe and sound in your LAN account. If you don't sync your messages after a trip, you will get really confused. For example, you may have been downloading messages to your laptop computer while on a trip. When you get back to the office and log on to your network account, you won't find those messages in your LAN account because they've already been downloaded to your mobile account.

How, then, do you go about restoring to your network account those messages that you downloaded while you were on the road?

Enter cc:Mail Mobile's Docking Mode. *Docking* occurs when you bring your ship of a traveling computer into the dock of the network so that information can move back and forth. When you use Docking Mode, cc:Mail Mobile allows you to log on to both your LAN account and mobile account simultaneously so that you can copy or move messages, attachments, and even entire folders between the two. Cool, huh?

Here's the procedure, assuming that you have your computer turned on, running Windows and cc:Mail Mobile:

1. Choose Mobile⇨Docking Mode.

You see the Lotus cc:Mail Docking dialog box, as shown in Figure 19-3.

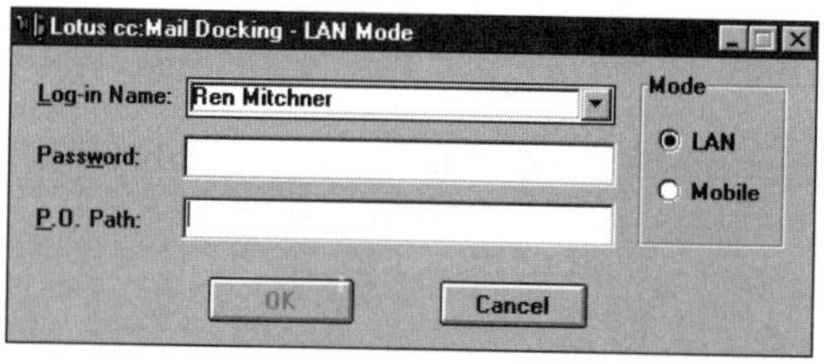

Figure 19-3:
The Lotus
cc:Mail
Docking
dialog box.

2. If you started cc:Mail Mobile in mobile mode, select the LAN radio button here to log on to that account as well. If you originally logged on to cc:Mail Mobile in LAN mode, select the Mobile radio button. Just select the mode that you are not already using.

3. Enter your password, and make certain that the correct DOS path is listed for the cc:Mail Post Office in the P.O. Path field; then click OK.

cc:Mail Mobile pops up a message box to inform you that you're now in docking mode. This message box also lists your user name and the post office path of the docked account.

4. Do that Docking Mode stuff!

Highlight the messages or folders that you want to move or copy to the other account, and then select Mobile⇨Copy to Docked Account or Move to Docked Account.

Copy leaves a copy of the message on both accounts, whereas Move deletes the message from one account and adds it to the other.

5. Click Exit Docking Mode when you've finished your docking chores.

The following are a couple of additional comments about using Docking Mode:

- ✔ Although you can move messages and attached files and folders via docking mode, unfortunately you cannot do the same trick with your mail directories. If you access your mail from two machines — say a desktop system in the office and a laptop computer while you're traveling — you have to periodically request directory updates from your administrator to keep the directory on your Mobile system up-to-date.

- ✔ Note that, when you copy messages to a docked account, the messages are marked as having been read in both accounts, whether or not you have actually read them.

Chapter 20

Troubleshooting

● ●

● ●

*U*nfortunately, trouble and remote connections to your e-mail go hand in hand. Although cc:Mail Mobile is one of the easiest and most reliable of all remote access solutions, so many different obstacles can crop up that at some point, usually at the worst time, you're almost bound to have problems. This chapter shows you some of the diagnostic tools that you have at your disposal and introduces you to possible solutions to the problems.

Keep in mind that there's always a good chance that any problems you're experiencing with your mobile connection aren't your fault, nor is there anything you can do about them. The first time that you connect from a given location, any problems that crop up are, in fact, probably due to your connection; you must work with your system administrator to resolve them. However, after you've successfully connected a couple of times from a specific location, problems rarely just occur out of the blue.

Problems with later connections often happen because one or more of these items occurred:

✔ You changed something.

✔ Your system administrator changed something.

✔ Technical difficulties exist between where you are and where your post office is.

If you didn't change your configuration, add or remove hardware or software, or let your 12-year-old "tweak the performance" of your computer, you're probably off the hook. Call your system administrator, and check to see if there are known problems on his end. If there aren't, assume the third solution, and wait a few hours.

For example, those massive blackouts that plagued the western United States a while back wreaked havoc with cc:Mail Mobile connections. There really wasn't anything to do but wait until business hours on the Monday after the blackouts for the system administrator to come in and fix things.

The following sections provide you with ways of finding and fixing problems that you (hopefully won't) encounter.

Using cc:Mail Background

cc:Mail Background is that extra window that pops up whenever you send or receive mail. Its job is to transfer your mail messages to the post office and from the post office back to you. "Background" is in the name because the software, theoretically, works in the background, and you don't need to pay attention to it. When everything works well, you can indeed safely ignore it. However, it provides lots of useful information about your connection, so it should be the first place to look if you're having difficulties.

cc:Mail Background, seen in Figure 20-1, tells you almost anything that you need to know about your connection.

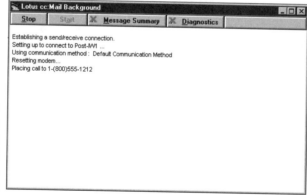

Figure 20-1: cc:Mail Background in action.

Here's how to diagnose a problem with cc:Mail Mobile by using cc:Mail Background:

1. **To retrieve your mail, click the Send/Receive SmartIcon or choose Mobile⇨Send/Receive Mail.**

   Twiddle your thumbs until the call is finished. If you're relatively sure that you should have new mail, wait until you get a notification of your mail, or click on the Inbox icon or press Ctrl+I to bring up the Inbox. No mail? Either nobody loves you anymore, or you have a problem.

   It's time to troubleshoot!

2. **Bring cc:Mail Background to the foreground, either by pressing Alt+Tab or by selecting cc:Mail Background from the Taskbar if you use Windows 95.**

   The horizontal lines separate each connection attempt. Between the lines is information about the connection, including the communication method, error messages if applicable, and the outcome, including the messages that were sent and received. Take a look at Figure 20-1 again.

3. **If you see lines with *Error* in them, write down the error message and number and contact your cc:Mail administrator for help.**

   Otherwise, look for a sign that something went awry. This could be a message like "Call not established," which indicates that something probably went wrong at the post office end.

4. **If everything looks normal, and you see messages like "0 Messages Sent" and "0 Messages Received," you're left with the inescapable conclusion that your e-mail works, and no one cared enough to send you a message. Try sending yourself one to cheer yourself up.**

   That's it! If you didn't solve the problem using these steps, take a look at the following section.

Using the Session Log

Another way to find and fix problems is to use the Session Log. The Session Log is Lotus's attempt to provide you with a "black box" that includes important information about your mobile connection (or lack thereof). From the session information, you may be able to tell what went wrong (or what is going wrong) so that you can begin fixing the problem.

Actually, the Session Log is nothing more than a transcription of the cc:Mail Background window for a specific connection, but it does give you a way to check your connections. It's particularly useful for taking a look at scheduled connections that may happen when you aren't sitting in front of your computer, so you don't necessarily know how they work.

The Session Log can tell you when you connected, how many messages were transferred or rejected, and if there were any problems or errors.

The following are instructions on enabling and using your Session Log, and how to make sense of it.

1. **From your cc:Mail Mobile session, select Mobile⇨Mobile Setup.**

   Enabling your Session Log is one of those Mobile Setup options, as shown in Figure 20-2.

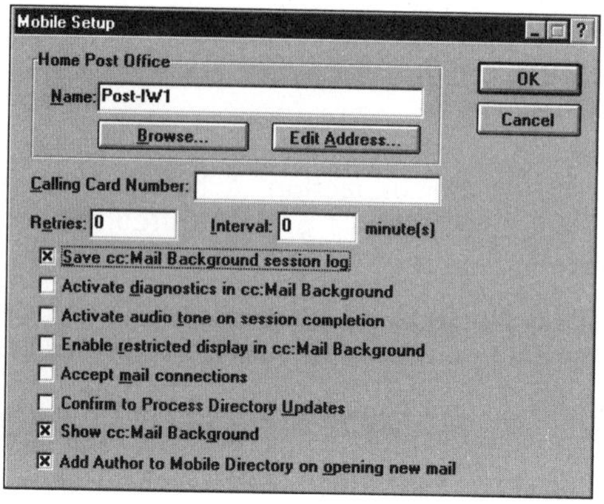

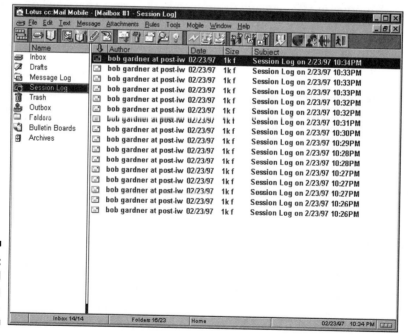

Figure 20-2:
The Mobile
Setup
dialog box.

2. **Select the Save cc:Mail Background session log check box and click OK.**

3. **Make several connections so that you have session logs to examine.**

   Choose Mobile⇨Send/Receive Mail to connect and get your mail. After doing this a couple of times, proceed to the next step.

4. **Double-click on the Session Log container in the container pane.**

   Figure 20-3 shows the cc:Mail Session Log container.

Figure 20-3:
The cc:Mail
Session Log
container.

Each of the session logs looks like an individual message, but instead of holding communications from someone else, it's just a progress report, as it were, from cc:Mail Background.

cc:Mail Background is that extra window that pops up whenever you send or receive mail. Its job is to transfer your mail messages to the post office and from the post office back to you. If you enable the Session Log, cc:Mail Background sends you a message telling you about what it did each session.

5. Open a Session Log message by double-clicking it.

Figure 20-4 shows a sample session log, albeit a fairly boring one.

This session log reports several lines with date, time, and the activities that cc:Mail Background was performing. You don't need to worry about any of these unless you aren't getting mail messages or unless there's some other problem.

The lines that may be important are the "Using communication method" line, so you can tell exactly how cc:Mail Background is trying to connect to the post office, and any lines that have the word *Error* in them.

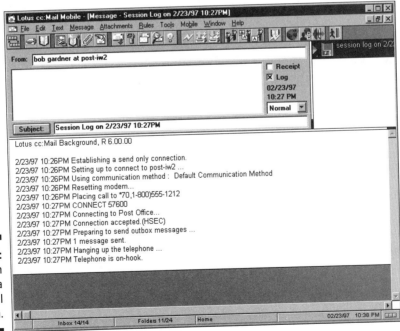

Figure 20-4:
A session log from a successful session.

If the call wasn't successful, that is, if you see a line like "Call not established," but you don't have any error messages, the problem likely lies with the main post office, not with you. Sigh with relief, wait a while, and then try again.

All lines that start with *Error* have an error code. Write that code number down, and tell your system administrator about it.

Figure 20-5 is an example of an unsuccessful session.

6. **After you're tired of scrutinizing the log, close it (press Ctrl+F4 or double-click the upper-left corner).**

   If you're having difficulties (rather than just examining the Session Log out of curiosity), check out the "Troubleshooting" section of this chapter.

Here are some additional notes about the Session Log:

✔ If you've found the error message number but can't contact your system administrator, or if you're really in a hurry and desperate for a solution, you still have an option. Choose Help⇨Search, and enter **error message** in the text box. Double-click cc:Mail Background Error Messages, and you get the full scoop. You get suggested possible solutions, but they're not for the faint of heart.

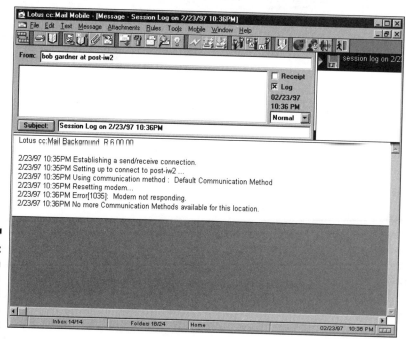

Figure 20-5:
A session log from an unsuccessful session.

✔ Session logs are great if you're on the road and get a call from your boss wondering why you haven't responded to his message. You just verify that your session logs show successful connections, and you can report that you've been checking your mail and he must have made a mistake. Otherwise, if your session logs show problems with your connections, report that you're experiencing technical difficulties and that you're working on them. Either way, you're in the clear.

Troubleshooting

As much as I would like to assure you that everything is going to work right all the time, it won't. This section presents some starting places to get you fixed up with relatively little pain when bad things happen.

What to do when your modem goes on strike

Don't panic. Close all of your open applications, exit Windows, shut everything down (including the modem), and turn off your computer. Count to 10, and walk around the (block, office, kitchen, conference room, rest room, smoke hole). Then power everything back up, including the modem, and try again. If it still doesn't work, don't panic.

In general, follow this procedure:

1. **Root around and find the information that you got from your system administrator about how your mobile post office was supposed to be configured.**

2. **Select Mobile⇨Locations and then choose Telephone.**

   Make sure that the location selected at the top of the screen matches where you are.

   Verify that the sample dialing string works from your location by calling it from a regular phone, just as shown, and waiting for a computer to answer (it sounds like a soprano jet engine).

3. **Select Communications and Enable the correct communication method.**

   The communication method that you're trying to use should have a check mark beside it. If it does not, click the communication method, and then click Enable. Click any other communication methods, and Disable them.

4. **Select the enabled Communication Method and click Edit.**

   Verify that all of the information visible, particularly Modem Type and Serial Port Settings, matches your computer's configuration.

5. **Select Mobile⇨Mobile Setup, choose Edit Address, and then verify that all of the information is in it, based on the information that your cc:Mail administrator provided.**

6. **Try again to send or receive mail.**

   If it works, great! If not, you still aren't allowed to panic.

7. **Check the most recent session logs in the Session Logs pane for error messages.**

   Now is a good time to call the system administrator and ask for help.

   However, Murphy's Law, the Garza cc:Mail Corollary, states that the cc:Mail administrator probably isn't available when you are having problems connecting. Thus, see Appendix D for help.

Lotus has a Web site!

The Lotus Web site has all kinds of good information that could be helpful if you're having problems connecting or using cc:Mail Mobile (or cc:Mail itself, for that matter).

You simply need a connection to the Internet and a Web browser (Netscape, Microsoft Internet Explorer, or the Webster browser that comes with Lotus SmartSuite, for example).

If you're connected to the Internet, you could choose from a couple of sites. Start your Web browser, and point it at http://www.ccmail.com/, or use http://www.support.lotus.com/ for a wider view of Lotus products. Browse around looking for Knowledge Base, product support, Frequently Asked Questions (FAQs), or anything else that looks helpful. Sorry to be so vague about this, but information at this Web site changes all the time.

Some companies provide Internet access but restrict access to the Web. (They probably don't want you spending all of your most productive hours at the Web sites of the Rich and Famous.) If so, just slip around the back door with the Lotus ftp site, and get the information that you need anyway. Again, just use your Web browser, and type ftp://ftp.support.lotus.com/ in the location line. The result isn't pretty or graphical, but the basic information is still there.

By the way, the information that you get on the Web site is generally fairly technical. Unless you're a certified cc:Mail power user, it isn't a walk in the park. Theoretically, the only reason that you need to use the Web site for support is if your own cc:Mail administrator can't help with your problem for some reason.

What do you do if you don't have a connection to the Internet? Pass the buck back to your cc:Mail administrator, who should probably be taking care of fixing your problems anyway. Copy this section of the book, highlight the addresses for those Web pages, describe your problem, and say, in the most kind and pleading voice you can muster, "Won't you please help me get this problem resolved?" Grovel if you must.

Maintaining Your Post Office

If you use cc:Mail Mobile quite a bit, your post office may need a quick tidying up to keep it running in optimal form. You can either maintain it when you feel like it — it doesn't take long — or wait for this ominous message from cc:Mail Mobile: "Post office database needs optimization." Now you are prompted by fear and anxiety into doing it.

I didn't know Lotus had a BBS!

A BBS, or bulletin board service, is a computer that is equipped with a modem and a ton of useful information. In this case, the Lotus BBS has information about Lotus products, including cc:Mail.

Because the phone call costs money for all of us except a few isolated readers in California's Silicon Valley, you're better off using the Web site if you can. Additionally, if you're not comfortable with using modems and dialing into bulletin board services, you may want to point your system administrator here.

Come to think of it, the biggest problems that you are likely to encounter with cc:Mail Mobile are with modems and communications. Modems and communications are required to connect to the BBS.

If, however, you just have to call in and check out the BBS because you love anything that's free, you can do so. Use Hyperterminal from your Accessories group if you're using Windows 95, or use Terminal if you're a Windows 3.x user. Set your communications software to call 415-691-0401, using No parity, 1 Stopbit, and a Length of 8. You can connect at speeds of 1200, 2400, or 9600 bits per second.

Here's the process:

1. **To optimize your post office, choose Tools⇨Optimize Mailbox on Exit.**

   You then see the Reorganize Post Office dialog box when you exit cc:Mail Mobile, as shown in Figure 20-6.

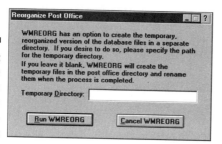

Figure 20-6:
The
Reorganize
Post Office
dialog box.

2. **Exit cc:Mail Mobile (press Alt+F4 or double-click in the upper-left corner).**

3. **Leave the Temporary Directory blank (it just causes you extra work), and click Run WMREORG.**

   "WMREORG" translates to Windows Mail REORGanization. No biggie.

4. **Don't panic! Your screen goes black, with a pop, and you see all kinds of warning messages before Windows returns.**

   A successful reorganization generates enough error messages to choke a frog. I don't have any idea how many you would get if it didn't work.

5. **This step is strictly optional, but if you want to know exactly what the reorganization process checked, you can use Notepad to look at the wmreorg.log file that is probably located in your ccmobile\ccdata1 folder.**

   If several people use cc:Mail Mobile on your computer, your log may be in ccdata, followed by some other number. You can see your name all over the file, so you know that it's yours.

6. **That's it! Pat yourself on the back.**

cc:Mail is kind enough to forget that you put a check mark beside Tools⇨Optimize Mailbox on Exit. The next time that you want to optimize your mailbox, just go back and put the check mark in and exit cc:Mail.

Part VI
Extra! Extra! Read All about It!

IF BOB DYLAN HAD PURSUED A CAREER IN COMPUTERS

"PUT HIM IN FRONT OF A TERMINAL AND HE'S A GENIUS, BUT OTHER-WISE THE GUY IS SUCH A BROODING, GLOOMY GUS HE'LL NEVER BREAK INTO MANAGEMENT."

In this part . . .

*I*t's here! It's on the market! It's cc:Mail 8!

What, you ask, is this information about cc:Mail Version 8 doing in a book that's ostensibly about cc:Mail Version 6? Good question, and one I was hoping you'd ask.

I've included this part in the book to kind of give you a preview of cc:Mail 8. Armed with this information, you'll be able to pester your administrator for the upgrade, and you'll have a good start on using it (when you walk in on a Monday morning with — surprise! — the new version of cc:Mail installed and running on your computer.

This part introduces cc:Mail Version 8 and gives you a brief overview of the similarities and differences between Version 6 and this new, upgraded, ready-for-Windows 95, and generally spiffy version. In particular, you get an introduction to the cc:Mail 8 interface, the basics of sending and receiving messages, and some techniques for managing your mail in cc:Mail 8.

Chapter 21

And Now, Heeeerrrre's Eight!

• •

In This Chapter

▶ Starting cc:Mail 8

▶ Getting familiar with the cc:Mail 8 interface

▶ Quitting cc:Mail 8

• •

Cc:Mail 8 is the newest, latest, and greatest version of cc:Mail. For those of you lucky enough to get your hands on cc:Mail 8, this chapter explains a little about what's up with cc:Mail 8 and introduces the interface and functionality of the software. The following chapters will get you actively involved in using cc:Mail 8.

Don't worry — fundamentally, it's just about like Version 6, so if you have Version 6 down, you won't have problems upgrading. It's kind of like upgrading from a Chevy (good, solid, reliable transportation) to a Porsche (still reliable transportation, but more fun when you're looking for real performance).

So, you ask, why aren't you covering Version 7 of cc:Mail? Well, Version 8 is only slightly different than Version 7. Version 8 is what's called a bug fix, which means that Lotus wanted a chance to fix some of the problems that it had with Version 7. cc:Mail Version 8 also has some enhancements over Version 7 that are sprinkled throughout the next few chapters, so you will be able to figure out what's in Version 7 and what's in Version 8. Don't worry, there are really only a handful of changes, and they're pretty cool. If you are currently using Version 7, it's likely that your company will soon upgrade to Version 8.

So, how can you convince your administrator to upgrade?

Right now, cc:Mail 6 (which looks just about exactly like cc:Mail 2) is the most popular version of cc:Mail in use. For most administrators, upgrading cc:Mail users from Version 2 to Version 6 was a no-brainer — there's no retraining or relearning for users (like you and me), and Version 6 offers some technical advantages on the administration side of things. See? Easy decision, right?

However, the next upgrade step, from Version 6 to Version 8, will likely give administrators pause. Why? Because it looks different, it acts slightly different for you the user, and all those cc:Mail users who don't have this book will have all kinds of questions. Additionally, cc:Mail 8 requires Windows 95, whereas cc:Mail 6 runs equally well on either Windows 3.1x or Windows 95. Administrators generally figure that they can either (1) run the e-mail system or (2) answer user questions. Given a choice, they'll do the former.

Before you pester your administrator too much about upgrading cc:Mail, consider what he or she is facing. First, the upgrade from Version 6 to Version 8 will most likely involve some system upgrades that can take time, ingenuity, planning, and money. Second, because the cc:Mail 8 interface is a bit different and has a few new features, your administrator will probably want to plan training time (or something similar) for users. So, the whole upgrade process could take some time, even after your administrator decides to do it.

Your administrator will probably upgrade to cc:Mail Version 8 sooner if he or she is adventurous and has faith in the users, and if most of the users have great training resources at hand (like this book, right?). Another reason that administrators may upgrade to cc:Mail 8 is if numerous influential bigwigs at your company ask for it. Politely, of course. And repeatedly.

But, (and this is a big but . . . not that your administrator is a big butt, er . . . has a big butt, but — oh, never mind) if your administrator is pretty conservative about upgrades and your training budget is as tight as the budget for raises, you'll probably not see cc:Mail 8 for a while.

As long as we're talking about cc:Mail versions, you may ask what happened to Versions 3 through 5. Good question — and one that I'm asking, too. I'd guess that it's because developers can't count (maybe they have fewer fingers than you or I), or perhaps developing cc:Mail was such a blur that they missed some numbers. Who knows?

Starting cc:Mail 8

Starting cc:Mail 8 is as easy as starting cc:Mail 6. In fact, the following instructions should look pretty familiar (you've been using them to start cc:Mail 6). If you need more details, you may refer to the first part of Chapter 1 in this book.

Start with your computer on and Windows 95 running.

1. Look for the cc:Mail icon on your desktop.

If you don't have a cc:Mail icon visible, you can start cc:Mail by going to Start⇨Programs⇨Lotus Applications and looking for *Lotus cc:Mail 8.0.*

2. Double-click the cc:Mail icon on your desktop (or Program Manager) or click the object once in your Start menu.

After your computer grinds for a few minutes, you should see something like Figure 21-1. Your cc:Mail login name should be in the Login/Profile name list box, and the flashing cursor should be at the Password: prompt.

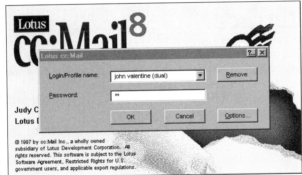

Figure 21-1. The cc:Mail 8 login dialog box.

3. Verify or enter the Login/Profile name in the dialog box and then type in your password in the Password box.

4. Click OK or press Enter when you're done.

If you haven't logged into cc:Mail from the current system, you'll see a dialog box like Figure 21-2 asking you if you want to create a new profile.

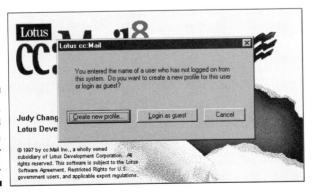

Figure 21-2. cc:Mail 8 requires a profile for each user.

You'll need to provide information about your post office location (Network or Mobile), post office path, password, post office name, connection type, other connection information (like a network address or phone number), and other administrivia. The best option is to have your administrator log you in for the first time, second choice is to log in with the administrator on the phone with you, and third is to get the administrator to provide all the information you need on paper.

Don't worry — it gets easier from here.

Getting Acquainted with the cc:Mail 8 Interface

At first glance, cc:Mail 8 looks somewhat different, complicated, and confusing. However, if you take just a minute to look at the window shown in Figure 21-3, you'll see that the differences are mostly cosmetic.

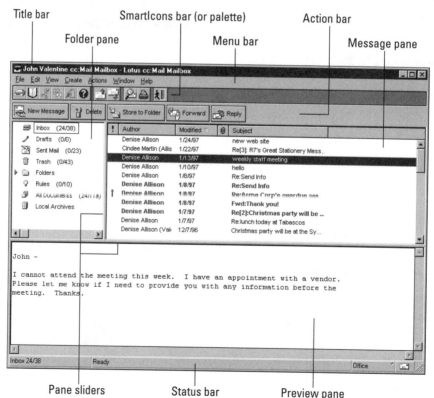

Figure 21-3:
The cc:Mail 8 main window.

See? The Action bar is new, but the rest of the cc:Mail 8 main window looks pretty much like the one in Version 6, only with pretty fonts and fancy buttons. The following sections briefly review (or introduce, as the case may be) these pieces.

Actually, the pretty fonts and fancy buttons are your tip-off that cc:Mail 8 is an application specifically designed and optimized for Windows 95, rather than one of those older Windows applications that merely runs under Windows 95.

The title bar

Just as in Version 6, the Title bar (shown in Figure 21-4) tells you what program you're running and gives you a place to boss around the cc:Mail main window (the application window, for those insistent on exact jargon).

Control menu   Title   Minimize button   Maximize/Restore button   Close button

Figure 21-4:
The title
bar.

John Valentine cc:Mail Mailbox - Lotus cc:Mail Mailbox

✔ **Control menu:** Click once to bring up a submenu with options to Restore, Move, Size, Minimize, Maximize and Close. It's called the control menu because it's where you control how the window appears (or doesn't appear, if you close it).

✔ **Title:** Click and hold to move the window around. Or, if you don't want to move the window around, just read the title to see the user name, the name of the program (like you'd forgotten), and the name of the container that's open.

✔ **Minimize button:** Click once to reduce cc:Mail to a button in your Windows 95 taskbar (so that it's not in the way).

✔ **Maximize button:** Click once to make cc:Mail fill the whole screen, or if cc:Mail already fills the window, click the restore button to reset the cc:Mail window to only a partial screen.

✔ **Close button:** Click once to exit cc:Mail.

The menu bar

The menu bar is the center of your cc:Mail 8 (or cc:Mail 6, for that matter) universe. Click a menu (File, Edit, View, Create, Actions, Window, or Help, or other menus that appear in specific contexts) to summon a submenu with commands that help you complete tasks. Although they'll probably never make really intuitive menus, these are pretty good, as software goes.

The following descriptions should give you a rough idea of what lurks under each of these menus. You'll rarely need to go poking through them, but it's often helpful to have a general idea of where to look for things. (I think of it like knowing what's under the hood of my car — the black greasy thing at the right is the air conditioner, the grungy thing at the front is the radiator, and the crusty box at the left is the battery.)

- **File menu:** Gives you a fairly standard set of options like saving or closing or printing, as well as options to attach files to messages or to export text to a file.

- **Edit menu:** Offers copy, cut, and paste options (as usual), along with options to find text and to undo a faux pas.

- **View menu:** Lets you choose which parts of the cc:Mail window are visible and to control how your containers appear. There's also an option to show the Search bar (to search for messages).

- **Create menu:** Lets you create messages, replies, forwards, folders, archives, and so on. (I think this one should be called the Genesis menu, but the developers didn't ask me.)

- **Actions menu:** Lets you do stuff like store or move messages, empty the trash, connect to the server (for cc:Mail Mobile users), go to the next message, and so forth.

- **Window menu:** Offers choices of which windows (for example, Mailbox, Address book, Bulletin Boards) should be open.

- **Help menu:** For the people who didn't get this book and who want to plow through online instruction about using cc:Mail. It's easier to read this book, I think.

The SmartIcons palettes

The SmartIcons (or buttons, if you will) palettes are very similar in both appearance and function to SmartIcons from cc:Mail 6. However, they seem to be somewhat smarter in cc:Mail 8 — that is, the bar does better at changing to offer common commands, depending on the context you're in. If you're writing a new message, you won't see icons to delete messages. By the same token, if you're reading messages, you won't have a spell check icon at your disposal.

Figures 21-5 and 21-6 show the two palettes from the Inbox window.

Figure 21-5:
The
SmartIcon
bar or
palette for
reading
messages.

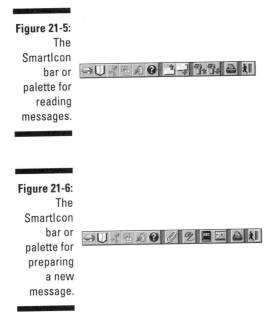

Figure 21-6:
The
SmartIcon
bar or
palette for
preparing
a new
message.

The Action bar

The Action bar, shown in Figure 21-7, is the coolest, most awesome, spec-
tacular, kick-butt part of cc:Mail 8. Just like the SmartIcons palette, the
Action bar changes, depending on what you're doing, and always presents
icons for the most common tasks in a given window. However, because of
the words on the buttons and much more limited selection at a given time,
the Action bar also provides a very good at-a-glance overview of what you
could do in a given window. As a matter of fact, unless you were doing some
pretty off-the-wall cc:Mail machinations, you'd be able to use cc:Mail 8 quite
effectively with only the Action bar to guide you.

Figure 21-7:
The Action
bar.

As shown in Figure 21-7, the Action bar gives choices for creating a new message, deleting a message, storing a message, and forwarding or replying to a message. If you choose to create a new message, the Action bar changes (see Figure 21-8) to offer options for Address and Save Draft, with a Send button that's grayed out (unavailable).

Figure 21-8:
The Action bar when creating a new message — no address yet.

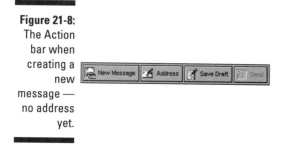

As soon as you address the new message, you also get the option to send it, as shown in Figure 21-9.

Figure 21-9:
The Action bar when creating a new message — ready to send.

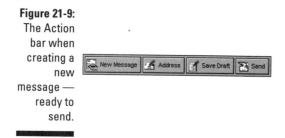

Pretty cool, huh? More on this later.

The Folder pane

Just in case you were getting complacent with the similarities between cc:Mail 6 and cc:Mail 8, those cc:Mail developers threw you a loop. The familiar Container pane from cc:Mail 6 is now called the Folder pane. There's nothing terribly different here — just double-click to open a folder and check out the contents in the Message pane. Check out the Folder pane in Figure 21-10.

Figure 21-10:
The Folder pane.

The Message pane

The Message pane lists the messages in the folder that you selected in the Folder pane. As you've come to expect from cc:Mail 6, the Message pane has several columns that list the author or recipient, date, and subject, as well as icons for the priority and attachments, as shown in Figure 21-11.

Each of these columns is called column width. You can enlarge or shrink column widths by positioning your mouse on the bar to the right of the column (the cursor will look like a double-headed arrow) and clicking and dragging the edge of the column into place.

Figure 21-11:
The Message pane.

!	Author	Modified	@	Subject
	Denise Allison	1/24/97		new web site
	Cindee Martin (Allis	1/22/97		Re[3]: R7's Great Stationery Mess..
	Denise Allison	1/13/97		weekly staff meeting
	Denise Allison	1/10/97		hello
	Denise Allison	1/8/97		Re:Send Info
	Denise Allison	1/8/97		**Re:Send Info**
!	**Denise Allison**	1/8/97		**Re:Acme Corp's overdue acc...**
	Denise Allison	1/8/97		**Fwd:Thank you!**
	Denise Allison	1/7/97		**Re[2]:Christmas party will be ...**
	Denise Allison	1/7/97		Re:lunch today at Tabascos
	Denise Allison (Val	12/7/96		Christmas party will be at the Sy...

The pane slider

No, the pain (er, pane) slider isn't a euphemism for that sticking window that lurches free and bashes your thumb. It's just the bar that separates the Folder pane from the Message pane. Again, you can position your cursor right over the bar so that the cursor turns into a double-headed arrow, and drag the slider to the left (to give more space to the Message pane) or the right (to give more space to the Folder pane). However you set it, cc:Mail will remember for the next time.

Exiting cc:Mail 8

To exit cc:Mail 8, you can use the same basic techniques you used to exit cc:Mail 6.

> ✓ Choose Alt+F4.
>
> ✓ Double-click the control-menu box (in the very-most-upper-left-hand corner of cc:Mail).
>
> ✓ Click the Close button (in the very-most-upper-right-hand corner of cc:Mail).

After using one of those methods, cc:Mail prompts you to be sure you really want to exit. Choose Yes or press the Enter key to exit. If you're having second thoughts, just click No.

Sometimes when you're trying to exit cc:Mail, you may get a pesky Modified Message dialog box, shown in Figure 21-12, telling you that a message has been changed and requiring that you make a choice, because you have an unfinished cc:Mail message (that you started writing but didn't send) floating around. You can

> ✓ Send the message,
>
> ✓ Save the message in the Drafts folder,
>
> ✓ Close the message and lose all changes, or
>
> ✓ Continue working on the message.

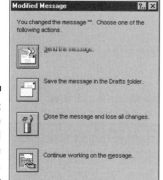

Figure 21-12:
The
Modified
Message
dialog box.

After you make your choice, cc:Mail will close.

 With Versions 7 and 8, you can exit the cc:Mail application with new or modified messages still waiting to be sent hanging out on your desktop. So cc:Mail never actually goes away until all of your messages have been closed. Kind of like a pesky bellboy waiting for a tip.

As with cc:Mail 6, don't *ever* quit cc:Mail 8 or Windows 95 by just hitting the power switch. You should know better by now.

Chapter 22

Experiencing the Difference: New and Noteworthy in cc:Mail 8

In This Chapter

▶ Using friendly names

▶ Delegating your mailbox

▶ Short-circuiting shortcuts

▶ Nesting folders

▶ Previewing messages

▶ Formatting messages with Rich Text

▶ Sorting messages by anything

▶ Grouping messages

▶ Synchronizing your mobile mailbox

Although the basics of using cc:Mail are very similar from Version 6 to Version 8, cc:Mail 8 does add some very convenient and useful features. This chapter outlines some of the most significant new features in cc:Mail 8. Rather than starting back at the very beginning (which isn't, in this case, a very good place to start), I'll assume you're at least superficially familiar with cc:Mail 6 and provide an overview of these features in that context. (The next chapter will get into the specific instructions for using cc:Mail 8.)

With that, up, up, and away to the newest and coolest of cc:Mail version 8.

Using URLS

With Version 8, you can now launch your favorite Web browser right from within cc:Mail. With Version 7, if someone sent you a URL (just a fancy acronym for the name of a Web site like http://www.ccmail.com) embedded into an e-mail message, you would have had to copy the URL, open your browser and paste the URL into the browser's search bar. With Version 8, all you have do is double-click on the URL, and cc:Mail launches your browser so that you can go to the Web site toot sweet.

Using Friendly Names

cc:Mail 8 enables you to create friendly names, or aliases, for any entry in your personal address book. These aliases free you from the tyranny of remembering Internet addresses like info@xmission.com. Instead, you can set the friendly name to something like "Information" and forget those @'s and !'s forever. Likewise, you can replace those cryptic numbers and letters of your mom's e-mail address with the much easier to remember "Mom."

You can only create friendly names for entries in your personal address book. Therefore, you may need to copy some entries from the public address book into your private address book before you get started with friendly names.

Copying public address book entries to your personal address book

1. Choose Window⇨Address Book.

This brings up the cc:Mail Address Book window, as shown in Figure 22-1, so you can manage your addresses.

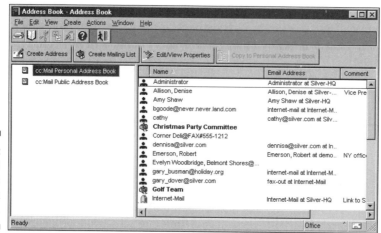

Figure 22-1:
The cc:Mail
Address
Book
window.

2. **Click to select the public address book in the Folder pane.**

3. **Select the public address you want to eventually create a friendly name for from the right pane.**

4. **Click the Copy to Personal Address Book button.**

   There! You just copied the address to your personal address book.

Creating or changing friendly names and address book entries

Personal address book entries contain, in addition to the actual address information, space for comments and a friendly name or alias for the entry. A logical time to create friendly names is at the same time that you add a new entry to your personal address book, although it's also easy enough to add or change the friendly names later. Here's the process for doing both at once:

1. **Choose Window⇨Address Book.**

   This brings up the cc:Mail Address Book window.

2. **Click the Create Address button on the Action bar (or select Create⇨Address Book Entry).**

   You see the New Entry dialog box, as shown in Figure 22-2.

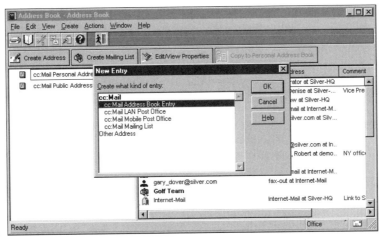

Figure 22-2:
The New
Entry
dialog box.

3. Select the top item in the list — cc:Mail Address Book Entry — and click OK.

The New cc:Mail Address Book Entry Properties dialog box appears, as shown in Figure 22-3.

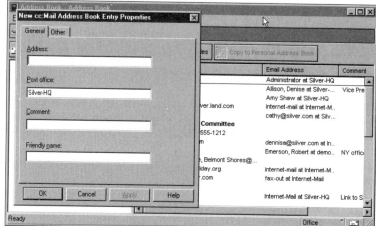

Figure 22-3:
The cc:Mail
Address
Book Entry
Properties
dialog box.

4. In the Address Book Entry Properties dialog box, enter the Address, Post office, a Comment (if you want), and the Friendly name.

- The address is generally either a cc:Mail address on your local system or an Internet address. For example, Ben Jonson may be a cc:Mail address, whereas bjonson@xmission.com would be an Internet address.

- The Post office field contains the name of your post office (provided by your administrator) when the address is a cc:Mail address. If you provided an Internet address in the Address field, you need to put the gateway address (also provided by your administrator) in the Post office field. For example, my local post office is post-iw2, but my Internet gateway is Internet (although I know people at other companies with gateways like SMTP or INET).

- Comments are optional. Have fun if you'd like.

- The friendly name is anything you want to use that helps you remember the address. Your spouse may be "sweetie" or your buddy Richard Roe may be just "Dick." The recipient of your message will not see the friendly name you use, so you could, I suppose, create a friendly name for your boss like "the jerk" or anything else you want.

5. **After you finish filling in the blanks, click OK to save the entry and close the dialog box.**

   The entry now shows up in your personal address book alphabetically by the friendly name.

Here are a couple more tidbits about creating friendly names and personal address book entries.

✔ If you have more lengthy comments to make than will fit in the Comment field on the General tab of the Properties dialog box, select the Other tab. There you'll find ample space for anything short of a biography.

✔ If you want to change the address book entry or friendly name, just click once on the entry to select it, then click the Edit/View Properties button to recall the Properties dialog box.

Delegating Your Mailbox

If you're out of the office or in meetings a lot and get tired of returning to the office to find piles of e-mail that someone else in the office could easily have dealt with, you'll be pleased to learn that you can now delegate your mailbox to someone else (which is much better than just giving out your password willy-nilly to the departmental secretary and your nearest and dearest acquaintances).

When you delegate your mailbox, your delegate gets limited authority over your mailbox. The delegate can access your mail and folders, but not archives. Similarly, your delegate can send mail, but not make changes to your personal address book. Any messages sent from your account by your delegate will show up with your name and your delegate's name on the message. For example, Sue Griffin, if you delegate your mailbox to David Anderson, the messages David sends will show up with "Sue Griffin (David Anderson)" in the From line.

How to delegate?

1. **Choose File⇨Delegate Mailbox.**

   You'll see the Mailbox Delegation dialog box, which is shown in Figure 22-4.

2. **Select your delegate's name from the address list.**

3. **Click Add to add the delegate to your list.**

4. **Repeat the last two steps to assign more delegates.**

   You can have as many delegates as you want (or as many as it takes to handle your mailbox).

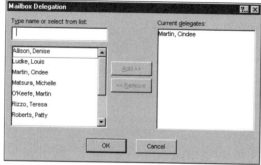

Figure 22-4:
The
Mailbox
Delegation
dialog box.

5. Click OK when you're finished.

Each of your delegates will receive a message telling them that they've been designated your delegate.

As soon as you've delegated your mailbox, your delegates can access it. It may be a good idea to drop the delegates an e-mail or give them a call to let them know what you want them to keep, delete, store, respond to, or ignore.

When you return from your trip or get off the list of official meeting attendees and have time to handle your own mail, you can remove delegates with the following process:

1. Choose File⇨Delegate Mailbox.

You see the Mailbox Delegation dialog box.

2. Select the name of the person you want to remove and click Remove.

Additional tidbits about delegating your mail:

✔ You have to delegate your mailbox from your LAN account. If you wait until you've already gone on a trip and you're using your mobile cc:Mail 8 client, it's too late.

✔ Only other cc:Mail 8 users can be delegates, so you need to check to verify that your potential delegate is using the right version of cc:Mail.

✔ After you remove someone from your delegate list, they still have full delegate authority until they've logged out of cc:Mail and logged back in.

Short-Circuiting Shortcuts

If you're a longtime cc:Mail user or if you've gotten accustomed to using the keyboard shortcuts in cc:Mail 2 or 6, you'll be in for an unpleasant surprise when you try those old familiar shortcuts in cc:Mail 8. This is hardly a biggie, but it's also not quite wonderful either. For example, Ctrl+S no longer sends a message; rather, it saves a draft. Likewise, Ctrl+A no longer summons the Address dialog box; rather, it selects all within an open message.

If you're a die-hard shortcut user, you'll want to take a look in the drop-down menus to verify the shortcuts that you use most often — the shortcuts are listed beside the commands they correspond to, but you knew that already.

Nesting Folders

If you're a cc:Mail user who uses folders extensively, you'll be pleased to learn that cc:Mail 8 adds the capability of having nested folders. That is, instead of having just a single list of folders, you can have sets of folders within other folders. You could have a folder for accounts, then folders within the Accounts folder for the Johnson account, Kyler account, and so forth.

1. **To create a folder, select Create⇨Folder.**

   You'll see the Create New Folder dialog box, as shown in Figure 22-5.

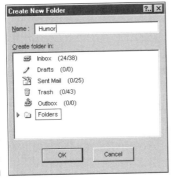

Figure 22-5:
The Create New Folder dialog box.

2. **Type the Name for your new folder in the field at the top of the dialog box.**

3. **Click the name of the folder you want to Create the new folder in.**

   Although cc:Mail makes it look as if you can create folders within your Inbox, Drafts, Sent Mail, Trash, or (if you're using Mobile) Outbox folders, that's not possible. Folders within the Folders folder (aargh!) is the only option.

   A triangle in the left margin indicates folders that have subfolders. You may need to double-click a main folder to open it and see the other folders within it.

4. **Click OK to create the new folder and close the dialog box.**

   You should see your new folder appear in the list in the Folder pane, as in Figure 22-6.

Figure 22-6:
The Folder
pane.

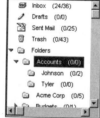

If you don't see the folder, you may need to expand the folder that contains it. For example, if all the folders are collapsed, you need to double-click Folders to expand it, then double-click Accounts. Alternatively, you could choose View⊅Expand All (Shift++).

After you've created and used a number of folders, you may start to run into problems finding messages. No problem! Just remember that you can summon the Search bar with Ctrl+Q or with the Search button (or choose View⊅Search Bar); you can read all about searching in Chapter 14.

Everything else about folders, including storing messages, retrieving messages from folders, and deleting stored messages, works much the same as it does in cc:Mail 6. No problem, right?

Previewing Messages

Previewing messages is the cc:Mail equivalent of holding an envelope up to the light so that you can see what's inside. cc:Mail 8 gives you a preview window, if you want, so that you can see the first few lines of each message in your Inbox or in a folder without having to go to all the trouble of opening it up. Using it is a snap (and you don't even need a bright light bulb).

1. **View the Preview pane with <u>V</u>iew⇨Show <u>P</u>review Pane.**

   You'll see the Preview pane across the bottom of your screen, as shown in Figure 22-7.

   If you don't like the Preview pane, just select <u>V</u>iew⇨Show <u>P</u>review pane again to turn it off.

2. **Wait just a second and the first few lines of the message appear in the Preview pane.**

Actually, if you want to, you could even scroll through the whole message in the Preview pane, but if you're going to that much trouble, you may as well just open the message.

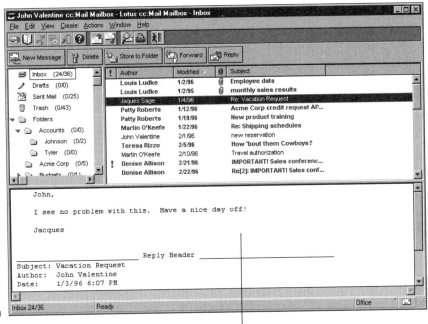

Figure 22-7:
cc:Mail 8
with the
Preview
pane.

Preview pane

Here is additional information about previewing messages:

✔ At your discretion, you can have cc:Mail mark previewed messages as read or not. Choose File⇨Tools⇨User Preferences, then click the Mailbox icon at the left side of the dialog box. Check or uncheck the box to Mark message read when displayed.

✔ Previewing a message does not return a receipt, even if the author has requested a receipt. The receipt is sent only if you actually open the message.

Sorting Messages by Anything

As you're digging out from that mound of new messages in your Inbox and trying to figure out what's the top priority to read and answer, you may consider re-sorting the messages to ease your work. For example, you may sort the messages by author so that all the messages from your boss are together and the messages from your significant other are together. After you've dealt with those high-priority messages, you could sort by date so that you can answer the oldest ones first and see the newest arrivals. Finally, you may sort the remaining messages by subject to make it a little easier to see what's there.

How do you do this? Just click the header of each of the column widths — Author, Received, Subject, or anything else you want. Click a header a second time to sort in reverse order. That is, clicking Received one time puts the newest messages at the top, and a second click puts the newest messages at the bottom. cc:Mail even provides a little up- or down-facing arrow in the column headings so that you can see which column the mailbox is sorted by and which direction (ascending or descending) it's sorted in.

Check out Figure 22-8 to see how it works.

Grouping Messages

If, and only if, you and all your frequent correspondents all use cc:Mail 8, you can take advantage of grouping messages together with the replies in your Inbox and folders. This feature, also commonly called threading, makes it much easier to follow an e-mail discussion without having to skip around in your Inbox for the other messages with a similar subject. Here's how to take advantage of it:

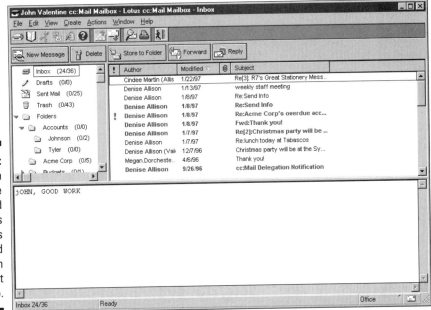

Figure 22-8:
A click on the Modified button sorts messages by received date with the newest at top.

If you have the group messages icon in your mailbox or folder view, just click it to organize your messages in groups. If the group messages icon isn't visible, you'll have to add it.

1. **Choose View⮕Design List View.**

   The Folder List View dialog box appears, looking very similar to Figure 22-9.

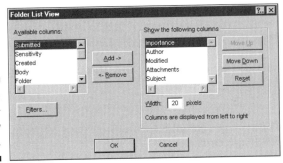

Figure 22-9:
The Folder List View dialog box.

2. **Scroll through the Available columns until you see and select Group Replies with Original.**

3. **Click the <u>A</u>dd button to add Group Replies with Original to the column widths in the mailbox.**

4. **Click OK to close the dialog box.**

And here's more about grouping messages:

- ✔ Grouping messages won't do you any good if you're corresponding with people who don't use cc:Mail 8, corresponding with people via the Internet, or trying to organize messages from Internet mailing lists. Sorry!

- ✔ As you may have noticed, the Folder List View dialog box gives you a whole slew of options for customizing the list. You can add or remove columns, move columns around in the list, and, most important, reset any changes you may make. Feel free to experiment here — <u>R</u>eset will rescue you if necessary.

Formatting Messages with Rich Text

As you've probably noticed, e-mail messages are generally pretty boring — just plain old text, generally in a font like Courier or another typewriterlike font. Fortunately (or not, perhaps), cc:Mail 8 lets you format your messages with Rich Text. Rich Text is just the fancy computerese term for "with fonts and sizes and italics and bold and underlines and colors." Pretty cool, huh? Not only that, it's easy to do.

Although formatting messages with Rich Text is fun and easy, you'll need to steer clear of all formatting for messages you're sending to Internet addresses or mailing lists or to anyone who isn't using cc:Mail 8. The formatting won't come through at all to people who aren't using cc:Mail 8. Moreover, your references to the "boldface formatting below" will look pretty silly as well. If you really need to send formatted text to non-cc:Mail 8 users, you must use file attachments and word processing documents.

1. **Start a new message by clicking the New Message Action bar button (or by selecting <u>C</u>reate➪Message).**

The New Message window appears, as in Figure 22-10.

2. **To get the full flavor of cc:Mail 8 formatting, start by formatting the page with <u>T</u>ext➪<u>P</u>age Options.**

In the Page Options dialog box, shown in Figure 22-11, you can set the page size (both width and height), as well as the page margins, measurement units, and whether the text should be automatically wrapped (as with a word processor) or not (as with a typewriter).

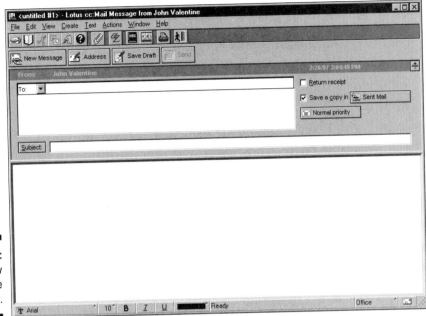

Figure 22-10:
The New
Message
window.

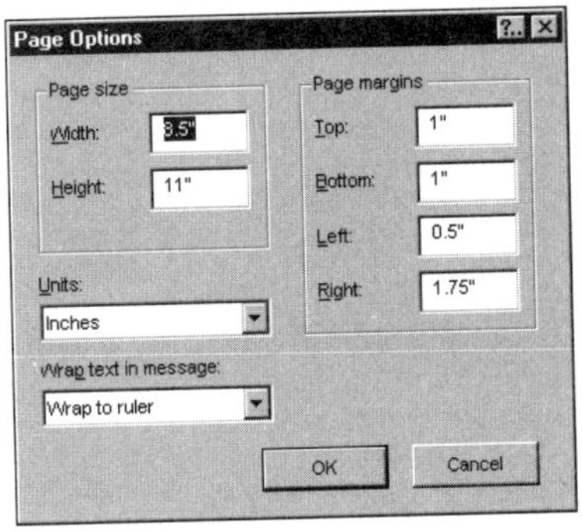

Figure 22-11:
The Page
Options
dialog box.

Other than setting the margins, you probably won't want to get too tied up in the rest of the formatting. After all, it's only an e-mail message. If you were doing something that formatting really mattered in, you'd use a word processor, right? Of course!

If you're pretty sure that your recipient will print the message, go ahead and set Page Options settings — they will apply to the document when it's printed.

3. Click OK when you're finished with the Page Options dialog box.

4. You can set the alignment (centered, left-aligned, or right-aligned) with Text⇨Alignment and the alignment option of your choice.

Your alignment setting can apply to the entire message (if your cursor is not in the message body and you haven't entered any text yet), just to the selected text, or just to the paragraph your cursor is in.

5. As you enter text, you can format it with the font, size, bold, italic, underline, and color buttons from the bottom of the New Message window.

Figure 22-12 shows the formatting buttons from the New Message window. Just select the text to format and click to select options. Bold, italic, and underline, apply formatting directly; the font, size, and color options each bring up a submenu from which you choose the text characteristics.

Figure 22-12:
Formatting buttons from the bottom of the New Message window.

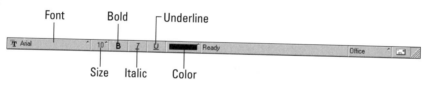

The menu options Text⇨Normal (or Italic or Bold or Underline) offer the same capabilities as the pop-up menus from the bottom of the window.

Inserting bullets into your cc:Mail message is equally easy — Text⇨Quick Bullet puts bullets at the beginning of each line you have selected.

6. Address and send your message as you usually would.

Fancy, huh?

Here are some additional notes about Rich Text formatting in cc:Mail 8:

✔ If you'd rather take care of the formatting from a dialog box, just select the text to format, and either click the button or choose Text⇨Text Properties to bring up the Properties dialog box. After you finish applying the formatting characteristics from both the Font tab (shown in Figure 22-13) and the Alignment tab, close the dialog box by clicking the close button at the top right of the dialog box.

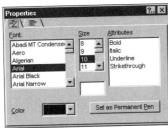

Figure 22-13:
The
Properties
dialog box.

✔ If you're very comfortable with the Windows 95 interface and like right-clicking objects to control their properties, you can do that with text in cc:Mail message windows as well. Just right-click to bring up the context menu, then choose Properties.

✔ Perhaps time will prove me wrong, but I think that elaborate text formatting in e-mail messages kind of defeats the purpose. Part of what's traditionally great about e-mail is that you can just dash off the message and the content is the only significant factor. If you start having to really format the message, you may as well just write and fax a memo. Sigh.

Using Stationery

cc:Mail 8 offers stationery, which is actually just a fancy term for a form or template messages. You can set up one or more standard message formats to use, rather than just using the plain old blank message.

For example, if you work at one of those companies that require you to submit weekly status reports, you may set up Status Report stationery. Likewise, if you send a lot of messages to Internet mailing lists and you have a somewhat hypersensitive legal department, you may set up External Message stationery with the obligatory disclaimers that you're not speaking for the company and that they'll deny ever hearing your name if you get sued.

Creating stationery is just about like making a new message and saving a draft. The only difference is that stationery is designed to be kept and reused, and that it's easy to choose from the Create menu. Here's the process:

1. Choose Actions⇨Stationery.

The Stationery dialog box, shown in Figure 22-14, lists the stationery you have and will also list the stationery you create.

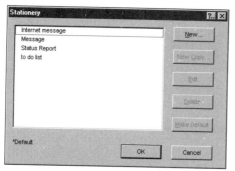

Figure 22-14:
The
Stationery
dialog box.

2. **Click New to create a new form.**

3. **Create the message or template you will use, just as if you were creating a new message.**

   If you're ever going to take advantage of the cc:Mail 8 Rich Text formatting capabilities, this is the time to do so, because the stationery you create will be reused repeatedly. (If it won't be reused repeatedly, what are you doing making stationery at all?!)

4. **When you've finished the stationery, spell check and proofread it before you click the Save Stationery button in the Action bar (although you can always edit it later).**

5. **Provide a descriptive name in the Name Stationery dialog box and click OK.**

6. **Back in the Stationery dialog box, note that you can create a new copy of the stationery you have selected, edit the selected stationery, or delete the stationery.**

   Additionally, if you have a specific kind of stationery that you use more than any other, you can choose Make Default to make that stationery be the stationery that is used for all new messages.

7. **When you're finished creating and editing your stationery, click OK.**

Using the stationery you've created is just like creating a new message, and almost equally easy.

1. **Choose Create⇨Other Message and choose your stationery from the pop-out menu.**

2. **Complete and send your message as you usually would.**

   Pretty neat, huh?

Stand still for other stationery tips:

✔ As you create stationery, try to include all the standard details that won't change from message to message — like your boss's address for status reports or your complimentary closing, "Best regards" (or the closing of your choice) and your name, on your messages destined for the Internet.

✔ Create stationery with a *signature,* which is a closing block of text including your name, contact information, and, optionally, the slogan or quotation of your choice. Then set that stationery as the default so that your signature will appear in every message you send.

✔ Generally you'll want to keep your signature to four lines or less, to avoid getting hateful messages from people who have nothing better to do than to critique your judgment. Think I'm kidding? Try posting a long signature on the Internet.

Synchronizing Your Mobile Mailbox

If you're a cc:Mail Mobile user, you'll probably be delighted to learn of the synchronization feature to keep your LAN and Mobile boxes marching in lock step. With cc:Mail 8, if you delete a message from your Mobile box, the synchronization will automatically remove it from your LAN mailbox as well. Furthermore, you can even choose which folders to synchronize.

Here's all you have to do to set up synchronization. Hypothetically, you use cc:Mail from your laptop at home and from your office computer in the office. You'll want to set up synchronization on your home computer (the computer running cc:Mail 8 in Mobile mode) to keep everything working.

1. **On the computer running cc:Mail in Mobile mode, choose Actions⇨Locations.**

    You'll see the cc:Mail Location dialog box, as in Figure 22-15. This dialog box, just as in cc:Mail 6, is the control point from which you can create New locations, or edit and delete locations for mobile use.

2. **Click to select your location (although it's probably already selected by default), then click Edit to edit the location configuration.**

    Figure 22-16 shows the Location dialog box for Home.

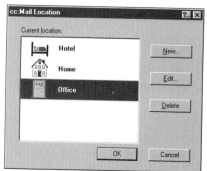

Figure 22-15:
The cc:Mail
Location
dialog box.

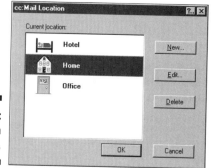

Figure 22-16:
The Location
dialog box.

3. **If you want, click the check box to Update Mobile Address Books with changes from the post office when you connect.**

   Updating mobile address books could take a while, so I don't recommend it if your connection will be a long-distance call on your nickel.

4. **Click in the check box to Synchronize LAN and Mobile Mailboxes.**

   This check tells cc:Mail to handle synchronization when you dial in, but there are some configuration options you'll want to attend to.

5. **Click Choose Folders to bring up a dialog box in which you choose which folders to synchronize.**

   As in Figure 22-17, you can either choose to synchronize All folders (recommended) or only Selected folders.

   To choose selected folders, just click the folder to synchronize and click Add. Watch for the right-pointing arrow to indicate that a folder can be expanded to reveal other folders within it.

   As with other cc:Mail lists, you can Ctrl+click or Shift+click to select multiple folders at once.

   Choose folders from the Selected folders list and click Remove if you don't want to synchronize them.

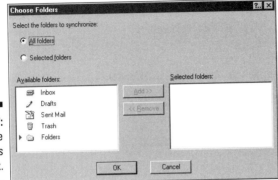

Figure 22-17:
The Choose
Folders
dialog box.

After you've selected your folders, click OK.

7. Now, click Advanced Options in the Location dialog box to specify how to handle potential problems in the synchronization.

The Advanced Options dialog box lets you specify how cc:Mail should deal with conflicting changes. That is, if you rename your Accounts folder to Big Accounts when you're at the office and you decide to call it Important Accounts at home, cc:Mail will get confused when trying to synchronize the mailboxes.

Select either Mobile Mailbox changes will replace LAN changes, or LAN changes will replace mobile changes to determine which changes win out.

Likewise, if you delete messages one place and not the other, cc:Mail needs to know how to deal with those. You can select either or both of the options: If deleted from Mobile Mailbox, delete from LAN mailbox, or If deleted from LAN mailbox, delete from Mobile Mailbox. Just to prevent confusion, I'd select both.

8. Click OK when you're finished, then click OK again to close the dialog box.

Read on for some additional tidbits about synchronizing mailboxes.

✔ Depending on how much time you have, you may want to change the options you choose here under Locations in the dialog box when you actually connect to the post office. For example, if you're trying to just send and receive mail in the five minutes you have before running to a meeting, you'll probably choose not to synchronize the mailboxes or address books. Likewise, if the call you're making is a long-distance call on your nickel, don't update the address book unless you absolutely have to.

✔ When you synchronize your mailboxes, cc:Mail will also automatically synchronize your address books.

Be my guest

Version 8 of cc:Mail offers what's called the Guest account. If you happen to be at someone else's desk and just want to do a quick check of your mail without having to go though all of the hoops of adding another account to that person's desktop, you can login as a Guest. This gets you right into using cc:Mail without having to create a profile on your coworker's computer.

Chapter 23
Doing the Basics with cc:Mail 8

. . . .

In This Chapter

▶ Sending messages using cc:Mail 8

▶ Reading messages using cc:Mail 8

▶ Replying to messages using cc:Mail 8

▶ Tossing messages using cc:Mail 8

. . . .

Although this preview can't cover all of the nuances of the cc:Mail 8, this chapter gives you a good start on doing some of the basics with cc:Mail 8. Keep in mind that these steps are very similar to those for Version 6, so in many cases the details provided in earlier chapters of this book can help you here.

Creating and Sending Messages

Actually, the blaring heading "Creating and Sending Messages" may be a bit anticlimactic, particularly if you're already a savvy cc:Mail 6 user. The differences between sending messages in cc:Mail 6 and sending messages in cc:Mail 8 are more or less cosmetic. cc:Mail 8 does offer more automation and additional ways to customize and automate the process, but the principles remain the same.

In the next few sections, you see the procedures for addressing a new message, providing a subject line, writing the actual message, and sending it away.

Creating a new e-mail message in cc:Mail 8 hardly qualifies as brain surgery. Grab the keyboard and mouse, fasten your seat belt, and follow the Action bar buttons.

1. Click New Message from the Action bar (or select Create⇨Message).

The new cc:Mail message window appears, as in Figure 23-1.

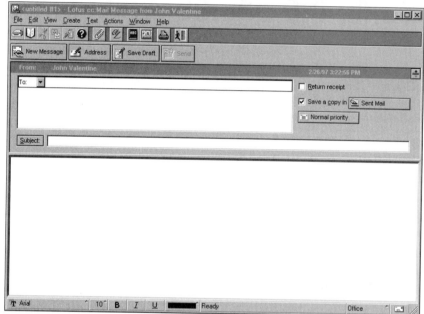

Figure 23-1:
The cc:Mail
8 New
Message
window.

2. Click the Address button from the Action bar (or select Actions⇨Address).

The Address Book window (see Figure 23-2) awaits your selection.

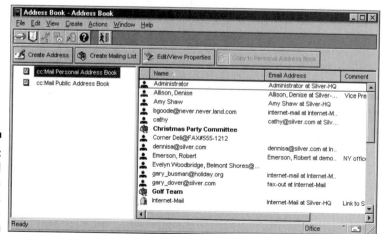

Figure 23-2:
The cc:Mail
8 Address
Book
window.

3. **Click to tell cc:Mail to <u>S</u>how Names from the public address book or personal address book (depending on who will be the recipient of your first message).**

   You may consider sending your first message to yourself, just so you know that everything is working as it should.

4. **In the Type Name or Select from List field, type the first few letters of the address and then click T<u>o</u>:, <u>C</u>c: or <u>B</u>cc: to add the address to the list.**

   Continue selecting names and adding them to the address list on the right side of the dialog box. If you add a name by mistake, just click the name in the address list on the right and press DEL to remove it.

   The process of typing just the beginning of the name and letting cc:Mail select the name for you is the same as Quick Search from cc:Mail 6.

5. **Click OK when you're finished addressing the message.**

6. **Optionally, check the boxes to request a <u>R</u>eturn receipt or to Save a <u>c</u>opy in Sent Mail.**

   You don't have to do either if you don't want to. If you're just sending to yourself, it probably doesn't really matter.

7. **Click the Priority button to toggle through Normal Priority, Urgent, or Low Priority identification for the message.**

8. **Click in the <u>S</u>ubject field and type in a descriptive subject for your message, if you want.**

   If your subject lines are predictable enough, you may click the Subject button and either select a prewritten subject from the list or add new subjects for use later. Click OK when you've finished massaging your subject lines.

9. **Type the text for your message.**

   If you've encountered a case of writer's block, don't sweat it. It's just a test message, after all. Something profound like "laksjd;flkajf;lakdfj" should be fine.

   If you want to format anything in your message, now is the time. Wait any longer and that baby will be gone.

10. **You could click the Save Draft Action bar button if you want to pause the message and return to it later, but don't bother for this sample message.**

11. **Click the Send Message Action bar button (or select <u>A</u>ctions⇨<u>S</u>end) to send the message.**

12. cc:Mail asks you if you're sure that you want to send the message, as shown in Figure 23-3. Just say Yes.

Bye, message!

Figure 23-3:
The cc:Mail
8 Send
message
confirmation
dialog box.

If you're sending a message to an Internet address or to people who do not use cc:Mail 8, the fancy formatting options like typeface, type size, boldface, italics, underlining, and colors won't make it to the recipient. Just the text itself can be effectively transmitted through most Internet gateways; the formatting will usually be stripped out automatically.

Reading Messages

Reading your first message in cc:Mail 8 is as easy as a quick double-click or two. You'll probably notice that the Folder pane (at the left in Figure 23-4) and the Message page (at the right) look very similar to their counterparts in cc:Mail 6.

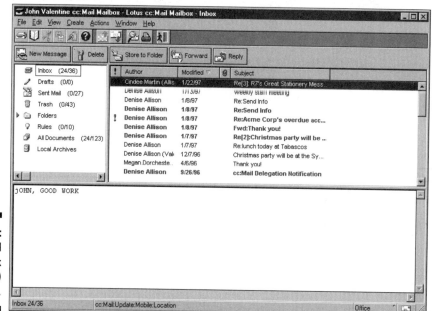

Figure 23-4:
The cc:Mail
8 mailbox
(Inbox)
window.

1. Double-click Inbox in the Folder pane to make sure the Inbox folder is open.

When you first open cc:Mail, the Inbox will be open by default. However, if you've been using cc:Mail for a little while, it's probably a good idea to double-click the Inbox, both to open it and to get cc:Mail to check for any additional mail that may have leaked in.

2. Double-click a message in the Message pane to open it and read it.

You could also click once to select the message, then press Enter, but that's more work than you really have to do.

The open message will look somewhat like Figure 23-5.

If you're wondering what all this stuff is, good question! Starting under the Action bar (which now has new buttons, appropriate to your task of reading messages, by the way):

- **From:** Tells you who sent the message, along with the time and date.

- **To:** Shows the names of everyone who received the message. You see your name in here, along with, possibly, others.

- **Subject:** Tells you (surprise!) the subject of the message.

- If the message you opened has an attachment, you see an Attachment button at the right side of the message header that tells you how many attachments you have.

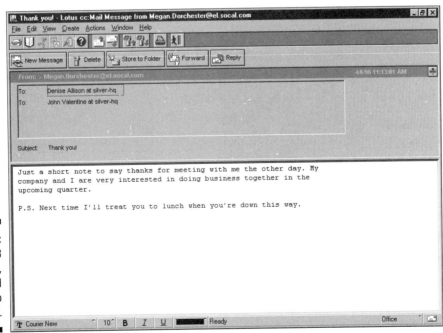

Figure 23-5:
A cc:Mail 8
Message,
open and
ready to
read.

- The remainder of the message is the actual text that you were sent.

- All the way at the bottom of the message, you see formatting buttons for font, size, boldface, italics, underline, and color. Those do you no good when you're reading the message but may be handy when you're forwarding or replying to a message.

3. **After you've finished reading the message, close the message by clicking the Close button at the top right of the title bar (or press Alt+F4).**

There you go! You've read your message.

Replying to Messages

Replying to a message is pretty much the same in Version 8 as it is in Version 6. Version 8, however, lets you reply to a message using the Action bar. The following steps show you how to do this:

1. **Open the message to which you want to reply.**

Actually, you can reply to a message that isn't open, but how often are you going to remember the content of the message accurately enough to be sure you want to reply to it?

2. **Click the Reply button from the Action bar.**

The Reply dialog box appears, as shown in Figure 23-6.

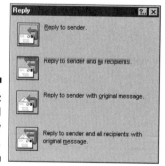

Figure 23-6:
The cc:Mail
8 Reply
dialog box.

3. Select who should receive the reply and how.

You can choose <u>R</u>eply to sender or Reply to sender and <u>a</u>ll recipients. Or you can choose to reply to the sender and include the text of the <u>o</u>riginal message, or even reply to the sender and the recipients, again including the original <u>m</u>essage.

You see the Message window with your reply, ready to be modified and sent, as in Figure 23-7.

If you choose to include the original text, you see the reply separator, in addition to the text that was sent to you.

4. Add recipients, request a <u>R</u>eturn receipt, Save a <u>c</u>opy, or change the priority if you'd like, using the same procedures used in creating a new message.

5. Write the text for your reply in the message window.

If you are sending the message to another cc:Mail 8 user, format to your heart's content.

6. Click the Send button on the Action bar (or choose <u>A</u>ctions⇨<u>S</u>end) when you're finished.

See how much easier that Action bar makes the process? Almost everything you need (except something to say, of course) is right there on the action bar.

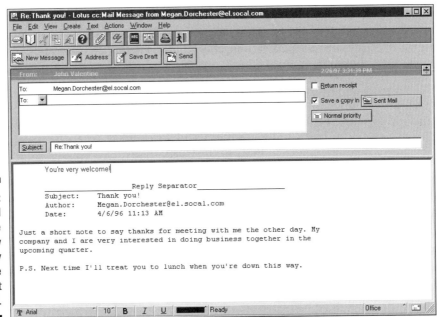

Figure 23-7:
The cc:Mail 8 Message window with a reply and the original text included.

Don't forget that the Save Draft icon is on the Action bar so that you can save an incomplete message. Just open the Drafts folder from the Folder pane, open the message, and finish sending it at your convenience.

Deleting Messages

The process for deleting a message is much the same in cc:Mail 8 as in cc:Mail 6. It's pretty complex, so bear with me:

1. Select or open a message.

2. Click the Delete button from the Action bar.

Whew!

If you delete something by accident, just head to the trash can and dig it back out. Good thing that's there, huh?

Alternatively, depending on which SmartIcon palette is visible, you may be able to click one of the following:

- ✔ The Delete SmartIcon
- ✔ The Delete and Move to Next Message SmartIcon
- ✔ The Delete and Move to Previous Message SmartIcon

The SmartIcons in Version 8 are very similar to the ones in Version 6. To customize the SmartIcons, check out the dialog box that appears when you choose File⇨Tools⇨SmartIcons.

An additional tip about deleting messages:

- ✔ New and nice in cc:Mail 8 is that you don't have to bother with enabling the Trash folder. It's there, and it's enabled. When you delete a message, it goes directly to the trash, where it stays for a while in case you really didn't mean to delete it. To check out (or change) how long your trashed messages hang around, choose File⇨Tools⇨User Preferences and then select Special Folders from the list on the left. You'll see a dialog box like Figure 23-8. The default setting is to Always empty the trash when you exit cc:Mail. However, I'd recommend a setting like the one shown in the figure — select Delete messages older than... and fill in the blank for about 10 days. That way messages will remain in the Trash purgatory for 10 days before they wither and blow away.

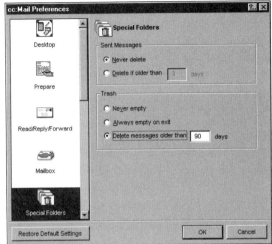

Figure 23-8:
The
cc:Mail 8
Preferences/
Special
Folders
dialog box.

Chapter 24

Putting Your Ducks in a Row

· ·

· ·

*T*his chapter provides an overview of some of the things you can do to help manage your cc:Mail messages, including creating folders, making rules, and using the Search dialog box.

Once again, you won't notice much of a difference in managing and customizing cc:Mail, but I have pointed out a few things that may interest you.

Managing Your cc:Mail 8 Messages

Just as the process of managing your life gets somewhat easier when you get a bigger office with more storage, the process of managing your messages gets somewhat easier when you upgrade to cc:Mail 8. The principles of moving messages into folders and archives is the same as it always has been, but it's easier to organize them now because you can have nested folders. For example, your Project X folder can now contain subfolders for Crises, Problems, Challenges, and MadBoss (now if that isn't an improvement, I don't know what is).

The fact that cc:Mail 8 is a Windows 95 application gives you a couple of extra-convenient tools, like the right-click pop-up menu. When you get a chance, try right-clicking a couple of things and seeing what sorts of options you get. Pretty cool, huh?

Automatically managing messages

If you're going to be a truly organized and efficient cc:Mail 8 user, you'll get accustomed to using folders to manage your e-mail. You could just keep creating folders with <u>C</u>reate Fol<u>d</u>er, as outlined in Chapter 13, and manually sticking your messages in them, but a better approach is to use cc:Mail 8 rules to do that filing for you.

Wait! Stop! Don't tell me! You've already tried using the damn rules from some other version of cc:Mail . . . and they were horribly confusing . . . and you couldn't do anything with them until you bought this book . . . but even so, they're anything but easy to use (breathe here!). Nolo problemo! cc:Mail 8 makes rules easy. Check this out! Follow along as we create the same rule that we created in Chapter 16 using Version 6, but it's easier now.

In case you haven't played with rules yet, they're just instructions to cc:Mail about how you want your mail managed. That is, you use a rule to tell cc:Mail to "take that incoming message from my boss and file it away under Daily Frustrations and beep at me so I know I got the message."

Creating a new rule

Here's the new-and-improved rule process, but make sure you have a folder to receive messages from your boss before you start.

1. **Choose <u>C</u>reate⇨<u>R</u>ule.**

   You'll see the cc:Mail Rule Viewer, as in Figure 24-1.

   In cc:Mail 6 you had to put all kinds of thought into the rule, but cc:Mail 8 makes even creating the rule pretty routine.

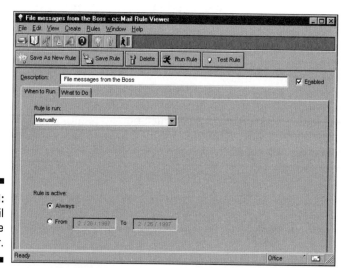

Figure 24-1:
The cc:Mail
8 Rule
Viewer.

2. **At the top of the window, just under the Action bar, enter a Description for the rule.**

    Because we're creating a rule to file messages from the boss, a description like "file messages from the boss" seems appropriate.

3. **Check to Enable the rule so that it will be able to run.**

    A rule that isn't enabled is like a ball-and-chain spouse with a muzzle on. The rule can't nag cc:Mail to do work for you.

4. **On the When to Run tab, choose when the rule should be executed.**

    Because we're filing incoming messages, On receiving message is the time to run it. However, you may shuffle through the other options, including new options like on daily or weekly schedules. Additionally, note down at the bottom of the dialog box that the rule can be active specifically between certain dates (for example, when you're going to be mostly out of the office on training, or whatever).

5. **Click the Whoop-tee-doo (What to Do) tab.**

    You'll see a new tab like the one in Figure 24-2.

6. **Tell cc:Mail to Find messages in some folder.**

    Depending on what you're doing, you'll have cc:Mail look in different places for messages, but we're going to choose Inbox because that's where new messages from the boss end up.

    If you want to look somewhere else, just click the Browse button, select the location, and click OK. You can look in multiple locations by clicking the next (currently blank) line and browsing to a location again.

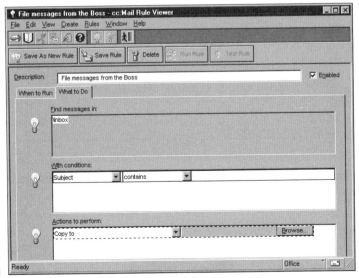

Figure 24-2:
The cc:Mail
8 Rule
Viewer's
What to Do
tab.

7. Under With conditions, tell cc:Mail how to know if it has found the right message.

The right message for this particular example is one from the boss, so you want to set Author, contains, and type in your boss's name.

You could, if you want, add other conditions to more thoroughly specify messages. Just complete the first row of the conditions and then click the second row and add another set of conditions.

8. Under Actions to perform, specify what cc:Mail should do after it finds a message from the boss.

We want to file the boss's messages away, so choose Copy to and then Browse to the folder you keep those messages in.

Your tab should look like Figure 24-3.

If you want to add another action, just click the next line and add, for example, Beep. On the third line, add Alert and type the text into the blank at the right.

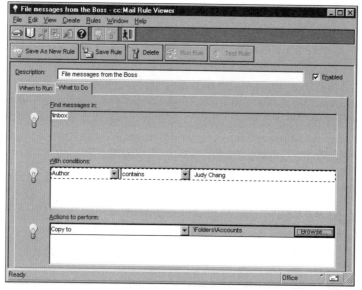

Figure 24-3:
The cc:Mail
8 Rule
Viewer
with a
completed
What to Do
tab.

9. Look up at your Action bar and choose Save As New Rule.

That's it!

Managing rules

Managing rules in cc:Mail 8 is just as easy as managing folders. As a matter of fact, the process is very similar. You can see your list of rules under the Rules folder in your Folder pane, as in Figure 24-4.

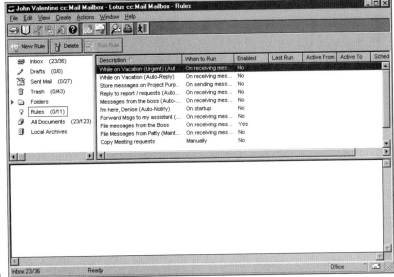

Figure 24-4:
The cc:Mail
8 Message
window
with the
Rules
folder.

Over in the right pane, you can see the list of rules and all the information you'd ever need about them, including

- ✔ Description
- ✔ When to Run
- ✔ Enabled
- ✔ Last Run
- ✔ Active Dates
- ✔ Schedule

If you need to edit a rule for any reason, from fixing a problem to disabling the rule to adding actions, just double-click the rule from the list to bring it back up in the Rule Viewer.

Because you're in the Rule folder, the Action bar agreeably cooperates and provides buttons to create a new rule, delete a rule, and run a rule. Now, isn't this easier than in cc:Mail 6?

Searching for lost stuff in cc:Mail 8

Losing messages and addresses is universal, and, at least for me, upgrading to cc:Mail 8 didn't necessarily help. As a matter of fact, those nested folders make it somewhat harder to track down the truly lost messages. However, the new and cool Search bar takes care of that in a flash.

1. **Choose View⇨Search bar (or Ctrl+Q) to display the Search bar.**

   The Search bar appears above the Action bar, as in Figure 24-5.

2. **If you just need to quickly find a message with some word in it, just type the word(s) and click Search.**

   cc:Mail rummages through all the messages in the folder you have selected and presents you with the list of everything that contains that word (or those words).

   To get the full list back, just click Reset to reset the search.

3. **Get more specific, if you want, by choosing the Conditions button and telling cc:Mail more precisely what you're looking for.**

   The Search Conditions dialog box lets you specify where to look (in the first field), that you want to include or exclude something (in the second field), and what you want to include or exclude (in the third field).

4. **Click OK to close the dialog box, then Search in the Action bar to find the messages.**

   Pretty slick, huh? Again, click Reset to get them all back.

cc:Mail Version 8 allows you to cancel a search in progress (as in Versions 2 and 6), which you can't do in Version 7.

Search bar

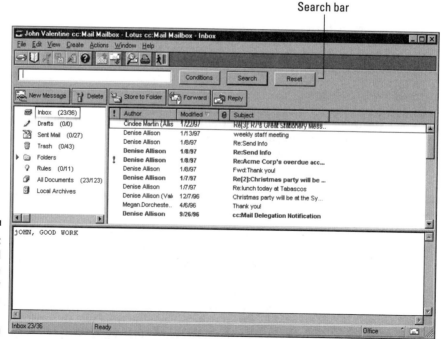

Figure 24-5:
The cc:Mail
8 Message
window
with
Search bar.

Chapter 25

Some Tidbits about cc:Mail 8 for Mobile Use

. . . .

In This Chapter

▶ Installing cc:Mail 8 Mobile

▶ Configuring mobile mode

▶ Customizing the mobile setup

▶ Receiving and Sending messages in cc:Mail 8

. . . .

T his section tells you all about (briefly, though) installing cc:Mail on your own and what's different about using cc:Mail 8 Mobile. Although the installation instructions are written for the benefit of those of you who are installing cc:Mail 8 for mobile use at home or on the road, they also work for just installing cc:Mail in the office. In my experience, administrators would rather do the installation themselves if they can possibly lay hands on your computer. It's only if they have to make a house call that they entrust you with the goods.

Installing cc:Mail 8 for Mobile Use

For those of us who get a set of disks for cc:Mail 8 from our system people with the expectation that we'll be able to proceed on our own, here's the procedure. It's quite similar to the procedure for installing cc:Mail 6 Mobile:

1. **Close all applications.**

   This isn't quite essential, but it sure makes the installation process more reliable and faster. I recommend it.

2. **Insert Disk 1 in the floppy drive, then choose the Start menu and <u>R</u>un.**

3. **Enter** a:\install **in the text box and click OK.**

Feed additional disks to the computer as requested. It's like feeding a whiny cat, but not quite as fun as visiting the petting zoo. Eventually, you see a dialog box like the one in Figure 25-1.

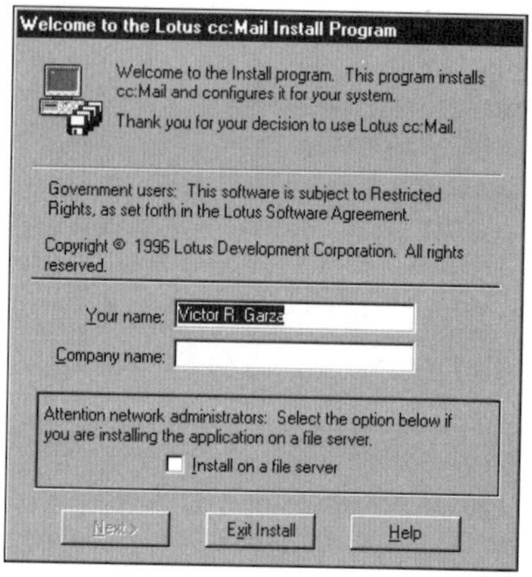

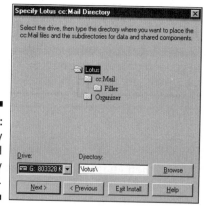

Figure 25-1:
The
Welcome to
cc:Mail
Install
Program
dialog box.

4. **Provide or verify the requested information and click Next.**

5. **cc:Mail Mobile asks again to verify that you didn't commit a typo. Just click Yes and proceed.**

6. **Click Next to accept cc:Mail 8's suggested directory.**

Unless you're sure you know what you're doing and have some really good reason to do so, just accept cc:Mail Mobile's suggestions on the cc:Mail Mobile directory, as seen in Figure 25-2.

Figure 25-2:
The Specify
cc:Mail
Directory
dialog box.

7. Select the cc:Mail Mobile applications you want to install by checking the boxes in front of the items. Click Next to proceed when you're done.

You certainly want to install cc:Mail 8 (that's why you're here, after all).

Organizer is personal-information-manager software. It's very good software and works well with your Day-Timer. If you want to try it, go ahead. On the other hand, if you don't plan to make any changes to your (already excellent, I'm sure) information-management system, don't worry about it.

8. Choose Default features — Automatic install or Minimum features — Automatic install in the Install Options dialog box (see Figure 25-3). Click Next to continue.

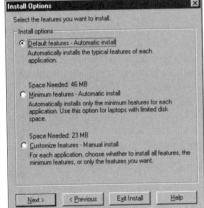

Figure 25-3:
The Install
Options
dialog box.

If you have loads o' disk space, choose the Default features option. If disk space is pretty tight, go for Minimum features.

The third choice, Customize features, is recommended only if you really want to take extra time to tinker with your computer or you really care about the particulars. Not recommended.

9. In the Select Program Folder dialog box, select where you want to find cc:Mail 8.

The default choice is, as usual, just fine. Click Next to continue.

10. Yeah, yeah, yeah. I've closed everything and am more than ready to Begin Copying Files to my hard disk.

On the other hand, maybe you just spent 10 minutes messing with this stuff because you were bored. In that case, answer No, don't install the files. I want to go back through these questions again . . . or *not!*

11. Wait and feed the computer disks if you need to.

After you see the Install Complete dialog box, click <u>D</u>one to accept the congratulations from the install program and get on with it.

12. Complete the registration dialog boxes, clicking <u>N</u>ext to move to the next one in the sequence, or just click E<u>x</u>it if you're tired of this process.

Sometimes your system administrator may specifically want you to register, and sometimes not. Just ask. If you aren't sure, choose E<u>x</u>it. You'll get another chance in two weeks.

Configuring and Using cc:Mail 8 in Mobile Mode

Actually *using* cc:Mail 8 in mobile mode isn't markedly different from using cc:Mail 8 in LAN mode. However, you need to provide some additional setup information. Ideally, you'll be able to con your cc:Mail administrator into setting up cc:Mail 8 for mobile use. However, if you had to install the thing, you probably have to configure it, too. Read on (this is kinda different from cc:Mail 6).

If your administrator really did set everything up for you, skip this next part entirely.

Configuring cc:Mail 8 for first use

The first time you log into cc:Mail 8, you have to wade through a wizard and provide all kinds of information. Before you start, make sure that you get a slip of paper from your administrator that has all the information you need, and that you get the administrator's phone number so that you can fill in the missing pieces.

1. Choose Start⇨Programs⇨Lotus Applications⇨Lotus cc:Mail Release 8.

If you installed cc:Mail in a different location, you have to adjust the above line accordingly.

You'll see the Lotus cc:Mail login dialog box, as shown in Figure 25-4.

Figure 25-4:
The cc:Mail
8 Login
dialog box.

2. **Type in your Login/Profile name.**

   This should be provided by your administrator.

3. **Type in your Password and click OK.**

4. **cc:Mail tells you what you already know — you've entered the name of a user who hasn't logged on from this system. Choose Yes, of course you want to create a new profile.**

   Now you see the cc:Mail Setup Wizard, as shown in Figure 25-5.

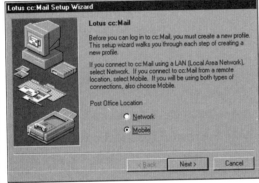

Figure 25-5:
The cc:Mail
Setup
Wizard.

5. **Choose Mobile for the post office location in the cc:Mail Setup Wizard dialog box and click Next.**

6. **Accept the default location for the mobile mailbox path and click Next.**

7. **Enter your post office name (from that handy-dandy sheet the administrator gave you) and click Next.**

8. **Presumably your Connection Type will use a modem, so verify that entry and click Next.**

   It's possible that you'd use a different type of connection, but the specifics would be radically different for each type of connection. If I were you, I'd punt and have the administrator do the setup if it's anything besides a modem connection — it's just not worth the frustration.

9. **Enter the country, area code, and phone number, then click Next.**

10. **cc:Mail offers to determine the modem type and appropriate settings, as shown in Figure 25-6.**

   By all means, accept the offer — it almost always works right and saves you the trouble.

Figure 25-6:
Let cc:Mail
determine
your
modem
settings.

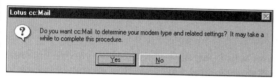

Wait. Wait.

11. **cc:Mail announces the modem and port it has found and asks you if you want to use it. If cc:Mail has guessed correctly, choose Yes. If cc:Mail is wrong, choose No.**

   If cc:Mail 8 missed the boat on your modem, you could either pick it out of the list or go with the generic selection, which should work fine.

   If you're really not sure, just go with the suggestion, see if it works, and call your administrator if you can't get connected.

12. **Click Next to move to the next screen of the Setup Wizard.**

13. **Fill in your post office path if you'll be using a LAN connection and click Next. Otherwise, do nothing and click Next.**

14. **Verify the information in the Setup Wizard (which looks very much like Figure 25-7) and click Next.**

Figure 25-7:
The cc:Mail
8 Setup
Wizard
confirmation
screen.

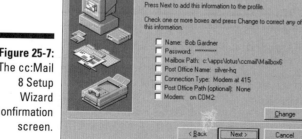

If some of the information is incorrect, just put a check mark by the information to change and click Change. You'll get a second chance to specify the setting.

Whew! That's it, though. You're done. cc:Mail will probably ask you if it should connect and get your mail. Beats me — I'm tired. Do what you want.

Customizing the cc:Mail 8 Mobile setup

After you have the basics taken care of, you still probably want to tweak the connection information to verify that everything happens as it should. You can customize many (noncritical) things about the way cc:Mail Mobile makes connections, and you do most of it in cc:Mail 8 from the Locations dialog box.

The procedure for tweaking your location follows:

1. **Select Actions⇨Locations.**

   You'll see a dialog box like the one in Figure 25-8. You can create New locations, Edit existing ones, or Delete locations. For now, I'll assume that you're at home and want to configure your cc:Mail 8 Mobile connection for there.

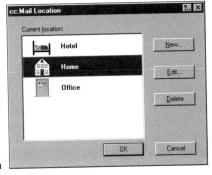

(You can come back later and take care of other locations — Vacation Home, Kid's House, Barely-Mobile Home, and so on)

2. **Double-click the location you want to edit (or select the location and click Edit).**

   If you just select a location and click OK, you'll change to that location. Hmmm. After rereading that last sentence, I think I'll set up a location called Aruba, select it, and click OK.

3. Take a gander at that dialog box now.

Is that *some* dialog box or what? Wow! (It's pictured in Figures 25-9 and 25-10.)

Seriously, this dialog box offers tons of choices because there's a lot that you can configure about your cc:Mail 8 Mobile connection. Frankly, I'm not going to go into all of it here because I don't have another 150 pages for a brief introduction to cc:Mail 8 Mobile.

However, you'll be happy to know that many of the settings are very comparable to those in cc:Mail 6, and many more of them are very intuitive (to us, that is; I'm sure the programmers thought they were *all* intuitive). Here's a quick tour, tab by tab.

Notice that at the top of the window, above the tabs, the dialog box reminds you what location you're modifying.

- Using the What to Do tab (shown in Figure 25-9), you can instruct cc:Mail about what to do each time you connect to the post office.

  These are all default settings that you can change when you actually dial in. If you'll be connected with a long-distance call on your dime or with limited time, you may check out the Filter Messages button. Under that section, you can tell cc:Mail to download only certain messages through your mobile connection. That way you won't have to pay to download your mother-in-law's digitized collection of Elvis songs. Heck, you can even make cc:Mail ask you for confirmation before downloading messages.

- Using the Dialing tab, select Use dialing rules. Click Edit Rule to modify them.

  Although you could manually Select the post office and number to call, or Dial manually, I don't know why you'd want to. These haven't changed at all since Version 6, so there won't be any surprises here.

- Using the Schedule tab (see Figure 25-10), you can click to select the schedule on which cc:Mail mobile should make connections.

  Generally, connecting on startup and on exit is sufficient, but you could construct a pretty elaborate schedule if that floats your cookies.

- Using the Connections tab, you can set up multiple types of connections (if your modem just isn't enough for you).

  Unless your administrator told you that there are multiple connection methods available and that you should set them up, don't worry about anything here. If you need to change the Modem configuration (after you get a newer, faster, and overall snazzier modem), you can do that by clicking the Edit button on this tab.

- Using the General tab, you can do a bunch of miscellaneous stuff, including controlling some notification and display options.

  You may revisit this tab after you've been using cc:Mail 8 Mobile for a while, because you'll have a better idea of what to change then. In the meantime, I'd recommend putting a check next to Don't display names or calling card numbers for security reasons. Also, leave the check on Confirm before processing address book updates because an unexpected update that processes automatically will bring you to a complete standstill until the update is finished, which can take a while.

4. Click OK when you're finished with the customization.

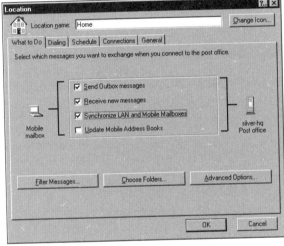

Figure 25-9:
The cc:Mail 8 Location mongo super-duper dialog box with the What to Do tab displayed.

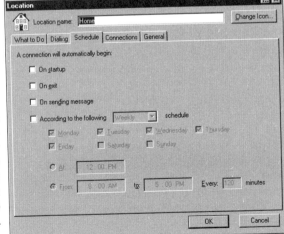

Figure 25-10:
The cc:Mail 8 Location mongo super-duper dialog box with the Schedule tab displayed.

Receiving messages

If you configured cc:Mail Mobile to send and receive messages on startup and on exit, you'll probably take care of most transfer obligations right there. However, you may want to check mail periodically just because. If so, do this:

1. **Select Actions⇨Connect.**

   You may see a dialog box asking you about getting a copy of the public address book. Just click in the Do not display this dialog box again box, and click No, muttering under your breath "Don't be a nag." We'll take care of the address book in a minute.

   You'll see the Connection Confirmation dialog box, as shown in Figure 25-11.

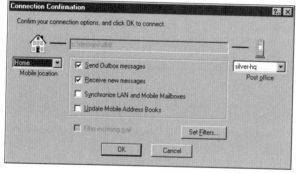

Figure 25-11: The cc:Mail 8 Connection Confirmation dialog box.

   Check to verify that cc:Mail remembered the correct mobile location (on the left) and post office (on the right).

   With lines connecting them. How cute.

3. **Check each activity you want to do on this connection.**

   - Send Outbox messages — Sends any messages you've sent but that have been sitting on your computer waiting for you to connect.

   - Receive new messages — Obvious, and the most fun.

   - Synchronize LAN and Mobile Mailboxes. It's useful but it may take a while.

   - Update Mobile Address Books — If you choose to synchronize the mailboxes, this happens anyway. Otherwise, go for it if you have a little time. If you got the nag dialog box after Step 1, you should probably do this now or you won't have any addresses to send mail to.

4. Click Set Filters if you want to specify what mail is downloaded during this session.

Transferring messages over a telephone connection is considerably slower than over a regular LAN connection. Unless you have an unlimited phone budget and lots of patience, you may consider filtering out unwanted messages without waiting for them to download.

5. Click OK when you're ready to go.

6. Wait.

Ho hum.

After all of your messages have been transferred to your computer (or rejected, if you filter your mail), cc:Mail Mobile disconnects from the post office.

All your messages are now in your Inbox (or elsewhere, if you've been getting creative with rules).

That wasn't so bad, was it? Read your messages at your convenience. Because they are all now on your computer, you don't have to be tied to the telephone or a specific location. Heck, you could even take your computer to the mountains and read your mail there.

Sending mail (Introduction to the Outbox)

As with cc:Mail 6, sending messages from cc:Mail 8 Mobile is almost the same as sending messages from cc:Mail 8 in LAN mode. Just remember, because cc:Mail Mobile doesn't maintain a full-time connection to the post office when connected in mobile mode, your messages cannot actually be sent immediately either.

As soon as you click Send, the message dives into the Outbox, where it lurks until cc:Mail Mobile connects to the home post office to send mail. Even if you think you've sent the message, until you connect to the post office and send your Outbox messages, that message remains, lurking in your mailbox. As a matter of fact, until you do the connection bit, your message in the Outbox is just like most checks in the mail.

Part VII
The Part of Tens

The 5th Wave   By Rich Tennant

Karl Malden as a young man

Are you gonna keep your nose glued to that screen all day again today?

In this part . . .

You've probably heard of David Letterman's top-ten list, where he lists ten reasons why Dennis Rodman wears a skirt, or ten reasons why Bill Clinton was re-elected. Well, you get the idea. I have my own lists, but they have nothing to do with Dennis Rodman or Bill Clinton. Well, almost nothing.

My lists will make you smarter, funnier, wittier, and more attractive to the opposite sex. But wait, there's more. They will also help you out in a bind and may very well save your bacon some day. And to think I included these lists for free with this book. . . .

Chapter 26

More Than Ten Ways to Make Yourself Look Like a Guru

In This Chapter

▶ Several suggestions that will save you time and effort

Use WinZip

Along your cc:Mail travels, you may find that instead of the normal attachments that you get with your e-mail messages (like .doc files, which are Microsoft Word documents, or .xls files, which are Microsoft Excel spreadsheets), you may find that every so often one of the people that you work with will send you a file that has a .zip extension at the end of the filename. These files are called compressed files, and the person sending them to you probably figured that you would rather get a single, compressed file than 50 different Word documents, or he or she may have decided that compressing a ten-megabyte Excel spreadsheet down to one megabyte would make for easier transport.

Compressing a file squeezes it down to it's component parts — oftentimes shrinking the file considerably. Compression software can also be used to take a whole bunch of files and not only compress them but mush them into one big file instead of a whole bunch of little files, making it easier to attach them to e-mail messages.

Well that's all fine and dandy, except now you're probably stuck with a file that you can't look at or work on. What to do now? Go out and get a program like WinZip (shown in Figure 26-1) from Nico Mak Computing, which allows you to uncompress that file and use it on your machine. WinZip also allows you to make compressed files of your own, which enables you, in many cases, to save hard disk space on your machine. You can also use compression programs to create what are called *self-extracting* files. When the recipient of this type of file runs the file, it automatically uncompresses, preventing the hassle of having to get the same compression program that you have. (Now wasn't that was nice of you?)

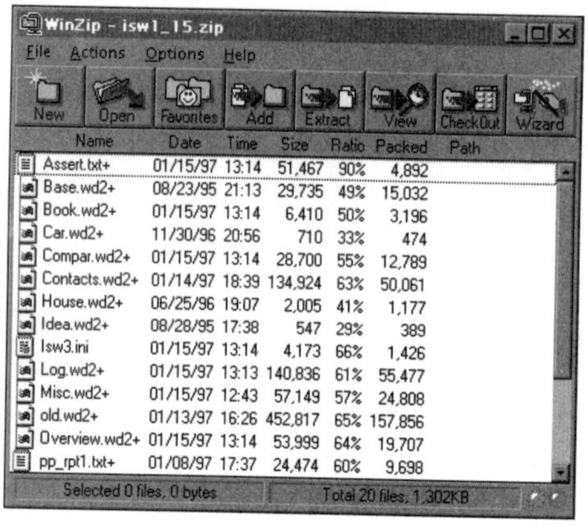

Figure 26-1:
WinZip is
an
indispensable
utility.

Take Security Seriously

Now you've probably heard how information (like e-mail) that you are sending across the Internet is inherently insecure, and that almost any malicious person with the right tools can read and capture all of the information that you are sending (not trying to make you feel insecure or paranoid). You can use a compression utility in conjunction with a password to make sure that any files that you send via e-mail are safe from prying eyes.

You can also use a program like DataSAFE from Authentex to make sure that the data you are sending is secure. Now, making things secure usually requires that both you and your message recipients need to have the same type of security software. That is not the case with DataSAFE, where all that you do is create a self-contained "safe" that has all of your files in it. You transport the safe to the person whom you want to receive it. All the person on the receiving end needs to know is the combination for the safe, and the contents of the safe are spilled out his or her desktop.

The only problem with this type of security method is that the person on the receiving end needs to know the combination of the safe. Now, it wouldn't be a good idea to include the safe's combination in the e-mail that you are sending with the safe. It also wouldn't be a good idea if you were to send the combination before or after you sent the safe in an e-mail because if people are gathering information on your e-mail, they would acquire the same information (and the combination). It's probably best to call the person up and give that person the combination over the telephone or agree on a common number that only the two of you know (like someone's birthday) to make sure that this type of information stays safe.

This type of security only works if you are sending information that is somewhat sensitive. It is by no means foolproof. If you really want to keep e-mail secure, you should be using an industrial-strength application that your administrator has probably installed.

Know about the Cryptic privdir.ini File

Here's an important one. You should know by now how to save your friends and colleagues' Internet addresses (if you don't, check out Chapter 7). But I'll bet that you didn't know that all of those Internet addresses were saved to a file on your local hard drive. So what, you ask? Well, unlike files that are on a network (like most cc:Mail files), the files on your local hard drive are seldom, if ever, backed up to a floppy or tape drive. But I expect that a person of a caliber such as yourself always backs up data files or talks to their network administrator about doing this backup, right?

Well, back to the point, there is a file that holds all of those Internet addresses, and it's called the privdir.ini file. Its location is somewhat hidden, but you can use the Windows Explorer to find it. It is located at c:\windows\ccmail\cc1dir\privdir.ini. My method of safe backup is to copy this file to a floppy disk, label it "Internet addresses for cc:Mail," put the date on it, and put it in a safe place. It's a good idea to do this procedure about once every month to ensure that if there ever is a problem with cc:Mail on your computer and it has to be re-installed, you will have saved all of the addresses to the people that you correspond with on the Internet. This saves you mucho time if you ever find yourself in the predicament of having to enter all of those addresses again (like this author once did).

Use cc:Mail's Fax Features

If you find that you send and receive a lot of faxes and that most of those faxes you compose are at your computer, you may be interested to know that cc:Mail has the option to send and receive faxes. Of course, this is an option that your administrator has to install and maintain, but in many cases, it can save considerable time (not to mention paper) if the person that is composing the fax (you) could just compose it as if it were a traditional e-mail and then have the capability to just send the message to a fax machine. Real nifty if you can use it.

Set Up an E-Mail Virus Wall

Contrary to popular belief, there is no way to get a virus on your computer simply by reading an e-mail message. You normally have to receive an attachment to an e-mail and then launch, or run, that attachment before the virus can infect your computer. If you receive a lot of attachments via e-mail, it's probably worth your while (and your company's) to get some virus protection. If a virus does get attached to a file that comes along with an e-mail, a virus protection program can stop the e-mail and try to disinfect the message. Such programs are not cheap, but they save your company in lost time if viruses are a big problem. A program called E-Mail VirusWall from Trend Micro Inc. is one such program.

Use cc:Mail with Your Pager

Are you one of those people who are tethered to a pager? Did you know that cc:Mail can send messages to most regular and alphanumeric pagers so that if a specific person sends you a message, or if you get a high-priority message, you can get paged with that message (and sometimes even send small messages back to the sender of the message)? This feature can definitely make many people's lives easier.

Enable the Drafts and Trash Folders

If your Drafts or Trash folders aren't enabled, ask your administrator to enable them at the server. If these folders aren't enabled, they won't work, which means that you won't get the advantages of saving those jewels of your wisdom when you are called away from your desk in the middle of an inspiration, and you won't get a message back when you accidentally delete it.

Know the Difference between LAN Mode and Mobile Mode

With LAN mode, you can install cc:Mail as a LAN (or networked) version only. However, if you install cc:Mail as a Mobile version, you can use it as a pure mobile setup (for example, on your laptop or home computer), or you can use it on a LAN to be mobile on the network (for the office-hoppers among you that have a docking station with their laptop or have a laptop with a network card that enables a connection to the corporate network).

Know the Rules

Know what a Rule does and how to use it. Having a Rule is like having a butler handle all the little details that make life so tedious. You can set Rules up to watch what comes into the Inbox, delete old messages (for example, those older than five days that you haven't read and don't plan on reading), alert you when a message from your boss comes in, and so on. Oh, but Rules won't do your laundry. Sorry. For all of the skinny on Rules, check out Chapter 16.

Know Your Search Tools

Searching is one of the most powerful features of cc:Mail. You can search any message by author, subject, file size, date, or full text of the message. So get familiar with the search capabilities of cc:Mail. It may one day help get you a raise when you're the only one in the company who can find that information on the Fioti account (because you know how to search in cc:Mail). For the skinny on searching, check out Chapter 14.

Learn What All of Those SmartIcons Do and Use Key Combinations

SmartIcons speed your actions by putting common commands within reach of a mouse click. Using those icons can save you time, and time is money (or at least that's what my boss tells me). If you're more inclined to use the keyboard, memorize the following keystroke combinations:

- **Ctrl+S** = Send a message.
- **Ctrl+N** = New message.
- **Ctrl+I** = Refresh Inbox. (The default time to automatically update your Inbox is six minutes. If you're itchy to get your messages, just use this key combo.)
- **Ctrl+E** = Spell check.
- **Ctrl+X** = Cut.
- **Ctrl+V** = Paste.
- **Ctrl+C** = Copy.

Think the Control key is your buddy now? Try these:

- **Alt+Delete** = Delete the current open message.
- **Alt+F4** = Exit cc:Mail (and get a life). Go see some people in person!
- **Escape** = Close any open window, except the Inbox, which it minimizes. (In Version 2, you used Ctrl+F4, but put that version out of your mind.)
- **F1** = Help. (Don't you wish they had one of these for life, too?)
- **Ctrl+Z** = Undo. When you can't get help, try to undo. (This also would be handy for real life.)
- **Ctrl+A** = Address message.
- **Ctrl+Y** = Reply.
- **Ctrl+R** = Forward. (Intuitive ain't it?)

Close the Inbox

Did you know that the Inbox in Version 6 doesn't automatically disappear anymore when you close it like it did in previous versions (Versions 2.0–2.2)? It minimizes. That's a very nice change. If you've ever used a previous version of cc:Mail, you know how frustrating it can be when you're left without an Inbox, or any box for that matter.

Four Words: "User Setup Dialog Box"

Choose Tools⇨User Setup. All of your user-definable options are here. Check out what you can do from this powerful dialog box. Don't try too much at once. Check out things a little at a time and see if you like them.

Refresh

The Inbox is refreshed every six minutes now, which means that if you're waiting for a message that has just made its way to the company's cc:Mail server, you only have to wait a maximum of six minutes before it gets to you. If you're really impatient, you can just click on the Inbox SmartIcon or use the Ctrl+I keyboard combination to force your Inbox to be refreshed.

Know Your Version Differences

So in a nutshell, what are the differences between cc:Mail Versions 2, 6, 7, and 8 anyway? Version 6 added more visual keys to 2, but both are 16-bit programs that can run under Windows NT and Windows 95 but were made for Windows 3.1. They pretty much look and act exactly the same. Versions 7 and 8 are true 32-bit applications (translation: 32-bit = faster and more expensive), and both work with more mail engines other than cc:Mail, including Lotus Notes and Microsoft Exchange.

Chapter 27

Roughly Ten Ways to Be Smart

Spell Check

Check the spelling of your message before you send it. Oooh, oooh. Hey, cc:Mail comes with a spell checker, so why not use it?

My personal philosophy is that if I'm sending a message to a friend or a coworker, I don't have to be sure that my *T*s are crossed or my *I*s are dotted. (I guess that's because I use a computer and they always are anyway.) But you get the idea: If I'm just sending a friendly e-mail, I don't check all of the spelling and grammar. But if I find myself writing to my boss or to a client, I will always check how my message reads, even if it takes a little extra time. Then I use the cc:Mail spell checking feature (Ctrl+E in Versions 2 and 6) to make sure that my message looks professional.

Check That E-Mail Address

Make sure you put in, or at least check that that you have put in, the correct e-mail address of the person to whom you want to send an e-mail message. With cc:Mail's type-ahead addressing, it's easy to get one Andre when you meant to get another. It could be doubly embarrassing if you accidentally send your boss David Letterman's most recent top-ten list instead of the projected financials for the next quarter that she requested.

Don't Overstuff Your Trash Folder

If you find that you have more than 15MB of messages in there and you haven't cleaned out the Trash folder in a while, it's probably a good idea to do so. Your cc:Mail administrator should let you know if you're using up too much space on the cc:Mail server, but it's best to be proactive in these matters and take things into your own hands. It'll help you stay on the administrator's good side. I once saw someone with 30 megs of e-mail messages in his Trash bring a cc:Mail server to it's knees. And he would have been in a heap o' trouble if he hadn't been a VP (rank hath its privileges).

Save Often and Frequently (And Don't Forget to Stamp Out Redundancy)

If you're writing a long e-mail document, copy and transfer it to the Clipboard, save it as a draft, or send it to yourself so that you don't accidentally delete or lose it if the server goes down or the power goes out. This has happened to me more than once, so I recommend caution wherever possible. To highlight and copy text (which automatically puts it in the Clipboard), click down on your left mouse button while dragging the mouse pointer over the text that you want to copy. Then Select Edit⇨Copy or use the Ctrl+C keyboard combination. Then paste it in another application with Ctrl+V. If you don't have the capability to send you message to the Drafts folder, just address the message to yourself and mail it. Better safe than sorry.

Check Attached Files for Viruses

As I mentioned in the last chapter (and it's worth repeating), you should always check e-mail-attached files for viruses. Keep a directory that is just for file attachments (Go to Tools⇨User Setup⇨File location). Save attachments to this directory and then run a virus check program on the files before you open them. If you don't know what your company uses for virus checking, ask your cc:Mail administrator and bring some donuts. That'll grease your admin's wheels.

Keep Track of File Attachments

With all of the different file viewers that cc:Mail has, it's probably going to be the exception rather than the rule that you'll actually have to detach a file from an e-mail message. But when you have to detach a file, make sure you know where your attachments are stored for later retrieval. They can be saved either to a temporary directory or to wherever you want. To find out where the save directory is located, go to Tools⇨User Setup⇨File location.

Watch for Pesky Dialog Boxes

Always be aware of dialog boxes when exiting cc:Mail — for example, that annoying, senseless message, "Do you want to lose your changes?"

These warning boxes ask questions but don't show you which messages they mean. (You may think this is basic stuff, but don't tell me you haven't accidentally lost a message at one time or another because you ignored some warning message.) So make sure that all the messages you care about are accounted for before you go clicking on the Yes button.

Never Send a Message When You're Hot under the Collar

Always reread a message before sending it. Check the tone, grammar, and clarity. And if you're upset at the person to whom you're sending the message, take some time out before you actually send it. It just may save you from some hard feelings later.

Use Your Neck Muscles

Don't forget to look both ways before you cross the street. (I just had to put this one in.)

Chapter 28
Almost Ten cc:Mobile Tips

· ·

In This Chapter

▶ Ways to make life on the road simpler

· ·

Minimize the Phone Bill

You can schedule when cc:Mobile calls the server to update your e-mail messages (once per day, when you exit cc:Mobile, every few hours — whenever you want).

You don't have to be online all the time. You can create and read messages offline and then connect to the server to send and receive messages.

Use Filters

You can set up your machine so that when you download your e-mail, it will reject low or normal priority messages, for example. You can also filter messages for certain subjects, by size of message, by date, or by sender (to make sure that you get the ones from your boss).

Use the Message Summary Feature

With this feature, you can view headers of messages before the messages are downloaded (it's like screening your calls on the answering machine) so that you save money by not downloading messages you don't want or need (look for the check box under Mobile➪Filters).

Get the Latest Directory Update

Going on a trip? Make sure you have the latest directory update form your cc:Mail administrator. This ensures that you have the most recent addresses for your company's employees. Also, if you receive a message from someone who is not already in your address book, the address will be updated automatically. (Like magic!)

If you can, take a copy of the cc:Mail Mobile CD with you. You never know when you may need to reinstall the program. (I know you hate hearing this stuff, but if I don't warn you, who will?)

Understand Location Setups and Communication Methods

Make sure you fully understand location setups and communication methods. Configure location settings for an office and hotel and test them before you leave on a trip.

If you're using a laptop in public (say, an airport) so that you can gain access to a cc:Mail server, enable the restricted display option (it's a check box under Mobile⇨Mobile Setup) to hide your home office, name, address, and phone numbers from being displayed. (That stuff can be copied over your shoulder in an airport just like phone card numbers.)

Don't Panic

If you have a problem, it's probably not as bad as you think (usually). When you do run into trouble, activate the diagnostics in the cc:Mail Background program so that you can troubleshoot the problem with your cc:Mail administrator. You can activate diagnostics on a case-by-case basis by clicking on the little button that says Diagnostics at the top of the cc:Mail Background program.

Appendix A

Installing cc:Mail without Giving Yourself a Migraine

• •

*Y*ou know those lion traps that they have in Africa with the palm leaves covering a deep hole in the ground? Consider yourself lucky that installing cc:Mail and cc:Mail Mobile is nothing like that. And if you're really lucky, you'll walk into the office one morning and find your desktop machine or laptop already set up, configured, and ready to go.

If your not so lucky and you have to install cc:Mail or cc:Mail Mobile yourself, then you should be on your way with just a few helpful tips to ease your installation woes.

This little appendix pertains to both cc:Mail and cc:Mail Mobile, but if you find yourself needing in-depth instructions on installing cc:Mail Mobile, check out Chapter 17. The installations for cc:Mail Mobile and cc:Mail are extremely similar. There is only one real difference, and that's the fact that you have to usually install cc:Mail Mobile yourself and your administrator will usually install the LAN version of cc:Mail for you.

LN:DI — Is It a Dessert Topping or a Floor Wax?

One of the programs that can be installed when installing cc:Mail or cc:Mail Mobile is called LN:DI. What LN:DI really stands for is the Lotus Notes Document Imaging product family. Included in this product family is the Lotus Image Viewer (LIV for short). Well, what does LIV do, you ask? It's a program for viewing and manipulating graphics and image files (including faxes) that you receive through cc:Mail.

If you have the LN:DI Mass Storage System set up, you can use Lotus Notes to store mass amounts of images and then use LIV to access and view them.

LIV also has the capability to store images that are received as faxes and to translate those images to text that you can edit though a process called optical character recognition (OCR for short).

The OCR option only works if something called the LN:DI WorkGroup OCR Option is installed on your network and you have an Image Processing Server (both of these things would need to be installed and maintained by your administrator, and the same goes for the Mass Storage System).

LIV can also send an image that you have opened to a fax machine for fax transmittal if the Lotus Fax Server is installed on your network (by, guess who?, your administrator).

You can do some cool things with images in LIV, such as zooming in and out on a particular area of an image, enhancing a particular image to increase the display quality, rotating an image in 90-degree increments, and reversing the contrast of an image (to make it look like a photographic negative). You can also use LIV to print and copy images or view text annotations that are made on the image.

The following image formats are supported by the Lotus Image Viewer:

- ✔ **Bitmap files (with the extension .BMP):** This image format is used by windows applications like Windows Paintbrush.

- ✔ **CompuServe Graphics Interchange Format files (with the extension .GIF):** A popular image format used for transferring images by people on CompuServe.

- ✔ **JPEG files (with the extension .JPG):** Used for many high-end color and gray scale images.

- ✔ **LN:DI files (with the extension .LIF):** Used by LIV's big brother, the LN:DI Professional Viewer.

- ✔ **PCX files:** This image format is used by many popular paint and graphics applications.

- ✔ **Photo CD files (with the extension .PCD):** This image format was developed by Kodak and used for storing photos and images on a CD-ROM.

- ✔ **Tag Image File Format files (with the extension .TIF):** This image format is used on a wide variety of desktop scanners and desktop publishing and image manipulation programs.

You'll notice that all of these formats are options when you install cc:Mail and cc:Mail Mobile. I'd suggest checking all of the boxes because you never know what kind of graphics files someone may send you via e-mail.

Potential Headaches

Getting the installation going in cc:Mail or cc:Mail Mobile is a fairly straight-forward affair, but even the smoothest roads have a few bumps. Take this bump for example: If you're installing the program from a floppy, the first step is pretty easy. If you're installing the program from a CD, however, you've got to dig deep in the directory structure to find the right program.

Inserting Disk 1 in the disk drive

If you use Windows 3.1*x,* select File➪Run from the Program Manager. Enter **a:\install** in the text box and click OK.

If you use Windows 95, choose the Start menu and Run. Enter **a:\install** in the text box and click OK.

Possible headache #1: After putting the cc:Mail CD in the CD-ROM drive

If you use Windows 3.1*x,* select File➪Run from the Program Manager. Enter **d:\winmail\r6dsktop\install** (or for those of you installing cc:Mail Mobile, enter **d:\winmail\r6mobile\install**) in the text box and click OK. If your CD drive uses some other drive letter than d:, substitute that drive letter at the beginning of the command.

If you use Windows 95, click the Start menu and choose Run. Enter **d:\winmail\r6dsktop\install** (or for those of you installing cc:Mail Mobile, enter **d:\winmail\r6mobile\install**) in the text box and click OK (see Figure A-1). If your CD drive uses some other letter, substitute that letter in the command.

Figure A-1:
The Run
dialog box.

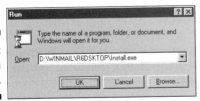

After a few seconds of furious disk or CD activity, the installation continues.

Possible headache #2

When you get to the Welcome to the Lotus cc:Mail Install Program dialog box, be aware that the installation program will not let you go any further until you have put something in the Company name: field (see Figure A-2). I usually stick with hitting the spacebar once there to make the program happy and then click on the Next > button with my mouse to move on. Don't click on the Install to a file server check box.

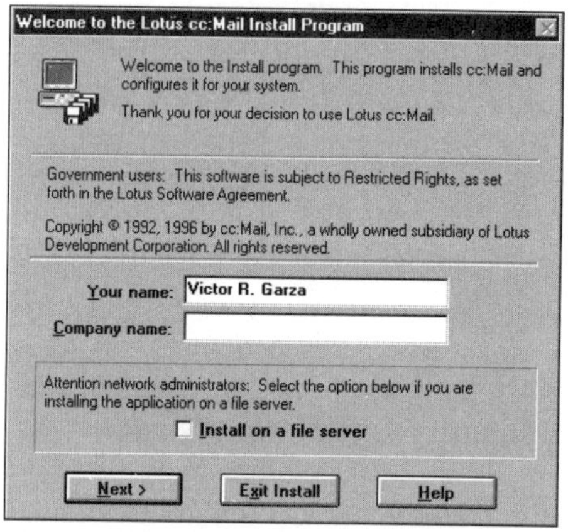

Figure A-2: Make sure that you provide a company name.

Possible headache #3

When you get to any dialog box that asks you to specify a particular directory for installing the program, it's in your best interest to stay with the default directory. Just keep clicking the Next > button.

Possible headache #4

Now you've probably come to a dialog box titled Select Lotus cc:Mail Applications, which is shown in Figure A-3. The question is, do you have an infinite amount of disk space for all of these applications? You certainly want to install the cc:Mail option, but the remaining applications are optional, depending on the space you have and if you want to have something else to tinker with on your computer.

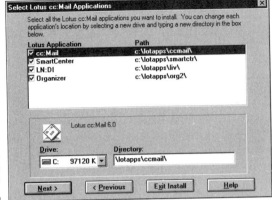

Figure A-3:
Do you
have room
to install all
of these
apps?

✓ SmartCenter is a different way of organizing and running the programs on your hard disk. Install it if you like, but it doesn't provide any new capabilities. You end up with these funky virtual file drawers at the top of your screen and programs in them. Maybe it works for some people, but an additional layer of complexity is the last thing I want on my computer.

✓ LN:DI is image- and fax-viewing software. Probably a good choice if you have the space for it. I talk about it in more detail earlier in this appendix.

✓ Organizer is the Lotus personal information manager software. It's very good software and works well with your trusty Day-Timer. If you can spare the space, go for it. If your time management system is as good as it gets, however, Organizer is expendable.

And just keep clicking the Next > button.

Possible headache #5

When you get to the Install Options dialog box (see Figure A-4), stick with either the Default features - Automatic install or Minimum features - Automatic install. Keep clicking the Next > button.

Possible headache #6

If you have elected to install LN:DI, you get the choice of which files will be associated with the Lotus Image Viewer (see Figure A-5). You can either leave the default (a safe bet) or click every file type.

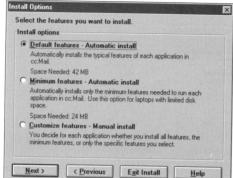

Figure A-4:
The Install Options dialog box.

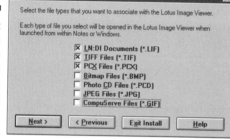

Figure A-5:
Stick with the defaults or click all of the check boxes.

Possible headache #7

It is possible that cc:Mail may detect a conflict with your modem that will not allow you to register automatically, as shown in Figure A-6. Don't worry, Lotus has been kind enough to allow you to register via other methods.

And as shown in Figures A-7 and A-8, cc:Mail will remind you every 14 days if you elect to skip out of the registration program.

Figure A-6:
No big deal. Just register via fax or mail.

Figure A-7:
You really
should
register.

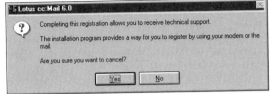

Figure A-8:
If you don't
register,
you'll get
pestered
every two
weeks.

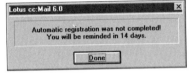

From Here on In...

Luckily, it's all pretty self-explanatory from here on in. And if for some
reason your administrator will not install cc:Mail for you, take a look at
Chapter 17. You should be able to get through the installation of cc:Mail by
following the steps underlined therein.

With these helpful tips, if you do encounter any problems, you should be
able to skate right over them. And remember, a good install is one you don't
have to do yourself!

Appendix B

Using the Menu Options

· ·

*T*he menus in cc:Mail for Windows give you access to all of the features available in cc:Mail. You can use keyboard shortcuts and SmartIcons to accomplish many tasks, but there is only one way to do everything, and for that you need to look at the menu bar. The menu bar contains a comprehensive list of all the cc:Mail options.

Sometimes the choice that you want on a menu may not be available and is grayed out. If you select the Edit menu, for example, and the Cut and Copy commands are not available, they are grayed out because you didn't select any text before opening the menu.

Each menu and each option have one underlined letter. To open the drop-down list on the menu bar, first press the Alt key and then press the key that corresponds to the underlined letter. Many pull-down menu options have keystroke combination shortcuts listed on their right. You can use these keystroke shortcuts rather than the menu. The keystroke shortcuts do not work if you open a drop-down menu first.

Some menu options have three dots, known as an ellipsis (...), after them. Options that show these three dots generate dialog boxes that contain more choices.

The File Menu

The File menu, naturally enough, gives you access to the file management options in cc:Mail. You can use this menu to save messages, print messages, and exit cc:Mail. The following list briefly explains each of the File menu options.

Open: This option opens the currently selected container or message.

New...: New allows you to create a variety of different things, including folders and archives, where you can store all of those messages that are filling up your Inbox. You can also add bulletin boards, public mailing lists, private mailing lists (you know, like those where everyone on it is an *X-Files* fan), mailing list participants (to add participants to an existing private mailing list), directory entries, and rules.

In Version 2 of cc:Mail, **New...** opens the Add New dialog box, which allows you to add a new folder or archive to the Containers pane. If the Address Book window is open, the Add New dialog box allows you either to add new addressees to an existing private mailing list or to create a new private mailing list.

In Version 2 of cc:Mail, **Rename** allows you to rename a currently selected folder. In Version 6, Rename has been moved to the Edit Menu.

In Version 2 of cc:Mail, **Store...** is used to either copy or move a message either from the Inbox to a folder or from one folder to another folder. You can copy, but not move, messages to a folder from an archive or bulletin board. This option brings up the Store dialog box. In Version 6, Rename has been moved to the Message menu.

Only in Version 2 of cc:Mail, **Save...** brings up the Save Options dialog box. This dialog box allows you to save an Attachment List item (such as a text from a message, a file, or a fax) to a disk or hard drive. If the Message window is open, the Save Options dialog box appears with the options to save an open item, save all items, or save selected items. When a file or fax attachment is selected, that attachment is saved in the default cc:Mail directory.

Save As...: This option brings up the Save As dialog box. This dialog box allows you to save a message with all attachments (such as a file or a fax) or just the attachments of a message to a disk or hard drive. If the Message window is open, the Save As dialog box appears with the options to save an open attachment or message text, save all attachments, or save selected attachments. When a file or fax attachment is selected, that attachment is saved in the default cc:Mail directory. This option also allows you to give a file attachment a different name before you save it. You also have the option to save part or all of the message header with any saved message text.

Print...: This option opens a dialog box in which you can make choices about printing the current Inbox, folder, message(s), file(s), or bulletin board list of messages.

Print Setup...: Print Setup displays a dialog box in which you can select different printers if they have previously been installed for Windows. You can also change paper orientation (portrait or landscape) and paper size (letter, legal, A4) here.

Import...: This option opens the Import dialog box, which allows you to bring text from text files into an open message. Import will not work on files larger than 20K in size.

Export...: Export allows you to save the text of an open or selected message as a text file.

Exit: Exit closes cc:Mail for Windows. If necessary, a prompt concerning open messages or changed messages appears.

The Edit Menu

The Edit menu contains some interesting time-savers and shortcuts for moving text from one application (like a word processing application) to another (like cc:Mail) or from one cc:Mail message to another message.

Undo: This command undoes your last action. If you want to undo something you did several or just two steps ago, you're out of luck. (For example, if you want to use Undo to undelete a word that you deleted two words back, Undo would only undo the last word deleted, not the one previous to that.) Don't always depend on Undo; it may not be there when you need it. A good thing to remember is that Undo can't undo a sent message.

Cut: Cut removes selected text (text that you have previously highlighted) and places the selected text in the Windows Clipboard. The Windows Clipboard acts like a storage buffer. You can cut or copy highlighted text to the Windows Clipboard and paste that text from the Windows Clipboard to another location in the document. When you cut or copy text to the Clipboard, the new text replaces whatever text was in the Clipboard. Cut can cut not only text but also messages from the Folders container or a message list.

Copy: This shortcut acts the same as Cut except that it doesn't remove the selected text from the originally selected area.

Paste: Paste is used to remove text from the Clipboard and put it in your document. Just place the insertion point (by clicking with the mouse) where you want to insert the text that's in the Clipboard. Whatever is in the Clipboard remains in the Clipboard until you either place something else in the Clipboard or close Windows. You can paste whatever is in the Clipboard to more than one place and to more than one document at a time. If there's information in the Clipboard, you can paste that information to wherever you want, however many times you want.

Delete: This time-saver deletes the selected message or highlighted text (or folder or archive). Delete also deletes a private mailing list or names from a private mailing list. Delete erases messages and text without saving them to the Clipboard.

Rename: Rename allows you to rename a currently selected folder. In Version 2, Rename is on the File menu.

Modify Mailing List: Allows you to add or delete a name from a private mailing list. This menu option does the same things that File➪New➪Mailing List Participants does.

Find/Replace...: This command brings up the Replace dialog box, which you can use either to search for text strings or to move quickly to a place in a message. This option also allows you either to replace a specific instance of specific text with some new text or to replace all instances of that specific text with some new text. You have to be careful with this option. If you want to globally replace the word *form* within a message, for example, and you forget to check the Match Whole Word Only option, you replace the text string form wherever it appears: *former, information, formal, reform,* and so on.

Find Next: Finds the next instance of the text that was selected in the Replace dialog box.

The View Menu

In Version 6, this menu item has been moved in its entirety to the Window menu. In Version 2, the View menu offers up a short set of options for viewing containers.

Expand: This command is used to expand a selected mail list or folder to see the individual containers that it holds.

Collapse: Collapse is used to collapse a selected, expanded mail list or folder to hide the individual containers that it holds.

Expand All: Expand All is used to expand all containers simultaneously in the current Containers pane.

Collapse All: Collapse All is used to collapse all the containers simultaneously in the current Containers pane.

The Text Menu

The Text menu offers options that allow you to play with the formatting of the text within a message (changing color, font styles, and paragraph formatting).

Fonts...: Fonts opens the User Setup dialog box. The User Setup dialog box shows the current font, style, and size of the characters of your message text. In addition, the User Setup dialog box can be used to change the fonts that are displayed in the container list and attachments list.

Colors...: This option opens the Color Highlighting dialog box, which allows you to change the foreground and background colors of texts and messages in the Item-View pane.

Margins/Tabs...: After you open a message, selecting this option opens the Margins/Tabs dialog box, which allows you to change the left and right margins and the number of tab stops in all mail messages in the Item-View pane of a Message window.

Use Default Margins: Use Default Margins sets the margins in a message to the default.

Ruler: This item turns the ruler in the Item-View pane of a Message window on and off. A check next to this item means that it's on; no check means that it's off. The ruler allows you to select the placement of margin markers. In Version 2, you can also use the ruler to change the position of tab stops.

Paragraph Formatting: This item turns on a feature that treats each line of text as a separate paragraph. A check next to this item means that it's on; no check means that it's off. It's best to leave this item on.

Message Menu

The Message menu offers up options for creating, addressing, and sending mail messages. The following list briefly explains each of the Message menu options.

New Message: This menu item opens up a New Message window for creating a new mail message.

Address...: This option opens the Address Message dialog box for addressing a new message.

Send: This command sends a mail message to the intended recipient(s).

Resend: This option resends a mail message to the intended recipients. This option is usually used if someone who deleted a message from you later asks you to send the message to him or her again.

Save Draft: This command is used to save a mail message to the Drafts folder. Save Draft is usually used when you have not yet completed a message and want to save it for completion later.

Store... Store is used to either copy or move a message either from the Inbox to a folder or from one folder to another folder. You can copy, but not move, messages to a folder from an archive or bulletin board. This option brings up the Store dialog box. In Version 2, Store is on the File Menu.

Reply...: This command opens the Reply dialog box. Reply is used to reply to a mail message. (Reply can be used only from the Message window.)

Forward...: Forward is used to forward a received message. This command opens the Forward Address dialog box, which allows you to address a message to be forwarded.

Delete Message: This command deletes the currently selected or open message.

Next Message: Next Message opens the next message in a list.

Previous Message: This option opens the previous message in a list.

Delete - Next Message: This command deletes the currently selected message and automatically displays the next one in a list. If you've selected a message from a list, the currently selected message in the list will be deleted and the next message in the list will be selected. If you're viewing a message in the Message window, the currently viewed message will be deleted and the next message in the list will be displayed. This command should really be called "Delete the Current Message and Move on to the Next Message," but then that wouldn't really fit on the menu.

Delete - Previous Message: This choice deletes the currently selected message and automatically displays the preceding message in a list. If you've selected a message from a list, the currently selected message in the list will be deleted and the previous message in the list will be selected. If you're viewing a message in the Message window, the currently viewed message will be deleted and the previous message in the list will be displayed. This command should really be called "Delete the Current Message and Move on to the Previous Message," but then the menu items would take longer to read than *War and Peace*.

In Version 2 of cc:Mail, **View Item** opens the currently selected item from an attachments list for viewing in the Item-View pane of a Message window. In Version 6, View Item has been moved to the Attachments menu and renamed View Attachment.

 In Version 2 of cc:Mail, **Run Item** is used to run an attachment rather than view it (from directly within cc:Mail). Running an attachment launches the application used to create the attachment directly from within cc:Mail. In Version 6, Run Item has been moved to the Attachments menu and renamed Launch Attachment.

 In Version 2 of cc:Mail, **Rename Items...** is used to rename a message item (the fancy name for the text of a message) or an attachment. This option brings up the Attachment Description dialog box. This option also allows you to change the name of an attachment from within a newly created message. In Version 6, Run Item has been moved to the Attachments menu and renamed Rename Attachment(s)....

The Attachments Menu

The Attachments menu offers up options on attaching items to mail messages. The following list briefly explains each of the Attachment menu options. By the way, in Version 2, this menu was called the Attach menu.

Text: This command attaches a text item to a newly created message. (I personally don't see any use for this command, but you may.) For example, some cc:Mail users choose to use the Text command to create text (such as lists of telephone numbers or client name-and-address lists) that message recipients may want to print separately from the message itself.

Files...: Files opens the Attach/Files dialog box. The Attach/Files dialog box allows you to select a file from your local drive or network drive and attach the selected file to a cc:Mail message. A maximum of 20 files may be attached to a single message.

Forms...: This choice allows you to attach an empty or filled in cc:Mail form to a cc:Mail message.

Clipboard...: This choice opens the Clipboard Item Types dialog box, which allows you to attach the contents of the Clipboard as a .CLP file to a message in cc:Mail.

Save Attachment(s)...: This option brings up the Save As dialog box. This dialog box allows you to save a message with all attachments (such as a file or a fax) or just the attachments of a message to a disk or hard drive. If the Message window is open, the Save As dialog box appears with the options to save an open attachment or message text, save all attachments, or save selected attachments. When a file or fax attachment is selected, that attachment is saved in the default cc:Mail directory. This option also allows you to give a file attachment a different name before you save it. There is also the option to save the part or all of the message header with any saved message text. The command is exactly the same as the Save As command on the File menu.

View Attachment: This command opens the currently selected item from an attachments list for viewing in the Item-View pane of a Message window. In Version 2, View Attachment is on the Message menu and named View Item.

Launch Attachment: This command is used to run an attachment rather than view it (from directly within cc:Mail). Running an attachment launches the application used to create the attachment. In Version 2, Launch Attachment is on the Message menu and named Run Item.

Rename Attachment(s)...: This command is used to rename a message item (the fancy name for the text of a message) or an attachment. This option brings up the Attachment Description dialog box. This option also allows you to change the name of an attachment from within a newly created message. In Version 2, Rename Attachment(s) is on the Message menu and named Rename Items....

Run Applications...: The Run Applications command opens the Attach New File dialog box and is used when preparing a new message. The Attach New File dialog box allows you to run any external application from within cc:Mail in order to create a file attachment for the message.

In Version 2 of cc:Mail, **Run Apps...** opens the Attach New File dialog box and is used when preparing a new message. The Attach New File dialog box allows you to run an external application from within cc:Mail in order to create a file attachment for the message. The dialog box usually allows you to create only a Windows Write (.WRI) file, a Windows Paintbrush (.BMP) file, or a text (.TXT) file.

The Rules Menu

If the Rules menu is missing from the cc:Mail menu bar, the Rules feature of cc:Mail for Windows has been disabled. See your cc:Mail administrator to have the Rules menu enabled.

Rules List: This choice opens a list of all the currently available rules within cc:Mail. Unless the Rules List window is open (enabled), the Run, Enable, Disable, and Move pull-down menu items are grayed out.

Create New Rule...: This option opens the Rule Editor dialog box for creating a rule to run within cc:Mail.

Run Rule: Use this choice to manually run a rule (or rules) currently selected from the Rules list. You can use this option to manually run any rule with the condition of Manual, On Startup, or On Exit.

Enable Rule: Use this option to enable a rule that is currently disabled.

Disable Rule: Use this option to disable a rule that is currently enabled.

Move Rule Position...: This choice opens the Move Rule dialog box and moves the numbered, highlighted rule to the position number selected in the Move Rule dialog box.

Run Rules as Scheduled: This option runs all currently enabled rules as scheduled. This menu item can be enabled or disabled. A check mark to the left of Run Rules as Scheduled indicates that this feature is enabled. No check mark to the left of Run Rules as Scheduled means that this feature is disabled.

To enable or disable a rule (or to use Run Rule or Move Rule Position), a rule must be first selected or highlighted. Disabling or enabling (or running or moving) only affects the currently selected rule.

The Tools Menu

The Tools menu allows you to check your spelling, search for text, and change the user setup properties of cc:Mail. The following list briefly explains each of the Tools menu options.

Spell Check...: This command allows you to spell check a message (or selected text) with the cc:Mail spell checker.

User Setup...: This choice opens the User Setup dialog box, which allows you to change a variety of different options in cc:Mail. You can change the way that the desktop looks, the conditions for preparing a message, the way in which you receive message confirmation, your message notification, various passwords, fonts, rules, and so on.

SmartIcons...: Select this command to open the SmartIcons dialog box, which allows you to change a variety of options with regard to the SmartIcons palette.

Search: This choice opens the Search window for performing searches on messages or addresses.

Empty Trash: Empty Trash manually empties the contents of the Trash folder.

Optimize Mailbox on Exit: Only in cc:Mail Mobile, this item is used to make sure that cc:Mail Mobile is running in tip-top shape every time you exit cc:Mail Mobile. When this option is on, a check mark appears to the left of the title.

Forms Filler: This option opens the cc:Mail Forms application. This application allows you to fill in premade forms and route or mail the forms to another person.

The Mobile Menu

The Mobile menu is available only to people who have cc:Mail Mobile for Windows installed.

Send/Receive Mail: This command sends all messages in the cc:Mail Mobile Outbox and receives messages from the cc:Mail post office. cc:Mail Mobile does this by making a phone connection to the currently selected cc:Mail post office.

Send Only: This choice only sends messages in the Outbox. It does not allow you to receive messages from the currently selected cc:Mail post office.

Receive Only: This option only receives messages from the currently selected cc:Mail post office; it does not send messages waiting in the Outbox to be sent.

Docking Mode...: This selection opens the Docking Mode dialog box. Docking Mode allows you to indicate whether you are a stand-alone mobile user or you are currently attached to a network.

Copy to Docked Account: Copies each mail message that matches certain conditions to your docked account.

Move to Docked Account: Moves each mail message that matches certain conditions to your docked account.

New Directory Entry...: This option opens the Directory Entry dialog box, which allows you to add a new addressee or a post office to the address directory.

Process Directory (or System) Updates: This command processes the system-update messages stored in the Directory Updates bulletin board. When this option is enabled on your network post office, this option can be configured to deliver directory-update messages automatically to synchronize your cc:Mail Mobile directory with your home post office directory. Your cc:Mail administrator decides whether to enable this option or not.

Locations...: This choice opens the Location Setup dialog box, which allows you to create and configure different locations (home, on the road, office) with different communication parameters and modem setup strings, as well as run scheduling events.

Mobile Setup...: Mobile Setup opens the Mobile Setup dialog box, allowing you to configure the home post office and enable or disable a variety of options and configuration information pertaining to the post office.

Filters...: Filters opens the Filters dialog box. The Filters dialog box allows you to place a variety of constraints on incoming messages from the post office.

The Window Menu

The Window menu offers helpful options for managing all of those renegade windows within the cc:Mail application. The following list briefly explains each of the Window menu options.

Go to Inbox: This command refreshes the screen to show you messages in the Inbox folder.

New Mailbox Window: This choice opens a new Mailbox window if you've accidentally closed a Mailbox window or if you want to have multiple mailbox windows open simultaneously.

New Address Book Window: This option opens a new Address Book window for addressing a mail message or working with private mailing lists.

Expand: This command is used to expand a selected mail list or folder to see the individual containers that it holds. In Version 2, it is on the View menu.

Collapse: Collapse is used to collapse a selected, expanded mail list or folder to hide the individual containers that it holds. In Version 2, it is on the View menu.

Expand All: Expand All is used to expand all containers simultaneously in the current Containers pane. In Version 2, it is on the View menu.

Collapse All: Collapse All is used to collapse all the containers simultaneously in the current Containers pane. In Version 2, it is on the View menu.

Cascade: This choice cascades all the currently open windows. Cascade places one open window on top of other open windows and allows you to see the upper-left corner of each open window (kind of like fanning out a deck of playing cards on a table).

Tile Horizontal: This option allows you to see all open windows tiled horizontally (above each other).

Tile Vertical: This choice displays all open windows vertically (beside each other).

Arrange Icons: This command arranges icons neatly across the bottom of the cc:Mail window when iconized windows exist or when the Mailbox window or Message window or Address window has been iconized.

Close All: This option closes all of the open cc:Mail windows within the cc:Mail application. Choose this command and the Message window, the Address window — all windows that have the possibility of being open at one time — are just gone — Poof! — leaving only the title bar, the menu bar, the SmartIcons, the Mailbox window (minimized), and the status bar visible.

Close Window: This option closes the currently selected cc:Mail window within the cc:Mail application (except for the Mailbox window, which just gets minimized).

The Help Menu

Need help? Look no further than the following list of cc:Mail options.

Guide Me: This option provides the major help topics available for cc:Mail for Windows. Replaces the Index option in Version 2 of cc:Mail.

Contents: This option is a great starting point for help in cc:Mail and lists the main help topics available allowing you to drill-down into any topic you need help for. Replaces the Expanded Index option in Version 2 of cc:Mail.

 Only in Version 2 of cc:Mail, **Mobile How Do I?** gives you an alphabetical index to commonly performed tasks within cc:Mail Mobile for Windows. (This option is available only for and can be used only with the mobile version of cc:Mail.)

How Do I?: This command provides an alphabetical list of all the help topics available within cc:Mail.

Search: This option brings up a dialog box that allows you to search the entire help system by index or by any word in the text of the help system itself.

 Only in Version 2 of cc:Mail, **SmartIcons** lists the iconized version of all available SmartIcons next to their key equivalents (key combinations). Clicking one of these little icons allows you to go directly to that help topic.

 Only in Version 2 of cc:Mail, **Terminology** provides an alphabetical list of all the commonly used terms in cc:Mail.

 Only in Version 2 of cc:Mail, **Key Equivalents** provides help in cc:Mail for using key combinations and lists all available key combinations for gaining access to all of the common functions within cc:Mail.

 Only in Version 2 of cc:Mail, **Using Help** actually gives you a definition of help and gives help topics for how to use help.

 Only in Version 2 of cc:Mail, **Tutorial** brings up a tutorial on how to use cc:Mail for Windows.

Mobile Tour: This choice brings up a tutorial on how to use cc:Mail Mobile for Windows. (This option is available only for and can be used only with the mobile version of cc:Mail.)

About cc:Mail: This selection brings up an About cc:Mail dialog box. Clicking anywhere within the area of the dialog box allows you to see a neat little screen show that displays the names of all the people who worked on bringing cc:Mail to you.

Appendix C
Keyboard Shortcuts

· ·

General Shortcuts

Command	Shortcut in Versions 2 and 6	Shortcut in Versions 7 and 8
Add New (folder or archive from the Mailbox window [or bulletin board — for you mobile users only])	Ctrl+N	none
Address a new message (with the New Message window open)	Ctrl+A	none
Cascade all of the open windows	Shift+F5	none
Close the currently selected window	Esc or Alt+F4	Esc or Alt+4
Collapse all open folders	Ctrl+–	Shift+–
Colors	Ctrl+H	none
Copy	Ctrl+C	Ctrl+C
Create a new message	Ctrl+M	Ctrl+M
Cut	Ctrl+X	Ctrl+X
Delete	Delete	Delete
Delete message	Alt+Delete	Alt+Delete
Delete the current message and move to the next message	Ctrl+Alt+right-arrow key	Ctrl+Alt+right-arrow key
Delete the current message and move to the previous message	Ctrl+Alt+left-arrow key	Ctrl+Alt+left-arrow key
Exit cc:Mail	Alt+F4	Alt+F4

(continued)

Command	Shortcut in Versions 2 and 6	Shortcut in Versions 7 and 8
Expand all folders	Ctrl++	Shift++
File attachments (from a New Message window)	Ctrl+F	none
Find next occurrence of a text string within a message	F3	F3
Forward a message (from the Message window)	Ctrl+R	none
Go to the Inbox folder	Ctrl+I	none
Help Index	F1	F1
Next Message	Alt+right-arrow key	Alt+right-arrow key
Next Pane (in clockwise order)	F6	F6
Open	Enter	Enter
Paste	Ctrl+V	Ctrl+V
Previous Message	Alt+left-arrow key	Alt+left-arrow key
Previous Pane (in counter-clockwise order)	Shift+F6	Shift+F6
Print	Ctrl+P	Ctrl+P
Reply (within a Message window)	Ctrl+Y	Ctrl+Y
Rules List window	Ctrl+L	none
Save As	F2	none
Save Window Defaults Now	Shift+F2	none
Search for addresses, messages, and text	Ctrl+Q	Ctrl+Q
Send message (within a Message window)	Ctrl+S	none
Spell Check	Ctrl+E	none
Store message	Ctrl+T	none
Switch to the next open window	Ctrl+F6	none
Tile all windows horizontally	Shift+F4	none
Undo	Ctrl+Z	Ctrl+Z
Use the default margins (within a Message window)	Ctrl+D	none

Navigational Editing Keys

When navigating within a mail message in cc:Mail, you can use the standard Microsoft Windows navigation keys. The following shortcuts work in all versions on cc:Mail.

Command	Shortcut
Move the cursor up one line	up-arrow key
Move the cursor down one line	down-arrow key
Move the cursor left one character	left-arrow key
Move the cursor right one character	right-arrow key
Move the cursor left one word	Ctrl+left-arrow key
Move the cursor right one word	Ctrl+right-arrow key
Move the cursor to the beginning of the current line	Home
Move the cursor to the end of the current line	End
Move the cursor to the beginning of the current message	Ctrl+Home
Move the cursor to the end of the current message	Ctrl+End
Delete the text from the current cursor position to the end of the line	Ctrl+Del

Keys for Selecting Text while Editing

When editing a mail message in cc:Mail, you can use the standard Microsoft Windows editing keys. The following shortcuts work in all versions of cc:Mail.

Command	Shortcut
Select one line of text up from the current cursor position (or if already selected, deselect the text)	Shift+up-arrow key
Select one line of text down from the current cursor position (or if already selected, deselect the text)	Shift+down-arrow key

(continued)

Command	Shortcut
Select the text one character at a time to the left of the current cursor position (or if already selected, deselect the text)	Shift+left-arrow key
Select the text one character at a time to the right of the current cursor position (or if already selected, deselect the text)	Shift+right-arrow key
Select the text from the current cursor position to the beginning of the current line	Shift+Home
Select the text from the current cursor position to the end of the current line	Shift+End
Select the previous word from the current cursor position	Ctrl+Shift+left-arrow key
Select the next word from the current cursor position	Ctrl+Shift+right-arrow key
Select the text from the current cursor position to the beginning of the message	Ctrl+Shift+Home
Select the text from the current cursor position to the end of the message	Ctrl+Shift+End

Appendix D

Selected cc:Mail Mobile Error Messages and Resolutions

 This appendix provides some last-ditch effort technical-type possible resolutions to cc:Mail Mobile connection problems. Refer to Chapter 20 before you start rooting through these suggestions — you shouldn't have to work this hard.

Some of the most obscure error messages were omitted from this list because they are just way out in left field. If you get errors that aren't listed here, contact your cc:Mail administrator and whimper. (If you don't want to whimper, just bring in two dozen donuts. That ought to do it.)

If you can contact your cc:Mail administrator and pass the problem-resolution buck off, do so. That said, dive into the errors, and may The Force be with you.

General Problems

Problem or Error Message	Possible Cause	Possible Solution
Anything didn't work once.	Just happens.	Try again before panicking.
[1002]: Data connection lost.	Good question.	Call back to see if the post office is shut down or if it just hiccuped on you.

Password-Related Problems

Select Tools⇨User Setup⇨Password and then check the following table. If nothing in the table works, contact your cc:Mail administrator.

Problem or Error Message	Possible Cause	Possible Solution
[1003]: Refused connection, wrong password.	Your Mobile password isn't the same as your LAN password.	Change your cc:Mail Mobile password to match your home post office password.
[1077]: Invalid length for new password.	Your password is not long enough.	Make your password longer.
[1078]: Pre-expired password or [1079]: Current password has expired.	Your password expired because of a decision your cc:Mail administrator made. Not your fault.	Change your password.

Problems with Communications

Choose Mobile⇨Locations⇨Communications. Select the Communications Method and then Edit. Verify the information to the best of your ability. If it all looks correct, contact your cc:Mail administrator and, politely, ask for help.

Problem or Error Message	Possible Cause	Possible Solution
[1022]: Invalid connection parameters.	Typo or incorrect information.	Check the settings for this communication method and correct the setting that doesn't match your computer's actual configuration.
[1023]: Problems initializing modem.	Your modem didn't respond to cc:Mail Mobile.	Check the modem settings (modem type, serial port, speed) for this communication method.

Problem or Error Message	Possible Cause	Possible Solution
[1028]: Invalid communication port setting	The COM port or speed setting isn't correct.	Change the communication port to COM1, COM2, COM3, or COM4 and set the speed to 9600 or the speed that your administrator suggested. If you've tried each of COM1 through COM4 and the right speed, and it still doesn't work, call for help!
[1029]: Invalid communication data rate setting.	The COM port speed setting isn't correct.	Set the speed to 9600 or the speed that your administrator suggested.
[1034]: Serial port not responding.	cc:Mail Mobile can't find the serial port specified.	Change the communication port to COM1, COM2, COM3, or COM4 and set the speed to 9600 or the speed that your administrator suggested. If you've tried each of COM1 through COM4 and the right speed, and it still doesn't work, call for help!
[1035]: Modem not responding.	Your modem is not turned on. Buy it a drink if necessary.	Turn on the modem or make sure that it is plugged in. There should be a light somewhere on the modem indicating that it's on.

(continued)

Problem or Error Message	*Possible Cause*	*Possible Solution*
You do not have a modem.	Uh, huh.	If this is obviously untrue, start trying other solutions in this part of the table. Attach a modem. The modem is not attached to the serial port you selected (COM1, COM2, COM3, or COM4). Bad cable, or it isn't properly plugged in. Move the modem cable to the serial port you selected or change the serial port setting. Make sure that the serial cable is plugged in all the way.
[1000]: Post office did not answer or Packet mismatch.	A bad connection.	Check that the correct modem type is selected. Lower the baud rate to 9600 if it's currently set above 9600. Verify the modem selection and phone number. Try again.
[1020]: No valid communiication methods are available.	You haven't enabled a communication method for this location or for the post office address.	Use Mobile⇨ Location, Communications to enable a communication method. Use Mobile⇨ Mobile Setup⇨Edit Address to verify that the post office address includes this communication method.

Problem with Post Office Address in Your Directory

Choose Mobile⇨Mobile Setup⇨Edit Address and make sure the information shown matches the information your cc:Mail administrator provided.

Problem or Error Message	Possible Cause	Possible Solution
The answering post office didn't respond.	Hard luck.	Check the phone number and then try again. If the phone number is correct, just wait a little while and try again.
[1007]: Wrong post office name requested.	The name or telephone number of the answering post office is not correct.	Check the spelling of the post office name and try again.
[1008]: Cannot generate phone number.	The post office phone number is not correct.	Check that the phone address, calling card number (if applicable), and outside line are correct.
[1061]: No carrier detected.	You called the wrong number, or the modem you called doesn't work right now.	Check the phone number, then try again.
[1063]: Voice call detected.	You called the wrong number.	Pick up the handset of your phone, apologize profusely, and then check the phone number, change it, and try again.
[1075]: No Home Post office defined.	You haven't set up your post office.	Set up a post office in the Mobile Setup dialog box.

Someone Else's Problem, No Action Required

Just wait these out or call your cc:Mail administrator and be mildly irritating. The administrator probably already knows about the post office being down but may not know about a problem with the post office not answering.

Problem or Error Message	Possible Cause	Possible Solution
[1016]: Post office is temporarily shut down.	The post office has been shut down. Surprise!	Try again later.
[1058]: Busy signal detected.	Huh. Let's think about this.	Try again later.
[1060]: No answer detected.	Well.	Try again later.
[1055]: Post office did not answer.	Gee whiz. I dunno.	Try again later.

Someone Else's Fault, Action Required

Check the suggested causes and, if you want, get on the phone with your administrator.

Problem or Error Message	Possible Cause	Possible Solution
[1068]: Message size too long.	cc:Mail rejected the message because it is too long.	Break into two messages or contact your cc:Mail administrator.
[1090]: You are not a user on this Post Office.	You have been moved to a different post office.	Ask your cc:Mail administrator for the name and location of your new post office.
[1076]: Mailbox is locked.	Your account is locked on the LAN.	Ask your cc:Mail administrator to unlock your account.
[1036]: Cannot access addresses for post office.	cc:Mail Mobile disagrees with the file access restrictions on the main post office.	Check with your cc:Mail administrator to verify that you have rights to access the post office directory.

Minor Error Messages

There are really no minor error messages, especially if you're the one getting them, but these aren't likely to be anything more than a nuisance.

Problem or Error Message	Possible Cause	Possible Solution
[1043]: No messages in Outbox to send.	You selected Mobile⇨ Send Only but there are no messages in the Outbox to be sent.	Write a message before you try to send it.
[1059]: No dial tone detected.	Your modem didn't receive a dial tone.	Make sure the modem is plugged into a working phone jack and that the phone cord is connected to the modem. Yell at the kids to get off the phone.
[1069]: Message priority too low.	cc:Mail rejected the message because its priority is too low.	Increase the message priority and resend.
[1070]: Maximum messages exceeded.	cc:Mail cannot accept all of your messages (probably more than 50) in one session.	Make another connection to send more messages.
[1072]: Unknown message termination code.	cc:Mail Background received an unknown error.	Try to send the message again.
[1081]: Message header is too big, canceling the operation.	You addressed the message to too many people, more than two. (Sorry, just had to work that in).	Remove some names from the recipient list.
[1082]: Sender name not in mail directory.	cc:Mail Mobile can't return a requested receipt to someone because his name is not in the cc: Mail Directory.	Add this person to the cc:Mail Direcory so that he can get his receipt — if you want him to.

Memory and Disk Space Errors

Really, these aren't cc:Mail Mobile specific errors, but they could crop up.

Problem or Error Message	Possible Cause	Possible Solution
[1065]: Message cannot be stored.	Message is too big to fit in the available space on the hard drive.	Make more disk space on your hard drive available by deleting temporary or unneeded files. Look in c:\windows\temp as a good place to start deleting files.
[1067]: Insufficient disk space for message.	Message is too big to fit in the available space on the hard drive.	Make more disk space available by deleting temporary or unneeded files. Look in c:\windows\temp as a good place to start deleting files.
[1086]: Not enough free disk space available, canceling operation.	There is not enough free disk space to do something.	Make more disk space available by deleting temporary or unneeded files. Look in c:\windows\temp as a good place to start deleting files.
[1092]: Not enough RAM, close another app and try again.	You have run out of memory.	Close other applications. Restart your computer, try again.

Index

7/29/9

Title	Author	ISBN	Price
The Internet For Macs® For Dummies® 2nd Edition	by Charles Seiter	ISBN: 1-56884-371-2	$19.99 USA/$26.99 Canada
The Internet For Macs® For Dummies® Starter Kit	by Charles Seiter	ISBN: 1-56884-244-9	$29.99 USA/$39.99 Canada
The Internet For Macs® For Dummies® Starter Kit Bestseller Edition	by Charles Seiter	ISBN: 1-56884-245-7	$39.99 USA/$54.99 Canada
The Internet For Windows® For Dummies® Starter Kit	by John R. Levine & Margaret Levine Young	ISBN: 1-56884-237-6	$34.99 USA/$44.99 Canada
The Internet For Windows® For Dummies® Starter Kit, Bestseller Edition	by John R. Levine & Margaret Levine Young	ISBN: 1-56884-246-5	$39.99 USA/$54.99 Canada

MACINTOSH

Mac® Programming For Dummies®	by Dan Parks Sydow	ISBN: 1-56884-173-6	$19.95 USA/$26.95 Canada
Macintosh® System 7.5 For Dummies®	by Bob LeVitus	ISBN: 1-56884-197-3	$19.95 USA/$26.95 Canada
MORE Macs® For Dummies®	by David Pogue	ISBN: 1-56884-087-X	$19.95 USA/$26.95 Canada
PageMaker 5 For Macs® For Dummies®	by Galen Gruman & Deke McClelland	ISBN: 1-56884-178-7	$19.95 USA/$26.95 Canada
QuarkXPress 3.3 For Dummies®	by Galen Gruman & Barbara Assadi	ISBN: 1-56884-217-1	$19.99 USA/$26.99 Canada
Upgrading and Fixing Macs® For Dummies®	by Kearney Rietmann & Frank Higgins	ISBN: 1-56884-189-2	$19.95 USA/$26.95 Canada

MULTIMEDIA

Multimedia & CD-ROMs For Dummies® 2nd Edition	by Andy Rathbone	ISBN: 1-56884-907-9	$19.99 USA/$26.99 Canada
Multimedia & CD-ROMs For Dummies® Interactive Multimedia Value Pack, 2nd Edition	by Andy Rathbone	ISBN: 1-56884-909-5	$29.99 USA/$39.99 Canada

OPERATING SYSTEMS:

DOS

MORE DOS For Dummies®	by Dan Gookin	ISBN: 1-56884-046-2	$19.95 USA/$26.95 Canada
OS/2® Warp For Dummies® 2nd Edition	by Andy Rathbone	ISBN: 1-56884-205-8	$19.99 USA/$26.99 Canada

UNIX

MORE UNIX® For Dummies®	by John R. Levine & Margaret Levine Young	ISBN: 1-56884-361-5	$19.99 USA/$26.99 Canada
UNIX® For Dummies®	by John R. Levine & Margaret Levine Young	ISBN: 1-878058-58-4	$19.95 USA/$26.95 Canada

WINDOWS

MORE Windows® For Dummies® 2nd Edition	by Andy Rathbone	ISBN: 1-56884-048-9	$19.95 USA/$26.95 Canada
Windows® 95 For Dummies®	by Andy Rathbone	ISBN: 1-56884-240-6	$19.99 USA/$26.99 Canada

PCS/HARDWARE

Illustrated Computer Dictionary For Dummies® 2nd Edition	by Dan Gookin & Wallace Wang	ISBN: 1-56884-218-X	$12.95 USA/$16.95 Canada
Upgrading and Fixing PCs For Dummies® 2nd Edition	by Andy Rathbone	ISBN: 1-56884-903-6	$19.99 USA/$26.99 Canada

PRESENTATION/AUTOCAD

AutoCAD For Dummies®	by Bud Smith	ISBN: 1-56884-191-4	$19.95 USA/$26.95 Canada
PowerPoint 4 For Windows® For Dummies®	by Doug Lowe	ISBN: 1-56884-161-2	$16.99 USA/$22.99 Canada

PROGRAMMING

Borland C++ For Dummies®	by Michael Hyman	ISBN: 1-56884-162-0	$19.95 USA/$26.95 Canada
C For Dummies® Volume 1	by Dan Gookin	ISBN: 1-878058-78-9	$19.95 USA/$26.95 Canada
C++ For Dummies®	by Stephen R. Davis	ISBN: 1-56884-163-9	$19.95 USA/$26.95 Canada
Delphi Programming For Dummies®	by Neil Rubenking	ISBN: 1-56884-200-7	$19.99 USA/$26.99 Canada
Mac® Programming For Dummies®	by Dan Parks Sydow	ISBN: 1-56884-173-6	$19.95 USA/$26.95 Canada
PowerBuilder 4 Programming For Dummies®	by Ted Coombs & Jason Coombs	ISBN: 1-56884-325-9	$19.99 USA/$26.99 Canada
QBasic Programming For Dummies®	by Douglas Hergert	ISBN: 1-56884-093-4	$19.95 USA/$26.95 Canada
Visual Basic 3 For Dummies®	by Wallace Wang	ISBN: 1-56884-076-4	$19.95 USA/$26.95 Canada
Visual Basic "X" For Dummies®	by Wallace Wang	ISBN: 1-56884-230-9	$19.99 USA/$26.99 Canada
Visual C++ 2 For Dummies®	by Michael Hyman & Bob Arnson	ISBN: 1-56884-328-3	$19.99 USA/$26.99 Canada
Windows® 95 Programming For Dummies®	by S. Randy Davis	ISBN: 1-56884-327-5	$19.99 USA/$26.99 Canada

SPREADSHEET

1-2-3 For Dummies®	by Greg Harvey	ISBN: 1-878058-60-6	$16.95 USA/$22.95 Canada
1-2-3 For Windows® 5 For Dummies® 2nd Edition	by John Walkenbach	ISBN: 1-56884-216-3	$16.95 USA/$22.95 Canada
Excel 5 For Macs® For Dummies®	by Greg Harvey	ISBN: 1-56884-186-8	$19.95 USA/$26.95 Canada
Excel For Dummies® 2nd Edition	by Greg Harvey	ISBN: 1-56884-050-0	$16.95 USA/$22.95 Canada
MORE 1-2-3 For DOS For Dummies®	by John Weingarten	ISBN: 1-56884-224-4	$19.99 USA/$26.99 Canada
MORE Excel 5 For Windows® For Dummies®	by Greg Harvey	ISBN: 1-56884-207-4	$19.95 USA/$26.95 Canada
Quattro Pro 6 For Windows® For Dummies®	by John Walkenbach	ISBN: 1-56884-174-4	$19.95 USA/$26.95 Canada
Quattro Pro For DOS For Dummies®	by John Walkenbach	ISBN: 1-56884-023-3	$16.95 USA/$22.95 Canada

UTILITIES

Title	Author	ISBN	Price
Norton Utilities 8 For Dummies®	by Beth Slick	ISBN: 1-56884-166-3	$19.95 USA/$26.95 Canada

VCRS/CAMCORDERS

Title	Author	ISBN	Price
VCRs & Camcorders For Dummies™	by Gordon McComb & Andy Rathbone	ISBN: 1-56884-229-5	$14.99 USA/$20.99 Canada

WORD PROCESSING

Ami Pro For Dummies®	by Jim Meade	ISBN: 1-56884-049-7	$19.95 USA/$26.95 Canada
MORE Word For Windows® 6 For Dummies®	by Doug Lowe	ISBN: 1-56884-165-5	$19.95 USA/$26.95 Canada
MORE WordPerfect® 6 For Windows® For Dummies®	by Margaret Levine Young & David C. Kay	ISBN: 1-56884-206-6	$19.95 USA/$26.95 Canada
MORE WordPerfect® 6 For DOS For Dummies®	by Wallace Wang, edited by Dan Gookin	ISBN: 1-56884-047-0	$19.95 USA/$26.95 Canada
Word 6 For Macs® For Dummies®	by Dan Gookin	ISBN: 1-56884-190-6	$19.95 USA/$26.95 Canada
Word For Windows® 6 For Dummies®	by Dan Gookin	ISBN: 1-56884-075-6	$16.95 USA/$22.95 Canada
Word For Windows® For Dummies®	by Dan Gookin & Ray Werner	ISBN: 1-878058-86-X	$16.95 USA/$22.95 Canada
WordPerfect® 6 For DOS For Dummies®	by Dan Gookin	ISBN: 1-878058-77-0	$16.95 USA/$22.95 Canada
WordPerfect® 6.1 For Windows® For Dummies® 2nd Edition	by Margaret Levine Young & David Kay	ISBN: 1-56884-243-0	$16.95 USA/$22.95 Canada
WordPerfect® For Dummies®	by Dan Gookin	ISBN: 1-878058-52-5	$16.95 USA/$22.95 Canada

Windows® 3.1 SECRETS™
by Brian Livingston

ISBN: 1-878058-43-6
$39.95 USA/$52.95 Canada
Includes software.

MORE Windows® 3.1 SECRETS™
by Brian Livingston

ISBN: 1-56884-019-5
$39.95 USA/$52.95 Canada
Includes software.

Windows® GIZMOS™
by Brian Livingston & Margie Livingston

ISBN: 1-878058-66-5
$39.95 USA/$52.95 Canada
Includes software.

Windows® 3.1 Connectivity SECRETS™
by Runnoe Connally, David Rorabaugh, & Sheldon Hall

ISBN: 1-56884-030-6
$49.95 USA/$64.95 Canada
Includes software.

Windows® 3.1 Configuration SECRETS™
by Valda Hilley & James Blakely

ISBN: 1-56884-026-8
$49.95 USA/$64.95 Canada
Includes software.

Internet SECRETS™
by John Levine & Carol Baroudi

ISBN: 1-56884-452-2
$39.99 USA/$54.99 Canada
Includes software.

Internet GIZMOS™ For Windows®
by Joel Diamond, Howard Sobel, & Valda Hilley

ISBN: 1-56884-451-4
$39.99 USA/$54.99 Canada
Includes software.

Network Security SECRETS™
by David Stang & Sylvia Moon

ISBN: 1-56884-021-7
Int'l. ISBN: 1-56884-151-5
$49.95 USA/$64.95 Canada
Includes software.

PC SECRETS™
by Caroline M. Halliday

ISBN: 1-878058-49-5
$39.95 USA/$52.95 Canada
Includes software.

WordPerfect® 6 SECRETS™
by Roger C. Parker & David A. Holzgang

ISBN: 1-56884-040-3
$39.95 USA/$52.95 Canada
Includes software.

DOS 6 SECRETS™
by Robert D. Ainsbury

ISBN: 1-878058-70-3
$39.95 USA/$52.95 Canada
Includes software.

Paradox 4 Power Programming SECRETS,™ 2nd Edition
by Gregory B. Salcedo & Martin W. Rudy

ISBN: 1-878058-54-1
$44.95 USA/$59.95 Canada
Includes software.

Paradox 5 For Windows® Power Programming SECRETS™
by Gregory B. Salcedo & Martin W. Rudy

ISBN: 1-56884-085-3
$44.95 USA/$59.95 Canada
Includes software.

Hard Disk SECRETS™
by John M. Goodman, Ph.D.

ISBN: 1-878058-64-9
$39.95 USA/$52.95 Canada
Includes software.

WordPerfect® 6 For Windows® Tips & Techniques Revealed
by David A. Holzgang & Roger C. Parker

ISBN: 1-56884-202-3
$39.95 USA/$52.95 Canada
Includes software.

Excel 5 For Windows® Power Programming Techniques
by John Walkenbach

ISBN: 1-56884-303-8
$39.95 USA/$52.95 Canada
Includes software.

...SECRETS®

INFO WORLD
TECHNICAL BOOKS

For scholastic requests & educational orders please call Educational Sales at 1. 800. 434. 2086

FOR MORE INFO OR TO ORDER, PLEASE CALL ▶ 800. 762. 2974

For volume discounts & special orders please call Corporate Sales, at 415. 655. 3000

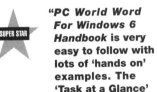

Order Center: **(800) 762-2974** *(8 a.m.–6 p.m., EST, weekdays)*

Quantity	ISBN	Title	Price	Total

Shipping & Handling Charges

	Description	First book	Each additional book	Total
Domestic	Normal	$4.50	$1.50	$
	Two Day Air	$8.50	$2.50	$
	Overnight	$18.00	$3.00	$
International	Surface	$8.00	$8.00	$
	Airmail	$16.00	$16.00	$
	DHL Air	$17.00	$17.00	$

*For large quantities call for shipping & handling charges.
**Prices are subject to change without notice.

Ship to:

Name _____

Company _____

Address _____

City/State/Zip _____

Daytime Phone _____

Payment: ☐ Check to IDG Books Worldwide (US Funds Only)

☐ VISA   ☐ MasterCard   ☐ American Express

Card # _____ Expires _____

Signature _____

Subtotal _____

CA residents add
applicable sales tax _____

IN, MA, and MD
residents add
5% sales tax _____

IL residents add
6.25% sales tax _____

RI residents add
7% sales tax _____

TX residents add
8.25% sales tax _____

Shipping _____

Total _____

Please send this order form to:

**IDG Books Worldwide, Inc.
Attn: Order Entry Dept.
7260 Shadeland Station, Suite 100
Indianapolis, IN 46256**

*Allow up to 3 weeks for delivery.
Thank you!*

IDG BOOKS WORLDWIDE REGISTRATION CARD

Visit our Web site at http://www.idgbooks.com

Title of this book: cc:Mail™ For Dummies®

My overall rating of this book: ❏ Very good [1] ❏ Good [2] ❏ Satisfactory [3] ❏ Fair [4] ❏ Poor [5]

How I first heard about this book:

❏ Found in bookstore; name: [6] _____
❏ Advertisement: [8]
❏ Word of mouth; heard about book from friend, co-worker, etc.: [10]

❏ Book review: [7] _____
❏ Catalog: [9]
❏ Other: [11]

What I liked most about this book: _____
_____
_____

What I would change, add, delete, etc., in future editions of this book: _____
_____
_____

Other comments: _____
_____

Number of computer books I purchase in a year: ❏ 1 [12] ❏ 2-5 [13] ❏ 6-10 [14] ❏ More than 10 [15]

I would characterize my computer skills as: ❏ Beginner [16] ❏ Intermediate [17] ❏ Advanced [18] ❏ Professional [19]

I use ❏ DOS [20] ❏ Windows [21] ❏ OS/2 [22] ❏ Unix [23] ❏ Macintosh [24] ❏ Other: [25] _____
(please specify)

I would be interested in new books on the following subjects:
(please check all that apply, and use the spaces provided to identify specific software)

❏ Word processing: [26] _____
❏ Data bases: [28] _____
❏ File Utilities: [30] _____
❏ Networking: [32] _____
❏ Other: [34] _____

❏ Spreadsheets: [27] _____
❏ Desktop publishing: [29] _____
❏ Money management: [31] _____
❏ Programming languages: [33] _____

I use a PC at (please check all that apply): ❏ home [35] ❏ work [36] ❏ school [37] ❏ other: [38] _____

The disks I prefer to use are ❏ 5.25 [39] ❏ 3.5 [40] ❏ other: [41] _____

I have a CD ROM: ❏ yes [42] ❏ no [43]

I plan to buy or upgrade computer hardware this year: ❏ yes [44] ❏ no [45]

I plan to buy or upgrade computer software this year: ❏ yes [46] ❏ no [47]

Name: _____ Business title: [48] _____ Type of Business: [49] _____

Address (❏ home [50] ❏ work [51] /Company name: _____)

Street/Suite# _____

City [52]/State [53]/Zipcode [54]: _____ Country [55] _____

❏ **I liked this book!** You may quote me by name in future
IDG Books Worldwide promotional materials.

My daytime phone number is _____

IDG
BOOKS
WORLDWIDE

THE WORLD OF
COMPUTER
KNOWLEDGE®

❏ # YES!

Please keep me informed about IDG Books Worldwide's
World of Computer Knowledge. Send me your latest catalog.

Macworld®
Books